THE POLITICAL THOUGHT
OF THOMAS G. MASARYK

by
ROMAN SZPORLUK

EAST EUROPEAN MONOGRAPHS, BOULDER
DISTRIBUTED BY COLUMBIA UNIVERSITY PRESS
NEW YORK

1981

EAST EUROPEAN MONOGRAPHS, NO. LXXXV

Copyright © 1981 by Roman Szporluk
Library of Congress Card Catalog Number 81-065163
ISBN 0-914710-79-6

Printed in the United States of America

FOR MARY ANN

CONTENTS

PREFACE

This book was written at the University of Michigan, Ann Arbor. I am grateful to the Center for Russian and East European Studies for supporting my research in many ways over the years. I wish especially to thank the Center director, Zvi Gitelman, and former directors, Morris Bornstein, Deming Brown, Alfred G. Meyer and William Zimmerman. I also wish to thank the Department of History and the Horace H. Rackham School of Graduate Studies for support of my studies. The latter has provided a publication subvention for this book.

My other debts include Ladislav Matejka, Svatopluk Soucek and Miloslav Jiran, all of the University of Michigan, who saved me from numerous errors and helped in other ways; Ezra Mendelsohn, of the Hebrew University of Jerusalem, who during his tenure as visting professor in Ann Arbor read an earlier version of this work; also Owen Johnson, Marta Johnson, John-Paul Himka, James Mace and Jo Thomas. Special thanks are due to Alice Gibson, whose remarkable editorial talents helped to transform this work into a much better product than it would have otherwise been. I am pleased to thank Connie Hamlin and Jeanette Ranta for their expert typing of several successive revisions.

More than twenty years ago I wrote a thesis at Oxford University (B. Litt., 1961) of which this book is a linear descendant. To Professor Sir Isaiah Berlin, thesis supervisor, I owe a lasting debt for the privilage of academic association with him and for his great personal kindness. While at Oxford, I was a student of Nuffield College, and I am grateful to the Warden and Fellows of Nuffield for electing me to a Studentship and for supporting me in other ways. My personal debts in Oxford are numerous and cannot be adequately discharged here, but I must thank the Warden (now retired), D. N. Chester, David E. Butler, Z. A. Pelczynski, the late John Plamenatz, and J. S. G. Simmons.

I have been fortunate to have had access to excellent libraries. I began to read Masaryk at the libraries of Maria Curie Sklodowska University, Lublin, and the Catholic University of Lublin; and I continued in Oxford at the Bodleian and the Taylorian, and at the college libraries of Nuffield and St. Antony's; at the British Museum and the School of Slavonic and

East European Studies, London; the libraries of Stanford University and Hoover Institution; University of California, Berkeley (The Masaryk-Benes Collection); the university and state libraries at Vienna; and at briefer interludes in New York Public Library, Library of Congress, and the Widener. The longest, however, has been my association with the libraries of the University of Michigan, and I am especially grateful to Joseph Placek for his expert assistance with this and other projects.

Over the years, I read papers and wrote articles on Masaryk. I am grateful to the following organizations and journals for providing me with opportunities to report on aspects of my work in progress: Oxford University Eastern European Society; St. Antony's College, Oxford; *The Slavonic and East European Review; Canadian Slavonic Papers;* Michigan Academy of Arts and Sciences; American Association for the Advancement of Slavic Studies; Ukrainian Research Institute, Harvard University; *East Central Europe;* and *Proměny.* I am grateful to those who responded with their comments, orally or in writting, as well as to those anonymous readers who evaluated my work before its publication.

This book is dedicated to my wife, Mary Ann.

INTRODUCTION

Thomas Garrigue Masaryk (1850-1937) is remembered today as the first president of Czechoslovakia (1918-1935) and as the leader and organizer of the Czechoslovak struggle against Austria from 1914 to 1918. His decision to confront Austria was the apex of a political involvement that had begun almost a third of a century earlier, when he first became a professor at the Czech University of Prague. More fortunate than his master Plato, Masaryk lived to see his political ideal realized, with himself in the role of a republican philosopher-king. It was a fitting end to a career that had begun with a dissertation on Plato and an essay on Plato's political ideal.

In retrospect, Masaryk's action may be seen as the most momentous Czech political fact since the independence of Old Bohemia had come to an end in 1620 with the defeat at White Mountain. In 1914, Masaryk challenged the rule of the Habsburgs over his people, and, when he organized the Czechoslovak forces abroad and thus became a "prophet armed," he did so in a way that no Czech had done in the preceding three centuries through armed struggle.

In 1914, notwithstanding his moral and intellectual authority, Masaryk had not been a recognized political leader. Yet, the success of his opposition to the Habsburgs led to his elevation to the presidency of the Czechoslovak Republic, and, indeed, more than any other Czech he was responsible for the rise of Czechoslovakia.

It might be argued that circumstances, a favorable constellation of forces, created the opportunity for Masaryk to seize the revolutionary leadership of his nation. This may be so, but Masaryk's claim to greatness is thereby not diminished: Prague was full of politicians, but it was he who concluded that the moment for action had come. The objective circumstances do not suffice for an explanation; its other component is the man's character, the subjective area. As R.H.S. Crossman has written:

> Good timing, we are told, is the secret of political leadership. But I suspect that being there at the right time is at least equally important. The statesman who *makes* the occasion—consciously planning his ascent to power and timing his great coup—is an invention of the novelist. In real life it is nearly always the occasion that makes the man. Winston Churchill was a brilliant, erratic outsider, with a very poor sense of timing; all his conscious efforts to achieve greatness failed—until the occasion made him great in 1940. . . . The kind of inspired leadership which wins a war or moulds a nation's history is hardly ever a matter of conscious calculation or timing. It is something much more personal—the uninhibited response of a whole man to a challenge exactly suited to call out the best that is in him . . . the secret of good leadership is the perfect matching of character and crisis. And that, of course, is a matter of luck.[1]

1914 provided for the sixty-four-year-old Masaryk what 1940 did for the sixty-five-year-old Churchill—a challenge exactly suited for him.

This study deals with the political thought of Masaryk. It does not endeavor to present, still less to explore in depth, Masaryk the politician. The author believes that if we are to comprehend fully Masaryk's actions in 1914 and later, an examination of his political thought is of equal importance to a survey of his political activity prior to the outbreak of World War I. Only by a study of his ideas can one understand how Masaryk perceived the condition of Bohemia, Austria, and the world at that time, and why he assigned the tasks he did to himself and to his compatriots. While we do recognize the significance of Masaryk's public career, this study does not cover it. After the biographical first chapter, only the most visible highlights of Masaryk's life and work, from his arrival in Prague in 1882 to his departure in 1914 and his return in 1918, are presented when appropriate and are used to facilitate the examination of his political thought and to suggest ways in which his actions can help one more fully to understand his principles. The same role is assigned to the general historical background and political setting, to which references will occasionally be made. In this work their function is auxiliary to the primary concern, a study of Masaryk's ideas.

This book argues that Masaryk's concern with the crisis of modern civilization was ever-present in his thought; and that to confront this crisis and its practical consequences was the dominant motive of his political activity and, indeed, of his life. The probing of this crisis in its diverse manifestations in culture, art, scholarship, politics, and in the daily life of the masses was the constant unifying theme of his thought.[2] A statement in *Modern Man and Religion* (1901) reveals his preoccupation in what he termed a "unified historical formula":

> Modern man has lost his unified religious world view; and the loss has led to intellectual and moral discontent and anarchy. For such a loss consists of a more or less violent rejection of the old world view; . . . a clash of the old view with a new one not yet fully delineated. Thus modern man is internally fragmented, disorganized, disintegrated, and inconsistent. . . ; he is incapable of enjoying his life truly and fully—and hence he despairs so easily and takes his own life. Thus our present age, our century, appears to be a time of crisis and transition. . . . To speak more concretely, the medieval world view as established and propagated by Catholicism has collapsed. Modern science and philosophy alike are opposed to Catholicism and this is why the present internal stress and weariness are manifested especially within the Catholic nations—and typically in French literature and philosophy. This clash of old and new appears also in the Orthodox nations, and here most characteristically in Russian literature and philosophy. . . . In Protestant nations there is another expression of the same internal conflict and modern fatigue, which corresponds to their different religious and ecclesiastical organizations.[3]

Thus Masaryk's political and social thought was dominated by his belief that the crisis of the modern world had been brought about primarily by the deterioration of traditional religious authority. When he

looked at the society of his time, he saw not only the decline of established authority but also the disintegration of traditional beliefs, ties,
and rules, and the rise of moral and intellectual conflicts within individuals and in social life. He related these negative phenomena to the rise
of secularism; the mass transition from rural to urban life; increased
widespread mobility; education that was often superficial—in short, to
social, political and economic forces that today's social scientists lump
under the heading of modernization. Masaryk did not use that term,
and his diagnosis of these diverse ills was not that of a political scientist
or sociologist. He identified problems within his own frame of reference,
and he sought his own solutions for them in a fundamental moral and
spiritual transformation that would overcome the crisis of modernity.
Deeply interested in religious, moral, and scientific authority, he believed
political authority to be secondary. He felt that social and political authority could not be secure and stable until man's moral and religious
life had a firm and systematic base. It is characteristic of his approach
that he treated all these kinds of authority as subject to one solution.

Masaryk's concerns were close to those of other nineteenth-century
European thinkers. The "crisis" which the young Masaryk described
was real: the phenomena he depicted actually had occurred during his
lifetime in Austria, and earlier in the century in Western Europe. Masaryk
was no doubt right in believing that what we now call modernization
was accompanied by the breakdown of traditional values and customs,
and that for many people this meant a sense of cultural loss and spiritual
disorientation so deep as to drive them at times to suicide.

In an earlier generation in Western Europe, men felt that a revolution
was taking place that was changing not only the political structure, but
also the total culture, of society. A new social structure was coming into
conflict with the traditional values of communal existence. There was,
as George Lichtheim wrote, a "very real sense of cultural dissolution
coming on top of the appalling social conditions created by early capit-
alism." Both conservative and socialist protests were raised; it was often
difficult to differentiate between them. The Saint-Simonians, as Lichtheim pointed out, criticized individualism, and proposed not only a new
social integration but a renovated religious faith. The "true" socialists
in Germany and the Christian socialists in England were faced with similar
problems; the same theme is found in Comte.[4] In this sense, Masaryk's

perceptions were in accord with what other Western writers and critics were observing in their own societies.

In like manner, Masaryk's focus on religious questions was not unique. Concern with "the nature of religion as the most critical and the all-embracing problem of man," of which Frank E. Manuel writes in *The Prophets of Paris*, is only one of the similarities to be found in Masaryk and Saint-Simon and Comte, both of whom influenced him either directly through their writings or indirectly through his high school teacher, Father Matěj Procházka. Saint-Simon was convinced that before humanity lay the prospect of a new religion that would fill the vacuum of contemporary disbelief. He believed at one time that the religion of the future would be nothing more than "generalized science"; later, he infused this religion with emotional and moral elements.[5] Of course, concern for religion was much wider. As Fritz Stern observed in his study on Lagarde: "The great minds of the nineteenth century all grappled with God, faith, and religion. Some sought to bury Christianity, others to revive it, many were brooding over the fate of a faithless world. The thought of a purely secular world was as intolerable as the thought of a controlled clerical society."[6]

These sentiments may be attributed to Masaryk as well. Chapter I examines the formation of his political thought and concentrates on his early preoccupation with religion and philosophy. It places this concern against the social and ethnic background of his native Moravia. Chapter II, "In Search of Authority: Religion or Science?," shows Masaryk's diagnosis of the ills of the modern world and presents his efforts to develop a new world view that would be able to replace the lost faith. At first, in the late 1870s and early 1880s, Masaryk believed that a new popular religion, one that was compatible with science, would replace the old. Gradually, he developed an alternative solution when he suggested that the antagonism between faith and science could be altogether abolished by the introduction of a scientific or philosophic religion. These reflections were connected with his ideas on leadership. While he was little interested in the practical problems of leadership and political authority in his own time, the young Masaryk had a very clear view as to what the ideal society should be like. In brief, Masaryk believed that politics ought to be a domain of experts, the scientists of society and government. Chapter III, "Leadership: Democracy versus Theocracy," taking as its point of departure Masaryk's early writings discussed in Chapter II, follows the evolution of Masaryk's thought on leadership from his first encounter with the intellectual and political Establishment of the Czech nation in Prague through his subsequent career as a writer, politician and statesman. It argues that throughout his active life Masaryk remained faithful to his early conviction that good government was government by the experts. This stand placed Masaryk in opposition to the dynastic, "theocratic" regimes of the Habsburgs and Romanovs, but it also prevented his full identification with those political currents that saw the basis of political authority in popular sovereignty.

Unlike those West European thinkers like Comte or Saint-Simon who had dealt with the decline of traditional religion, the rise of science, and the problem of popular belief, but who had been cosmopolitan in outlook and ignored ethnic nationalism, Masaryk had to face the latter issue directly, as a practical problem and as one that had to be taken into account in his Weltanschauung. Chapters IV, "Religion as Nationalism," and V, "Nation and State," present Masaryk's nationalist philosophy of history, which he first developed in the 1890s, and his view of the relation between nation and state. Masaryk's writings from the 1890s represent a new phase in his search for a world view that could provide a substitute for lost faith and offer intellectual, moral and emotional support to modern man. In these works one may observe Masaryk's transition from universalism, where religion and science are seen as worldwide phenomena, to nationalism. Masaryk had embraced universalism in his youth, after he had emerged from the village world of Moravia. By the 1890s, he had acknowledged that between the world whose fate so concerned him and the village that he had left in his youth there existed an intermediate structure of human association. He realized that one cannot become a citizen of the world directly and that moral, political, and social programs have to be adapted to particular circumstances.

These considerations, no doubt reinforced by Masaryk's practical experience in Prague after 1882, lie behind his adoption of a nationalist philosophy and interpretation of history. He did not abandon his old ideals—his concern for humanity or the search for a new religion—but he declared that the common goal of mankind should be pursued along separate, national roads. This recognition that universal values can achieve concrete realization only in accord with the precise conditions and needs of individual nations was formulated in the thesis that, since Providence had assigned certain tasks to each nation, it was the task of the Czechs to implement their own particular assignment. Masaryk's writings presented this assignment to his compatriots in the form of an historical analysis. Universal modern ideas, he hoped, would be more readily accepted if they were perceived by the people as messages originating in their national past.

If one were born in Moravia, as Masaryk had been, one was always aware of the fact that one had the choice of becoming either a Czech or a German, that ethnicities could not be bypassed in order to become a citizen of Europe, still less of the world. If an ethnic Czech chose not to become a member of the Czech community, he had no other choice but to end up as a German, even if he never consciously defined himself as such.

Masaryk made explicit theoretically what he had known empirically: mankind is divided into diverse groups with different languages, cultures, religions, traditions, ways of life. He now acknowledged that the crisis of modern civilization, which concerned him so profoundly, manifested itself in varying ways in different countries and peoples.

Also his study of Russia taught Masaryk that the antagonism between Catholicism and Protestantism—which he had earlier identified as a determining factor in differing manifestations of the crisis of Europe—did not make itself felt in all places at the same time and in the same form. For example, the crisis in Russia had been brought about and had accelerated under the impact of Western European ideas.

The uneven spread of the crisis of modern civilization, then, called for a response attuned to the individual and to particular local circumstances and conditions. Masaryk was no longer satisfied to point out abstract philosophical differences between Catholic and Protestant societies at large; he now applied these concepts to his interpretations of the specific political and cultural problems that beset individual nations.

His commitment to nationalism influenced Masaryk's conception of history, religion, education, culture and ultimately of politics. His conclusion was that national emancipation had to be a precondition of individual self-realization and progress in most areas of human endeavor. If men belong to different nations, live in different societies, under different conditions, and speak different languages, to require of them that they use a language not their own in their education and work means to deny their true selves and subject them to discriminatory treatment. It amounts also to depriving them of their legacy, their share of the cultural and spiritual heritage due them by virtue of their birth in a particular national community. The conclusion was inescapable that the political form of human community most compatible with an individual's spiritual and personal fulfillment was a self-governing nation.

Thus Masaryk eventually identified the nation not only as the unit best suited for individual fulfillment and as a vessel and bearer of supranational, universal content, but also as the sole locus of political legitimacy—challenging thereby the legitimacy of multinational states like the Habsburg monarchy. In 1914 he would proclaim a revolution against Austria in the name of national liberation. This revolution drew its justification, in his view also from the fact that the Habsburg monarchy (like the Empire of the Romanovs) was a theocracy, i.e., it represented the old, pre-scientific or mythical structure of authority. (Masaryk's arguments and specific policy recommendations drawn from them are examined in Chapter VI, "The Nationalist Revolution.") During the war Masaryk demanded the establishment of a national state of the "Czechoslovaks," considering the Slovaks to be a somewhat less developed branch of a single Czech nation which was nevertheless capable of becoming better educated in a future independent state. This position ignored the ethnic individuality and historical realities of Slovakia, even though Masaryk was invoking the principle of nationalism as the basis for his anti-Austrian program. He also claimed that Czechoslovak national aspirations constituted a concrete application of a universal humanitarian principle. It was not always clear how the Czech program promoted "humanity": without ever having embraced integral nationalism, which holds nationality as the sole basis of the social and individual ethos, Masaryk sometimes acted in 1914-1918 as if his operative consideration was national self-interest.

The final chapter, VII, "Masaryk's Republic: Nationalism with a Human Face," concentrates on two main themes: first, his solution to the problem of leadership in a democratic society (how did he reconcile his old ideas about political experts with his own role as a popularly elected president?); and, second, his position on the relationship between state and nation. How did Masaryk's view that the national state is the only legitimate state relate to the official ideology of Czechoslovakia, which was a multinational state containing besides the Czechs also Germans, Slovaks, Hungarians, Ukrainians, Jews, and Poles?

The chapter concludes with a brief look at Czechoslovakia after Masaryk. It assesses the legacy of Masaryk's republic in comparison with the other states in its own time and in a temporal perspective. Even though the leaders of the state professed nationalism as its official ideology, their policies, especially those of Masaryk himself, were guided by broader humanistic values. Similarly, Masaryk's perception of the role of expert leaders, one of whom he considered himself to be, was couched in strong moral terms: the leader had an obligation to promote morality and general welfare, not his own predilections.

CHAPTER I

YOUTHFUL PREOCCUPATIONS:
RELIGION, NATIONALITY, PHILOSOPHY

This chapter seeks to elucidate Masaryk's youthful ideas. It is to be hoped that the biographical facts selected for inclusion here will help to set the stage for the development of his political and social outlook and for the formation of his identity in relation to social, political, and ethnic factors. Thus the biographical data are set against the background of the prevailing social reality within which he grew to maturity.[1] Masaryk was born into the traditional world of rural Moravia, where imperial authority and the spiritual guidance of the Church were the dominant forces. His father occupied a place, albeit a very modest one, in that structure of authority. As young Masaryk began his formal schooling, he came into close contact with the Roman Catholic clergy; by the time he graduated from high school (at the rather advanced age of twenty-two), he had also come to know quite intimately the private world of the Austrian bureaucracy, having served for a number of years as a domestic tutor in the household of a high official in Brno and Vienna. High school also introduced him to the world of secular learning. He continued his studies at the University of Vienna and concluded their first phase with a doctorate when he was twenty-six. Finally, the formative influences of his youth included an exposure in various forms to the problems of ethnicity and nationality. He early observed the petty antagonisms between schoolboys who came from different villages, later the more serious Czech-German tensions and numerous instances of anti-Semitism. Religion, power, knowledge, nationality—these were, then, the principal areas of experience to which the young Masaryk was exposed and on which he reflected and wrote.

Thomas (Tomáš) Masaryk was born on 7th March 1850 in the Moravian village of Hodonín, the first child of Josef and Theresie Masaryk. Josef Masaryk had been born in 1823, the son of a serf and himself a serf until 1848, when he became a coachman on imperial domains. Theresie, whose maiden name was Kropatschek, was a domestic servant, and was ten years older than her husband; by language, she was German, not Czech. They were married on 15 August 1849.[2] Theresie's family lived in the more populous nearby town of Hustopeče; even after she had married and moved to the country she never forgot that she had come from the "city." It was she who insisted on sending Thomas to school. During his son's childhood Josef was promoted from coachman to supervisor over other hired laborers. He was interested in little outside his work, which was of a routine kind; he never questioned anything and obeyed his superiors to the letter.

Because of Josef's position as an imperial employee, the Masaryks ranked above ordinary peasants socially, and their son played for the most part with the children of estate officials and their servants; when he was nine, he made friends with the son of the estate manager, and together they read German children's stories. Hodonín had a two-grade school with parallel German and Czech classes; Thomas was sent to the German classes when he was six. Because Josef Masaryk and his family were often transferred from one estate to another, Thomas did not stay long in any one school. In 1861 he moved to a more advanced level when be became a pupil at the Piarists' school at Hustopeče. This step (which had to be approved by Josef's superiors) went beyond the education Thomas would have received had the matter been left only to the discretion of his father who, although he could read a little, had never gone to school at all.

In Hustopeče instruction was given in German, and the subjects included Czech, arithmetic, geometry, history and geography, physics and biology. Thomas was not an outstanding pupil, and his conduct left something to be desired as well. He did not make friends easily, preferring to read and reread his favorite book, a treatise on physiognomy according to Lavater's ideas, which had been given him by a former teacher. "I learned this book almost by heart," he said later, and "I used to watch my companions very closely, to see whether they had long fingers, round or pointed chins, and so on . . . ."[3]

Two years later Thomas completed the course, which had prepared him for teaching, and went back home. He was not allowed actually to teach until he was sixteen, except as a student teacher. Thomas took up this work, but left after a couple of months. Later he was sent to Vienna to learn the locksmith's craft. This was hard work, and the general conditions depressing: "The bustle of the city and my dealings with my new 'companions' soon became unbearable; the only pleasure I had was in the bookshops to which I used to make my way stealthily during the lunch hour—I had little to eat, sometimes nothing at all . . . ." He was clearly desparately homesick. "Perhaps I should have become reconciled to my fate if a trifling occurrence had not completely upset me; a fellow-boarder stole all my books, including my *Physiognomy* and sold them. From that moment onwards I was quite distraught; without much hesitation I made my way home."[4]

His father, much upset at the disgrace, apprenticed Thomas to the local blacksmith. But instead of the two years that had been agreed upon, Thomas lasted there only six months, months he found almost as hard to bear as the time in Vienna. He then became an assistant schoolmaster, receiving free lodging but no salary for his work. He devoted himself with great zeal to his new calling, feeling that God had led him to his predestined purpose.[5]

In addition to his school tasks, the young teacher served as church organist and assisted the parish priest, Father František Sátora, at funerals and weddings. But Masaryk's self-esteem was wounded because he knew no Latin and so had to learn the prayers by heart without understanding a word of them. His ignorance of Latin was also a handicap in his private reading. In an old Jesuit library he had found a seventeenth-century Catechism, and though he studied it eagerly, the numerous quotations in Latin and Greek made full appreciation of the work impossible. He decided to learn Latin; in short, to continue his studies. Father Sátora supplied him with a huge volume, a four-language dictionary (Latin-German-Magyar-Slovak), for the study of Latin, and also advised him to learn French. Himself a devout Catholic, Sátora encouraged Masaryk to read all the anti-Reformation pamphlets and treatises that could be found in the library. Thomas was particularly impressed by *"Vogel, friss oder stirb,"* an anti-Protestant tract, one of the many that he read. The net result was to make of him an ardent Catholic.[6]

Late in 1864 Masaryk was admitted to the high school at Strážnice— formerly a famous school but by then a mere *Untergymnasium*—but after a year there he moved to Brno, the capital of Moravia. Despite Sátora's continued financial assistance, Masaryk's situation was difficult. At first, as he recalled, he lived in "inexpressible misery"; only after he had become a top student did he begin to earn money as a private tutor. He found real security when the son of the Director of Police at Brno, Anton Le Monnier, became his pupil. The young Le Monnier was a boy from his own grade but, like most others, four years younger than Thomas. Masaryk was paid well enough not to need other income, and he was free to follow his interests. His employer was not only a leading bureaucrat but also a highly educated and cultured man. As a recent Czech writer observed, Le Monnier represented an old Josephinist tradition of Austrian officialdom, which combined power with knowledge and a sense of service to those it governed.

Masaryk discovered, through the example of Le Monnier, that it was "possible to *combine knowledge and political activity*—finding in this human justification."[7] He was allowed to use the Le Monniers' library, where he read the works of Lessing, Schiller, Goethe, Balzac, George Sand, Hugo, Dumas, as well as the scientific writings of the Humboldts. In the Brno periodicals he followed the controversy raging over Darwin's *The Origin of Species.* The authors of some of those articles were his teachers: the most remarkable among them, Father Matěj Procházka, taught divinity and philosophy and was a popular author as well. From Procházka, Masaryk received books that interested him no less than those he read at the Le Monniers'. Like Procházka, he was particularly enthusiastic about *Fabiola* by Cardinal Wiseman (a Czech translation appeared in Brno in 1857); among their favorite books were also *The Martyrs of Tilbury* and *Glaubenskraft und Liebesglut* by a Mme. Polko. He became filled with a fervent ardor for the missionary effort and the faith expressed by the martyrs.[8]

Yet, in spite of the priest's influence on him, religious doubts began to creep in. "I came across anti-Catholic books which exposed the Church's absolutism, her exclusiveness, and acts of violence . . . . I was growing up at a time of increasing liberalism and its fight against authority, both ecclesiastical and political."[9] He confided his thoughts to Procházka and found in him a man of understanding and compassion. It was largely owing to Procházka that Masaryk remained a religious man even after he had lost faith in the dogmas of the established church.[10] In his child-hood and adolescence he had seen the powerful role the church played as a source of social order and stability—for hers was the spiritual authority that the masses of people obeyed unreservedly. On the ground of his own experience of rural communities, which he regarded as universally valid, he firmly believed that to establish a stable basis for their lives men must have religion. Masaryk's belief that religion was essential to society no doubt developed under Procházka's influence; it withstood not only the attack of the skepticism and liberalism that Masaryk faced in Brno, but it was reinforced and deepened by his encounter with socialism, as ex-pounded by Procházka in his lectures, sermons, and articles.

"What is needed," Procházka wrote, "is only love, moderation, fair-ness and justice on the part of capitalists . . . then the antagonism between labor and capital, a deplorable phenomenon in the industrial world will disappear."[11] Procházka was conversant with socialist ideas and move-ments in Europe. He had read Marx and Engels, and he was the first Moravian to write about the Internationale. But the writer whose views most attracted him was Saint-Simon, although, as a faithful Catholic, he could by no means share the latter's view that religion should be stripped of all dogma. Procházka's conviction that society was essentially subordinate to religion, from which any effective reform must stem, provided the foundation on which Masaryk was later to build his own world outlook. When Masaryk criticized Marxism in the 1890s, he was proceeding from the premises laid out by Procházka.

In 1869 Masaryk was expelled from school. We do not know the precise reason, and Masaryk himself gave conflicting versions, but in any case he seems to have physically assaulted the headmaster.[12] Owing to the powerful protection of the Director of Police, and to a certain amount of luck, for Le Monnier at precisely that time was promoted to a high post in Vienna, Masaryk's lot improved; he was admitted to the famous Vienna high school, the *Adademisches Gymnasium.* As in Brno, the school life in Vienna was distasteful to him; again he was older than the other boys in years and experience, and he had to earn his own living.[13] His diligence in the study of the school subjects progressively declined;[14] very often he was absent, and when he came he was late. Accordingly his conduct, originally "praiseworthy," was for the last two years only "adequate," the lowest mark that would still permit its recipient to remain in school. His best subjects were religion, Greek, German, followed by Latin and natural history. His achievements in history and philosophy were "satisfactory"; in physics and mathematics—"sufficient."[15] "In Vienna I continued my high school studies and plunged deeper into my philosophical work," he wrote in 1875. "I worked through the writings of Lavater and Reichenbach and a good deal of mystical nonsense. The school logic and philosophy did not satisfy me in the least. My favorite work then was to translate into Czech Lange's *History of Materialism,* which I glossed with my own humble opinions."[16]

In 1870 Masaryk witnessed the fall of the worldly power of the Roman Catholic Church. Shortly after the dogma of papal infallibility was promulgated, Catholic France was defeated by Protestant Prussia, while the seat of the Pope himself was occupied by Italian troops, an action accepted with remarkable indifference by the powers of Europe. Already shaken in his faith, he still remained a Catholic, but he was deeply impressed by the fact that no one in Europe rose against the Italians.[17] If the Church was failing, and another indication of it was the renunciation of the Concordat by Austria, it made no sense to remain a member of it. A few weeks after the occupation of Rome by the Italians, Masaryk declared to his divinity master, Father Berlinger, that he would be Greek Orthodox, not Roman Catholic. He chose a denomination no less authoritarian, but one that, unlike the Church of Rome, showed no signs of collapse.[18]

Masaryk hoped to enter the renowned Oriental Academy and to pursue a diplomatic career. But it proved impossible for him to get in, and he never forgot the disappointment caused by this failure. He enrolled instead in the philosophical faculty to major in Classical philology, with the idea of becoming a high school teacher, even though he did not relish the prospect.[19] He was not interested in the subjects listed in the official syllabus; they did not stimulate in him that free "philosophizing" he was longing for, and they seemed remote from current issues. "At the Exhibition [Vienna World Exhibition 1873] the whole world with its progress and vitality was being revealed to me, while Vahlen croaked about Catullus. In the conflict between the two worlds, the new world of reality had won in me over the old one of the philologists."[20] Toward the close of his first year at University, Masaryk began to consider changing his subject. He wanted to understand "Life," to know its meaning and purpose, and having lost his faith in the dogmas and his confidence in the practical ability of the Church to provide direction to man's life and stability for society, he felt an urgent need to find a system that would take the place of his lost faith and provide an answer to all the questions that so disturbed him. Philosophy above all seemed to be the source to which he might look for help: the well-known philosopher, Robert Zimmermann, advised him to read the history of philosophy; accordingly, he embarked on a chronological study of the philosophers. From the first, it was Plato who exerted the strongest appeal.[21]

His uncertainty and doubts became sharper and all his questioning more pressing when his brother Martin died in 1875. Everything seemed then to have lost sense and value. "I went home and flung into a corner the blameless Catullus and the even more blameless Tibullus and Propertius . . . and that was the end of my philology. . . ."[22] From then on, he wrote in 1875, he would put his trust in philosophy, in which he found consolation.[23]

Philosophy to him meant Plato. He was not interested in Plato's theory of knowledge or the "ideas"; if he later claimed that Plato had exerted the strongest influence on him it was because Plato dealt with his own interests: religion, ethics, and politics. Masaryk admitted that in science Plato had become obsolete. This did not matter, just as it did not matter that Plato's ideas and epistemology were to him unacceptable. Masaryk was attracted to the striking uniformity of Plato's world outlook and his "particular blend of theory and practice." He set himself the task of working out a uniform world outlook that would constitute a guide for thought and action but would be free from the shortcomings he found in Plato's system. One fault was that in Plato's time the various branches of learning had not been clearly separated.[24] Fortunately, this was no longer true, Masaryk felt, because science had made such remarkable progress and had furthermore been classified by Auguste Comte, whom he called a "giant spirit of our century."[25]

Masaryk probably first learned about Comte from his professors, Theodor Gomperz and Robert Zimmermann, though he did not actually read Comte until 1875. He read *about* him in Mill's *System of Logic,* although he was unaware of Mill's work, *A. Comte and Positivism.* Even after 1875 he did not study Comte at first hand but rather through *The Positive Philosophy of Auguste Comte,* which had been condensed and freely translated into English by Harriet Martineau in 1853 and which Masaryk read in a French translation.[26] In addition to the scientific aspect of Comte's work, which to Masaryk seemed like a revelation, the personality of the French scholar, the similarities between Comte's social background and personal fate and his own, and most of all his Catholicism, made Comte seem even closer to him.[27]

Of the writings of John Stuart Mill, he studied the *Logic,* and in 1875 he read *The Subjection of Women.* He found himself so warmly in accord with the message of the latter work that he decided to review it in a journal; subsequently he wrote an article on the women's question himself. Theodor Gomperz and Franz Brentano, though differing in their interests and philosophies, each had a firsthand knowledge of Western thought, and it was through them that Viennese undergraduates learned about Mill and Comte. Masaryk, eager to become apprised of the recent trends in the West, attended their lectures, but he was interested not so much in strictly philosophical questions as in sociology, philosophy of history, psychology, and even physiology, for these he believed might be of practical use.[28]

Early in 1875 Masaryk decided to present his ideas to a wider public. He sent first to V. Vlček, editor of *Osvěta,* then the only Czech monthly review for the intelligentsia, an article directed against Schopenhauer as a representative of the "dangerous trend of pessimism," and when this article was rejected he sent a second article, this time on suicide. In the covering letter to the editor he wrote in rather awkward Czech:

> I occupy myself with philosophy: I wish to attain a professor's chair, at a higher school, maybe at ours, I think that I might, like anybody else, in some way be useful to my country. I have, to some extent, my own views; I am of the opinion that philosophy is not yet worthwhile as a science, and that it is necessary to lay the foundations if philosophy is to survive at all. . . .[29]

In 1875, having successfully completed his undergraduate courses,

Masaryk decided to work for a doctorate in philosophy. Early in 1876 he submitted a thesis in German, "The Essence of Soul in Plato," and, along with the official documents accompanying his application, he enclosed an autobiography ("Curriculum vitae") written in 1875. It concluded with the following sentence: "The promise I once made to myself will, with the help of God, be fulfilled."[30] Professor Franz Brentano, one of the official examiners of the thesis, was less than impressed, stating that Masaryk was too much of an apologist for Plato's doctrines. "Indeed," Brentano continued,

> Masaryk has read Plato's writings with great diligence; besides he has shown a really broad reading of modern philosophical literature: but this does not always benefit his thesis. When he has to admit the total indefensibility of some of the statements by Plato, he attempts to make Plato's mistake appear less objectionable by placing beside it similar or even greater errors of later philosophers who were concerned with the same matter. This often brings about digressions which lead the author away from his proper subject . . . .[31]

Brentano remarked also that Masaryk's style was poor, that his phrases were strange, often incorrect, even misleading, and he attributed these faults to the fact that German was not Masaryk's own language.[32] Nevertheless, because he was satisfied that Masaryk was capable of research in the history of philosophy and of dealing with problems in an original speculative way, he did accept the thesis. In March 1876 Masaryk passed the oral examination and received his doctorate.

Acceptance of the dissertation did not mean the end of Masaryk's interest in Plato. As early as September 1875, when he was still composing it, Masaryk conceived the project of writing a piece about Plato and patriotism. He returned to this as soon as he had passed the last examination, and in July 1876 Masaryk's article on "Plato as a patriot" appeared in *Zora,* a yearbook published by a group of young Moravians.[33] The article was a refutation of the opinions of Niebuhr, who had denied Plato's patriotism and found him an unsatisfactory citizen. As his theme Masaryk took the only nonnationalistic passage from an otherwise highly patriotic poem by Čelakovský: "Thou who maketh thy mother immortal in the memory of mankind—thou art our brother, thou art a patriot."[34]

Plato, wrote Masaryk, has been accused of criticizing Athens, but it is not lack of patriotism to disagree with one's compatriots and abstain from participation in public life in order to pursue one's own interests; great men are usually in conflict with their times. We could judge and condemn Plato if his views were wrong; but were they? Masaryk presented what was in his opinion must valuable in Plato's political doctrine; in the end he concluded that the whole of Plato's doctrine was sound. He supported his stand by pointing out that mankind continues to learn from him and that he did more to make his motherland famous than had anyone else: obviously he was a patriot. Therefore he felt that Niebuhr was mistaken in considering the patriotism of modern times identical with the ancient understanding of it. He added that in general Niebuhr had no clear idea what patriotism really was, an error common to most historians, statesmen and philosophers. Scholars have suggested that the article on Plato was above all a statement of the views of Masaryk himself.[35] The article, which was an indirect rejection of Czech nationalism and a statement of the primary importance of a world view, was published in Czech. Nejedlý has suggested that in this case Masaryk must have been motivated by the desire to place before the Czech people his views on matters that he felt were of great practical importance; for instance, the dangers inherent in Schopenhauer's pessimism and in the modern prevalence of suicide, matters with which the Czechs in particular had not been sufficiently conversant.[36]

Masaryk's road to a Czech national identity, which would in the next several years after the publication of this article lead him to a professorship in Prague and thus to a position first in the Czech intellectual establishment and then to politics, was not a straight or simple one.[37] During his childhood, even in his immediate family, two languages had been spoken and thus two "nations" represented. Masaryk's father was linguistically a Slovak, and his dialect was spoken at home; his mother was German (although her family may at one time have been Czech), and in her youth she spoke German much more correctly than Czech or Slovak. "My father knew German pretty well," Masaryk remembered, "but we children never spoke German to him, only to our mother." What he said about himself could equally well have been said by most of his Moravian peers: "Until my fourteenth year I had no national consciousness at all. I regarded it as quite natural to speak two languages."[38]

In the part of Moravia from which Masaryk's family came and where he himself was born, the local Slavic population spoke a Slovak dialect. In any gathering of people, some spoke this language, others that, but the difference in tongue was nothing but a simple natural occurrence, requiring no more thought than the fact that some people had fair hair while some black or red hair. Indeed more often than not preference was given to German. Although the Moravian peasant did not care much about the education of his sons, seeing no benefits likely to result from it, he made an exception when it came to learning German, for this knowledge constituted a visible asset. Quite often and without any compulsion the common people, and not only those richer and more prominent in the community, changed their Slav surnames to German ones.[39]

While hostility between the inhabitants of different villages or parishes was common,[40] a sense of belonging to a greater national unit could not be found in the *Slovacko,* the Slovak-inhabited part of Moravia, as distinct from Slovakia proper, or *Slovensko.* The people did not even consider themselves Moravians, nor were they aware that the Czechs from the "Kingdom of Bohemia" and the Moravians constituted a single nation. Vienna was the city of cities and to Vienna their thoughts were turned: it was there that one went to work and study, and from there the masters came. Brno, though capital of the province, appears to have been ignored in popular consciousness while the more distant Prague was always held in mind: country people believed that one day that seat of sin would perish. The common people did not preserve in their memories any of the great men of Czech history: if any name survived among them, it was that of the famous Austrian general, Radetzky.[41]

Such were the conditions under which Thomas Masaryk spent his childhood; he was himself not unlike those among whom he lived. He read about Prague for the first time in a book borrowed from Father Sátora. A beautiful and remarkable town it might be, but it did not evoke in him any nationalist visions or emotions; it belonged to the same remote category as those other fairy tale places, Budapest and Vienna. "He was not a Czech, he was a Slovak—a quite natural thing, which all the Moravians and particularly Slovaks know from their youth," wrote Masaryk's fellow-Slovak and friend, Jan Herben.[41]

Masaryk's biographer, Zdeněk Nejedlý, commented upon what he called the special characteristics of the Slovaks to explain Masaryk's subsequent development and his attitude towards nationalism. All true Slovaks, Nejedlý points out, are first of all cosmopolitans: wherever they go they feel at home. Since for a Slovak his motherland (*vlast,* used also as a synonym for the German *Heimat*) is his village, what is left is the whole world, no matter whether it is close or distant, Bohemia or America, Austria or France. When he is no longer a villager, a Slovak becomes a citizen of the whole world. Nejedlý's general observation may be applied to Masaryk: Masaryk's *vlast,* in his youth, was neither Moravia nor Slovakia, only the much smaller Hodonín and its vicinity, the Hodonínsko. While for Nejedlý this fact provides a clue only to Masaryk's cosmopolitanism, it may also shed some light on the origin of Masaryk's later idea of Czechoslovakia. It helps to explain why Masaryk was able so easily to move from "Czechdom" (after he had acquired it) to "Czechoslovakism," a wider concept of the national unity of the Czechs and Slovaks. Having never had an early and strong emotional attachment to Moravia or to Bohemia-Moravia, it was not difficult for him to add one land or another to the distance that lies between the Hodonínsko and the world. He retained an emotional attachment only for the places of his youth; much later he rationalized this attachment. "An abstract and narrowly political love for the fatherland was not enough for me. Since childhood I have felt my Czechdom concretely, through an understanding of the character, thoughts and life of my compatriots, there in the Slovacko and Slovakia, and, with the passage of time, in Moravia and Bohemia."[43]

Father Sátora, who helped and supported the young Thomas in his studies, was a zealous Czech nationalist, and from him Masaryk learned nationalist hatred. Sátora, born in 1826, belonged to a generation whose outlook had been formed before 1848, and, though a man with a strong sense of justice and equality and scornful of privilege confered by wealth, he directed his hostility against the Germans, in all of whom he saw bearers of social evil. From Sátora Masaryk caught his first glance of true national allegiance.[44]

In addition to the Germans, there were also Jews in Moravia. Masaryk had encountered anti-Semitism from early childhood. Hostility toward Jews was instilled in him particularly by his mother, a deeply religious woman, which in Moravia meant that she was strongly anti-Jewish. Father Sátora as well was anti-Semitic. As Masaryk recalled:

In the fifties of the last century every little Slovak grew up in an atmosphere of anti-Semitism which was inculcated in him by his family, school, church and general surroundings. My mother would not let me have anything to do with some Jews named Lechner, because, she said, Jews made use of Christian children's blood. . . . In sermons I was always hearing warnings against the Jews, and at school as well. The superstition about Christian blood became so ingrained in me that whenever a Jew happened to come near me . . . I used to stare at his fingers, to see whether there was any blood sticking to them. I kept up this stupid practice for quite a long time.[45]

The only exception to the general treatment of Jews was made for a certain Mr. Fixl, who from time to time arrived in the village with various wares for sale, some of which Thomas's mother bought. He told funny stories and anecdotes and was always a welcome visitor, so that the boy Thomas was quite unaware that he too was a Jew.[46]

When in 1865 Masaryk went away to high school in Brno, he was certainly not a Czech nationalist. He had no positive image of the motherland (wider than Hodonínsko) and his anti-Jewish and anti-German feelings arose from religious and social motivation. When the Austro-Prussian war broke out in 1866, Masaryk, along with some of the Czech pupils at the grammar school in Brno, wanted to enlist. They were, however, more against the Prussians than enthusiastically pro-Austrian.[47] When he recalled these events in later years, the President of Czechoslovakia did not wish it to be thought that he had once intended to fight for the Habsburgs. But it would be fair to imagine that, apart from being anti-Prussian because of his Catholicism, if for no other reason, he must have been a loyal subject of the Emperor. He had been brought up in a Catholic environment, and this certainly included loyal attachment to "His Apostolic Majesty."

In school there was a certain amount of antagonism between Slav and German boys, probably basically not unlike the conflict between the Čejkovíce and Podvorov boys, though age differences also contributed to the conflict. German boys, who did not have to spend additional years in the study of the German language, were as a rule two or three years younger than the Czechs in the same classes. But in Brno Masaryk encountered for the first time in his life both a more sophisticated form of Czech nationalism and the Slav-German conflict. "In Brno I began to understand my Czechdom; before that, at home, I had felt a primitive kind of socialism. It was through getting to know history that my consciousness crystallized . . . . Once we thoroughly understand our history we must realize that nowhere in the world can one find a greater one."[48]

A Polish schoolboy enlightened him on the Polish question, about which he had read in the newspapers during the Polish insurrection of 1863 and had heard more when Polish refugees began to arrive in Moravia. His sympathies, he recalled, had been fully on the Polish side, as they had been with the Danes during the war over Schleswig-Holstein.[49]

His departure to Vienna removed the two sources of tension and conflict in Masaryk's school life in Brno. He turned away from the Catholic Church toward his own idea of Protestantism without encountering any obstacles on the part of his school authorities, and the nationality conflict did not exist for him. In a class of fifty pupils there were only four Czechs, including Masaryk. Still it does not follow that there were no manifestations of nationalism among them: when news of German victories in France arrived, the *"Wacht am Rhein"* was sung in the school, and when his form joined in the singing Masaryk and his Czech friend, Kamaryt, left the room. Everybody knew they were Czechs, so their act was regarded as a natural one.[50] Here it was also regarded as quite natural for the Czechs to speak among themselves in their own language, although this had not been the case in Brno.[51]

Certain romantic nationalist ideas and sentiments he had first experienced at Brno remained with Masaryk in Vienna.[52] They were nourished by a youthful enthusiasm for romantic heroes like those he had discovered in the books of J.K.R. Herlos, the "German Walter Scott." But the great champions of modern Czech nationalism he did not know until later; he became acquainted with the writings of some of them only as a university student and as a graduate student in his mid-twenties. Masaryk's early nationalism, including his awareness of differences between the Slavs and Germans and a resentment of the German pretense of superiority, seems to have been restricted to the borders of Moravia and contained no political anti-Austrian sentiment. In his recollections, published in 1917, Masaryk jokingly recalled that he and the other Slovaks had preferred singing Slovak songs to anything else in the Czech students' club in Vienna. At that time he thoroughly approved of Slovak and Moravian "childish separatism."[53] This separatism Masaryk attributed to the influence of his Brno teachers and to the Moravian writers he had read. The literary and cultural separatism of Slav Moravia was not directed against Vienna but constituted an assertion of the traditional and distinctive character of Moravia in opposition to the main center of Czech life, Prague, which aspired to the role of the sole capital of the nation.[54] If his nationalism was manifested chiefly in a preference for Slovak songs, it is not surprising that his fellow-pupils remembered him as a cosmopolitan, even though everybody in the school knew that Masaryk was a Czech and spoke Czech as other Czechs did. A classmate later remembered him as "nationally indifferent."[55]

That political nationalism was alien to him, at least during the earlier part of his residence in Vienna, is also made plain by his choice of a career. When he first went to Vienna, his fondest wish was to become a diplomat, and this meant attendance at the Oriental Academy. To be admitted there, he had first to sit for language examinations. But as he said, only the sons of aristocrats seemed to get in, and thus his aspirations of becoming a diplomat were gone forever.[56] It is probably correct to assume that such a plan could have been conceived only by someone who was loyal to the existing state and fully intended to work for it while abstaining from its internal political struggles. (Is is possible to imagine Piłsudski or Lenin aspiring at a comparable stage to a career in the service of the Romanovs?) This was an understandable career choice for someone who had spent years as a member of the household, perhaps even as an adopted spiritual child, of a high official of the Imperial bureaucracy like Le Monnier.

Masaryk appears to have been indifferent to the dramatic events relating to Bohemia during those years. The year 1867 witnessed the Hungarian Compromise and the grant of a constitution to the Austrian part of the Dual Monarchy. On 22 August 1868, the Czech members of the Bohemian Diet issued a constitutional declaration restating the reasons for their earlier withdrawal from the Reichsrat. When Masaryk was twenty, attempts were made to reach an agreement between the Emperor and the Czech leaders whereby the Emperor would recognize "the rights of the Bohemian Crown." By his appointment of the Hohenwart Ministry on 7 February 1871 and issuing of the *Reskript* of 12 September 1871,

Francis Joseph declared himself ready to settle the position of the Bo-hemians in Prague in a new way. German and Hungarian opposition combined with the unrealistic demands of the Czechs caused the failure of negotiations and the dismissal of Hohenwart.

In none of the known autobiographical writings of Masaryk can re-ference be found to any of these events. Nor does he speak of them, nor indeed of himself between the ages of nineteen and twenty-two (the three years he spent in the *Akademisches Gymnasium*), in the fullest account of his life of which he can be regarded as part author, his *Con-versations* with Karel Čapek.[57] On the other hand, we know from Mas-aryk himself that the topics most important to him at that time were the Vatican Council, the dogma of Papal Infallibility, the occupation of Rome, and the failure of the European Catholic powers to defend the Pope's rights.

The first indication of serious interest in the question of nationality is to be found in a passage of his "Curriculum vitae" written in the sum-mer of 1875 for the university. Having first stated that it was Father Sátora who had won him over to the national cause, Masaryk added in a footnote that through a study of Roman history and culture he had modified his views on nationality and had come to share the opinions of Cicero. He had also come to agree by and large with the judgments of J.S. Mill as presented in his *Logic,* Book VI, chapter 10.[58]

"Modification" was rather "supplementation": the Moravian or Slovak nationality, as Masaryk understood it, reflected an attachment to the region where one's family lived and where one had been born; he had no need to change his outlook when he discovered the concepts of Cicero and John Stuart Mill and accept them. From Cicero and Mill he did learn something new: the idea of the political nation like that created by Rome, which, in spite of tyranny, "succeeded in establishing the feeling of a common country among the provinces of her vast and divided empire," and was a state in which "one part of the community do not consider themselves as foreigners with regard to another part." Mill's and Cicero's concept of nationality was contrasted by Masaryk with the concept of "nationality in the vulgar sense of the term"—"a senseless antipathy to foreigners," indifference to the general welfare of the human race, and so on.[59] Since "nation" for both Mill and Cicero was coextensive with the "whole of the citizens of the State," was the reader to infer that

Masaryk's nation (since he claimed to agree with Mill and Cicero) now embraced the whole of the citizens of Austria? Was the Habsburg monarchy in Masaryk's view that *res publica* of which he would be able to say, as Cicero did, that "the noblest use of virtue is the government of the Commonwealth?"[60]

It is easier to answer the second question. Masaryk seems to have accepted Austria as the state within whose framework the political life of all "Austrians" should be lived and their interests pursued. He had no wish at that time for a major reform of the monarchy or some special status for the Bohemian lands. Great political discussions and dissensions among the Czechs in Bohemia and Moravia took place in the 1870s; but the struggles between Old Czechs and Young Czechs and between Passivism and Activism did not engage him personally and remained largely unknown to him.[61] On the other hand, he openly declared himself in favor of Czech participation in the Vienna parliament, simply because, as he saw it, *all citizens* and groups of citizens should take part in the government of the State.[62] By politics he meant, as did the Greeks, the government of the State, and he saw action as the basic principle of political science. Thus Masaryk answered the argument that the Czech deputies "cannot come to Vienna."[63]

Every state, Masaryk argued, has to have one city as its capital: Vienna was the capital of Austria, a unifying link for the diverse peoples of the state. It was neither a German nor a Czech but an Austrian, i.e., a multilingual, city. Vienna ought to be on a smaller scale what the Austrian state should be as a whole. Masaryk drew an analogy with the parts of a man's body, which must cooperate with each other as all parts of the State must work together. Differences should be resolved by mutual concessions. He concluded that "universal federalism" was the "only reasonable goal of mankind."[64]

To return now to the first question: did Masaryk's idea of a nation comprise all the citizens of Austria? Friedrich Meinecke's distinction between *Kulturnation* and *Staatsnation* might be helpful here. It is clear that Masaryk was conscious of his Slavdom and did not deny it, but he accepted Austria as the political form, the *Staatsnation,* within which the Czechs lived. He did not regard politics as the primary sphere of human life and concern, however, and his interests lay primarily in religion, psychology, philosophy, sociology, and literature. He tried to detect and comprehend the ills and evils of modern civilization and to discover ways of restoring it to health, but he did not expect politics to provide salvation. His attention was not limited to any particular segment of mankind. In some ways he stood nearer to the people among whom he had been born; he understood their ways and therefore was able to see more easily what might be done to help them. He was not a political nationalist, nor could he be called a cultural nationalist, for nationality and nationalism found little place in the intellectual system he was striving to construct. He would eventually realize that he must take national factors into account; then his *Weltanschauung* would be redrawn and remodeled. But when Masaryk first began to seek a consistent, scientific and comprehensive solution to the crisis that was destroying modern civilization, nation and nationalism were playing no role in his efforts.

In the fall of 1876 Masaryk, accompanied by his pupil Alfred Schlesinger, traveled to Italy,[65] and a few weeks later he left Vienna for Leipzig. From Leipzig he sent to the journal *Koleda* an article on spiritualism that was never published. He also wrote to inquire about the publication of *Suicide,* an unpublished article written in 1875 which he had now expanded into a book. He had been considering an essay on Comte, but gave that up to write instead an essay on Funck-Brentano's *Civilization and Its Laws.*[66] A friend translated it into Czech from Masaryk's German. In spite of his best efforts, no journal to which the essay was offered would accept it. Another article, also inspired by Funck-Brentano, "On the Science of Morals," was rejected as well. In late 1876, Masaryk began to write an article "On Progress, Evolution and Civilization," to be included in a volume honoring A.V. Šembera, professor of Slavic philology in Vienna, whom Masaryk had met the year before. Indeed Šembera's daughter Zdeňka had become one of his closest friends. This article was published in March 1877,[67] and that summer *Moravská Orlice,* a Brno periodical, accepted the other article inspired by Funck-Brentano's book: it was entitled "Laws of Civilization and the Future of the Slavs."[68]

There was a Czech society in Leipzig to which workers, artisans and students belonged, but Masaryk did not like their simple vulgarity and preferred to avoid the place where they met.[69] He was aroused by the so-called Woltmann Affair, about which he learned from newspapers and from his correspondents in Moravia. Alfred Woltmann, professor of history of art in Prague, had told a students' club that Czech art had a distinctly German character. This led to a demonstration of protest, and Woltmann was put out of his classroom by angry Czech students. The incident became widely known, and Woltmann was offered a post at Strasbourg University. Masaryk considered such protests likely to hurt the Czechs' reputation abroad, and he condemned the use of force which, he said, always brings about an opposite reaction: "Our nation works for its own fall; if it perishes, it will be due to its own guilt, not that of foreign nations."[70]

His acquaintances in Leipzig included several Czech students, a Serb from whom Masaryk learned much about the character of South Slavs in the course of conservations carried on in French, and a few Romanians with whom he regularly held lengthy discussions. Masaryk's friendship with J.B. Pjech, publisher and author, gave him an opportunity to learn about the Lusatian Serbs, who were said to be in the process of Germanization.[71] Masaryk's friends also included a small circle of university men with whom he shared intellectual interests: his landlady's son, Dr. Göring; the Englishman Justus Lockwood; three German students; and Alfred Schlesinger, Masaryk's former student who had come to Leipzig with him to study law.[72] Another of Masaryk's acquaintances (but not a member of the circle) was an eighteen-year-old Moravian from Prostějov, Edmund Husserl, who, though now of German persuasion, was Masaryk's compatriot. They attended lectures and meetings at the philosophical society and Masaryk talked to him about Vienna and Brentano; they discussed religion and politics.[73]

Masaryk had gone to Leipzig wiht no definite program of study, and his interests were divided among psychology, physiology, philosophy, and theology. He sat under Drobisch, Zollner, Wundt, Roscher, and the divinity professors Luthardt, Kanis, and Fricke, concentrating at this time more on theology than on philosophy. He had previously read a good deal of literature on the occult, and in Leipzig he became interested also in spiritualism; from this he was led to a careful study of hypnotism.[75]

Probably the strongest personal influence on Masaryk in Leipzig was exerted by Gustav Theodor Fechner. Fechner was at this time over seventy-five years old and had long ceased lecturing, but he remained a popular and much revered figure. In private conservations he continued to expound his ideas on "psychophysics," a doctrine based on the relations between the body and spirit and their immortality (there is no death, was his thesis) and on the compatibility of science and religious faith. Masaryk was a frequent visitor at his house. He did not accept Fechner's theological views in their entirely, but he was impressed by the general example of a great scholar and scientist who professed religious faith in an age of materialism, as he was by his argument that religion must be essential to man because of its appearance everywhere within mankind's history. Fechner's conviction that religions, like everything else, develop and perfect themselves in the course of adapting to new needs and conditions provided inspiration for Masaryk's later determination to discover a religion that would be in concord with science.[76]

Masaryk did not change his essentially pro-Catholic and anti-Protestant attitude during his stay in Leipzig (an attitude, it must be added, combined by that time with personal disbelief in the teachings of the Roman Church and occasional doubts about the future of religion),[77] but nonetheless he realized that Catholicism was not the only religion that could be a source of social cohesion and stability. He identified what he considered to be the characteristic features of Protestant theology: individualism and subjective inquiry, free search and free thought, unhampered by the objective and universalist orthodoxy of the Roman Church, but in these various components he detected a danger for faith and, as a corollary, for the social order.[78]

The time spent in Leipzig provided Masaryk with an opportunity to make comparisons in another sphere as well. Germany in the 1870s, after its victory over France of a few years before, was rapidly developing its industry, trade and communications, while in political and social life the influence of organized labor was becoming increasingly felt. It was difficult for Masaryk to abstain from making comparisons unfavorable to Vienna and Austria, and even to the Czechs. He applauded the strong influence of a unified and united nation.[79] The thought of the superiority of a single national state over the amorphous, characterless multinational Empire may first have occurred to the cosmopolitan Masaryk at this time.

Masaryk had always been a devout reader of fiction. When an illness combined with a general nervous and mental crisis befell him early in the spring of 1877 (the nature of this affliction is unclear, but it lasted for several months), he found himself unable to continue his philosophical and scientific studies; but he spent weeks walking and reading novels. English literature was his favorite: he read a great deal of Dickens, urged a correspondent to get hold of *Lalla Rookh* by Thomas Moore, and could find no words to describe *A Life for a Life* by Mrs. D.M. Craik, which moved him deeply. He felt that no reader could help but identify with the characters.[80] He also read Turgenev's *Smoke* and *Virgin Soil* and *Kinder der Welt* by Paul Heyse.

In the middle of June a guest, Charlotte Garrigue, arrived to stay with Masaryk's landlady. She was twenty-seven years old, daughter of the president of the Fire Insurance Company Germania, New York, and her family had long been friendly with Masaryk's landlady, Mrs. Göring. Masaryk was impressed from the very first moment by her intelligence, knowledge, artistic interests, manners and family background. Her arrival coincided with his convalescence, and the two spent many hours together reading and discussing Goethe, Shakespeare, Mill's *Subjection of Women* and Buckle's *The History of Civilization in England.* They made excursions into the country; they attended concerts and plays in Leipzig. Two months after they met, Masaryk proposed and after a short time was accepted.[81] Charlotte Garrigue went back to New York, and Masaryk, who had decided to apply for a university lectureship, returned to Vienna. Soon thereafter Masaryk learned that his fiancée had suddenly taken ill, and he went to New York. She had recovered by the time he arrived there and they were married in Brooklyn on 15 March 1878. In a gesture unusual for a Central European, Masaryk adopted his wife's maiden name as his own middle name. A week later they sailed for Europe. But before they did, Masaryk seriously considered the possibility of remaining in America and finding a post as a professor or journalist.[82]

Charlotte Garrigue was an outstanding personality in her own right and it is strange that no biography of her has yet been written, for it could be an extraordinary book. In his conversations with Čapek, Masaryk reminisced about his late wife:

> She was beautiful to look at; she had a magnificent intellect, better than mine. . . . She loved mathematics. All through her life her desire was for precise knowledge: but she did not lack feeling on that account. She was deeply religious; death was to her as the passage from one chamber to another, so unshakeable was her belief in immortality. In regard to morals she had not a vestige of that moral anarchism which was so widespread in

Europe . . . ; for that reason, too, she was decided and firm on
political and social questions. She was absolutely uncompromising, and utterly truthful: these two qualities had a great influence on my own development . . . .[83]

It is perhaps only a speculation, but it would seem that this highly
talented woman influenced Masaryk even more than he seemed to be
able to acknowledge himself. He recalled that she helped him in his political battles and in "all my political activity" but this might be understood to mean that she adopted his political position for her own. This
was not the case. Charlotte Masaryk joined the Social Democratic party,
not Masaryk's own Realist party, and as Masaryk recalled—with approval,
of course—"when, in 1906, the workmen made a demonstration demanding free and equal suffrage and secret ballot, my wife walked in their
procession."[84] While there no doubt was a very close intellectual and
spiritual collaboration and companionship between them, it is quite
possible—this is a question for the biographer—that Charlotte exercised
a subtle but nonetheless profound influence in the evolution of Masaryk's
politics. As we suggested in the introduction (and as we will show in
later chapters), in his earlier years Masaryk was preoccupied with a search
for a comprehensive solution of the crisis of modern civilization. Charlotte, we may assume, shared his view that something was profoundly
wrong with the modern world—but, from what we know, she tended
to go about improving the world in a more realistic, matter-of-fact way.
Perhaps it was she who helped turn Masaryk toward a recognition of the
critical importance of the practical issues of the day, of concrete individual
actions, measures, reforms? The young Masaryk was scornful of reforms
and "little reforms" (*Reförmchen*)—the mature man recognized them as
useful. Could it have been also owing to Charlotte's inspiration and example—did she not join the reform-oriented Social Democracy, did she not
believe in the crucial importance of politics (*vide* her support of suffrage
reform)—that Masaryk moderated the scope of his designs without in any
way sacrificing his moral commitment?

Before we resume the story of Masaryk's academic career, let us run
ahead of chronology and digress briefly on his family story in the following years.[85] The young couple made their home in Vienna from 1878
to 1882, and there two children were born to them: Alice, in 1879, and

Herbert, in 1880. In Prague, where the family went from Vienna, Jan was born in 1886, Eleanora, in 1889 (she died the same year), and, last, Olga, in 1891.[85]

The life of Charlotte Masaryk was overshadowed by her family and her husband's public career, but it did nevertheless have a public dimension too. She wrote and published on music (she knew and admired the work of Czech composers) and, as we have noted, took strong interest in social and political questions. During the war she suffered from a nervous breakdown from which she never recovered. She was a patient in a clinic when her husband returned to Prague in December 1918. She died in 1923.

The decision to return to Europe meant that Masaryk would seek an academic appointment in Vienna. To receive one, a candidate had to fulfill several requirements, the most important of which was the writing of a dissertation. Before he left for America, Masaryk had submitted a thesis entitled "The Principles of Sociology—Part One," with which he enclosed a formal application and a second autobiography. "Concerning my philosophical tendency," he wrote in it, "I started from Plato and proceeded via Aristotle in the new empirical direction. Together with Plato and Aristotle, Hume, Comte, Mill were my teachers."[86] This thesis was examined by Professors Zimmermann, Brentano, Gomperz and Vogt.

Once back in Vienna, he learned that his thesis had been rejected,[87] but he was determined not to give up his hopes of a university appointment. He supported himself and his wife as a private tutor and temporary teacher of German in a high school while he worked on a new thesis, a study of suicide as a mass phenomenon of modern civilization. This dissertation he duly submitted late in 1878. The examiners (the same four who had rejected the first) seemed rather confused by it; several times the announcement of their verdict was postponed. Finally they decided to admit Masaryk to further examinations on the strength of the first part, which they felt had been worked out with great precision.[88] The examiners also agreed that their decision should be based not so much on the intrinsic merit of Masaryk's contribution as on his personal qualities. The committee decided that the biography (*Curriculum vitae*) which Masaryk had written in 1875 should be enclosed with the set of documents related to his application. On 7 March 1879 the final favorable decision was taken.[89] Two weeks later Masaryk delivered a trial lecture on "Plato's Doctrine of Anamnesis" and was examined orally. Soon thereafter his appointment was confirmed by the Minister of Education. In April he delivered his first lecture for undergraduates; the course he offered in his first term was "A History and Critique of Pessimism."[90]

Masaryk also continued his own philosophical studies, read Hume, and was much occupied with the question of scepticism and with the foundations of knowledge, science and religion.[91] In Hume's reasoning processes he saw grave dangers to religious belief. Although Masaryk had not surrendered to certain arguments that he nevertheless considered unanswerable, clinging to his conception of religion as an indispensable requisite for the individual and for society, Hume had deprived him of an inner conviction that he would never regain. Masaryk found some consolation in Hume's doctrine of morals, in the fact that the great sceptic had professed a degree of sympathy and humanity. The characters of men interested Masaryk no less than what they wrote, and to his bewilderment he found that Hume, "and this is a serious thing—with his scepticism, is *calm*."[92] In his years of teaching in Vienna, Masaryk also read widely: Goethe, Grillparzer, Lenau, and German writers from Bohemia, Hartmann and Meissner;[93] Tolstoy and Turgenev, and later Dostoyevsky.

On the invitation of the Czech Academic Union, Masaryk delivered a lecture on hypnotism in 1880, which appeared in print in Prague.[94] The following year his dissertation was published under the title *Der Selbstmord als sociale Massenerscheinung der modernen Civilization* (Suicide as a Social Mass Phenomenon of Modern Civilization). Masaryk regarded it throughout his life as his most important work. "We need religion, we need religious spirit," he insisted as he surveyed the crucial problems of his contemporary world.[95]

The author himself, as we have said, was at this time nominally a Catholic but in fact an agnostic. But to reject religion entirely was something Masaryk could not do: religion was to him the supreme and ultimate basis of everything in life.[96] Catholicism with all its dogmas (the latest of which proclaimed papal infallibility) was obviously out of the question; the only practical alternative was Protestantism.[97] Masaryk decided that he would formally become a Protestant. He knew a minister at Klobouky, F. Císař with whom he had often had lengthy discussions during summer holidays spent in Moravia, and he asked him for admission to the

Reformed Presbyterian Church (Helvetian Confession). Císař was un-
successful in his efforts to dissuade Masaryk, although he did all he could:
it was obvious to him that Masaryk was not a true Protestant and saw in
Protestantism, quite wrongly, a purely rationalist religion, that was
supposedly free from the elements of pure faith. As a last resort, he
required Masaryk to recite the Apostolic Creed. Knowing that Masaryk
did not believe in its articles, Císař hoped thus to avoid having to take him
into the church. But Masaryk did as he had been asked and on 31 August
1880 was formally signed into the church register. While his friends in
Vienna described his Protestantism as very free indeed, family evenings
at the Masaryks were now dedicated to reading the Bible; to exhibit the
proper democratic attitude, Masaryk also invited their housemaid to join
in. It was only with great difficulty that Císař persuaded Masaryk to give
up his expressed hope of becoming a Protestant minister.[98]

When it was announced in the course of the following year that Prague
University was to be divided into separate German and Czech universities,
the question of his future plans became particularly pressing to Masaryk.
His lectureship in Vienna was a temporary post. The prospect of a regular
professorship in Vienna was negligible, and the only German-language
university that appeared within reach was that at Czernowitz (the present
day Chernitvsti) in far-off Bukovina. Since Prague seemed to offer better
opportunities, Masaryk decided in its favor, though not without weighing
the odds first. Whatever his interests, views and beliefs might be, they
were not subordinated to nationalist considerations. By going to Prague
he would have to submit to having his words and deeds scrutinized by
Czech society, where national issues, in particular the struggle against the
Germans, were of foremost concern. Masaryk also feared Prague for the
provincial atmosphere he imagined he would find there, with its narrow-
mindedness, lack of tolerance, and dull intellectural pretensions.[99] There
was one thing, however, that probably made Prague appear preferable even
to Vienna. Had he been primarily interested in knowledge for its own
sake, an academic inquirer and a seeker after objective truth, Prague would
not have been the place to go. But Masaryk was committed to action,
not theory—he wanted to be a preacher, a guide, a popularizer and a
teacher. Who could possibly need him more than the Czech people?

The issue also had practical and more personal aspects. As Masaryk's
academic troubles had made clear, Vienna University was not the most

congenial place for a man of his outlook. Prague, on the other hand, offered not only more promising opportunities for action but financial security for Masaryk and his family in addition. We must not ignore the prosaic fact that in Vienna he had a family to feed, but no job, while Prague offered financial stability and even a measure of comfort. The Ministry of Education wanted Masaryk to go to Prague, but first a university committee there would have to agree to the appointment. That body, after having received the opinions of Professor Kvičala (Prague) and Zimmermann (Vienna), supported the nomination.[100] Submitting the appointment to the Emperor, the Minister expressed the hope that Masaryk would exert a moderating influence on his Czech colleagues.[101] (Since Masaryk's Czech colleagues presumably lacked, in the Minister's judgment, "moderation" in nationalist feeling, the government must have regarded him as free of this particular emotion.)

Masaryk's decision to accept a professorship at Prague conclusively removed from the realm of practical consideration all the other options he had considered at various times: his early hopes for a diplomatic career or for an academic post at an Austrian university outside Bohemia; ministry in a Reformed church; or even emigration overseas. Masaryk was going to Prague as a relatively new man in Czech national life and clearly as an outsider in the Prague society he was about to join by virtue of his official position. This was a momentous event. Masaryk had finally chosen his profession—and had made a definitive commitment to Czech nationality.[102]

CHAPTER II

IN SEARCH OF AUTHORITY:
RELIGION OR SCIENCE?

Can one speak of Masaryk's political thought at that point in his life when he was about to leave Vienna for Prague to become a professor of philosophy? We remember that his doctoral thesis was a technical work on an aspect of Plato's philosophy (but not his political philosophy) and that his longer monograph on suicide, which qualified him for university teaching, was a philosophical or sociological, but not a political, treatise. What were Masaryk's politics then at the time of his move to Prague?

Our biographical outline provided a partial answer when we noted that Masaryk accepted the political structure of the Habsburg Monarchy as something given and did not question the fact that the Czech lands were ruled by the Habsburgs. Clearly he was not a political nationalist, nor can he be called a cultural nationalist, despite certain mild expressions of Moravian or Czech ethnic feeling. This chapter will examine Masaryk's political thought by focusing on his Vienna articles on Plato and on progress, and on his thesis on suicide. Later our discussion will move to an analysis of Masaryk's book on concrete logic as an expression of his views as they developed in the 1880s in the Prague period. These works will be treated as statements of Masaryk's political thought, an outgrowth of his search for authority. The Czech scholar, Milan Machovec, in our view has acutely observed: "Philosophy or politics? This was *not* Masaryk's question. Ever since his youth . . . politics was for him identical with philosophy."[1]

There is a common theme, then, in all the writings of Masaryk: an analysis of the problems of the modern world and a search for their solution, based on his conception of human nature, of man as a moral and a political being. Masaryk's search for the salvation of man rather than for abstract truth found frank expression in a book ostensibly devoted to logic and philosophy in general. He quoted an early Father of the Church, St. Ambrose, as saying "non in dialectica complacuit Deo salvum facere populum suum," which may be rendered, "not through philosophy has it pleased God to save His people." Masaryk was making it plain that his concern was not at all with pure philosophizing.

In *Suicide*, Masaryk revealed that his utmost concern was with a faith for the people, and the same theme ran through the book on logic. In the former he had not yet clearly stated that faith entailed not only belief but also a leader or group of leaders who would formulate and interpret faith authoritatively. He did not yet link the problem of faith with the problem of leadership, although he had discussed leadership in very general and abstract terms in an essay on Plato's patriotism. His *Concrete Logic*, written in Prague, came closer to making this linkage when he proposed a scientific outlook and recommended vesting the authority to formulate it in a scholarly corporation, the Academy. He was becoming aware that, as he would put it still later quite explicitly, "To believe means to believe something and somebody—there is no other authority but knowledge and the knowing man."[2]

It is not our task here to define authority exhaustively, but simply to scrutinize it within certain limits. One definition might be that authority implies "the voluntary acceptance by one man or group of men of some decisions of another,"[3] or we might say that "authority is useful to society only when it possesses an ethical foundation, which alone distinguishes it from mere might."[4] We may feel that "obeying a command because of its authority entails obedience without considering the case which could be advanced to justify the command. If one does what somebody else wants only after deciding that there are good reasons for doing this, one is not acting in obedience to the other's authority."[5] Masaryk believed that the imperative challenge to the thinkers of his day was to construct a system that would give meaning to man's life and provide him with an authority to replace that time-honored authority which had lost its effectiveness. Our concern here, therefore, is primarily with his search for an all-embracing synthesis of thought as a guide to the good life.

Suicide as a Social Mass Phenomenon of Modern Civilization, published in German in 1881, was presented as a piece of sociological and philosophical research.[6] Its originality, in the view of the contemporary scholar Anthony Giddens, lies not so much in its statistical documentation as in Masaryk's attempt to provide a sociological interpretation of suicide "on the basis of the crucial importance of religion as a source of moral control in society." Giddens argues that Masaryk's work contributed to the development of a "distinctively sociological theory of suicide," influencing, among others, the work of Emile Durkheim.[7] But Masaryk's interest in the subject was not, initially at least, purely academic. There is a revealing autobiographical statement in his later article on "Modern Tendency to Suicide" (1896; Masaryk called it "Suicidism"):

> I was not ten years old when, for the first time, I began to think a great deal about suicide . . . . I can still see before me that gate leading to the stable, on which a farm-hand from our neighborhood hanged himself. . . . from that time for the gate . . . became taboo . . . a place of horror . . . . even now, as in my childhood, suicide is to me something horrible, something darkly unnatural, something inconceivable . . . . I regard the act as . . . something terrible, unthinkable, something that pollutes the brain and burdens and darkens the soul . . . .

Here Masaryk related two rather horrible tales of men who were buried alive, and concluded: "For a long time this prevented me from sleeping quietly, and, even now, it sticks in my brain like a sting in an open wound."[8]

Masaryk argued that in recent times the number of suicides had been steadily increasing and that indeed a mass tendency toward suicide could be detected. He sought to prove that the real causes for this phenomenon lay in the spiritual, i.e., intellectual, moral, and religious, deficiencies of the culture.[9] Although a higher educational level did not in itself lead men to commit suicide, it made their lives so much more refined, rich, and diversified that an intellectual choice between being and not being seemed open to them. Those who had no education whatsoever on the other hand, in the narrowness of their intellect, their simplicity and modesty, were satisfied with life. This was so because the education of the time was not *genuine* but *semi-education (Halbbildung).* Masaryk found a casaul relation between the growth of public instruction that provided such semi-education and the tendency to suicide; other things being equal, suicide was most prevalent in those countries where an unsystematic and impractical educational system obtained.[10]

Masaryk supported his contentions by statistical data. Although he granted that some of his figures were old, he explained ingenuously that this did not matter, because suicide was always the same. This was not a scientific position, of course, but in any case it would be incorrect, in our opinion, to treat Masaryk's work as a piece of empirical research, even though we may agree with Giddens that Masaryk made a contribution toward a sociological treatment of the problem of suicide. Rather than to check Masaryk's facts and the inferences supposedly based on them, we would tend to agree with a recent scholar who carefully examined *Suicide* and concluded that Masaryk had based his conclusions on very flimsy evidence. "One could almost say that Masaryk decided in advance that irreligiosity was the key to modern suicide, and that *Suicide* was written to justify this position."[11] If one looks at Masaryk's work in this way, one simply accepts most of his statements, like the following one, as expressions of his political and philosophical tenets, without worrying about whether evidence did, or even could, support or refute them. Thus Masaryk claimed that his figures proved that the motives for which men and women killed themselves were "predominantly immoral," and that suicides, with few exceptions, were victims of moral weakness and instability.[12] He believed that the tendency to suicide sprang not only from "half-education" but also from a lack of moral restraint. He claimed to see in the mass phenomenon of suicide modern society in its fully correct light: a civilized society whose weariness with life originated in a deficient intellectual and moral culture. That is, its world view is not sufficiently harmonious and good to make life satisfying. With this, he returned to the need for spiritual guidance, in short, for religion.[13]

It is not our concern to inquire what religion is and how it grows in man; it is enough for us to know that it is there and

and it invests men, like the invisible scent of a flower, with
its own value: wipe it away and the flower will delight your
eye but you will no more find it so fine; take away the religious
feeling from man and you will have made of him a being which
you can esteem and perhaps also admire but can love no more
with a full heart.[14]

With his whole heart Masaryk believed that religion would bring consolation in all life's circumstances, hope in time of hardship, and would
strengthen the love of mankind and the belief in immortality. A religious
man in all conditions of life remains joyous; if religion is absent, if the
authority of the Church decays, then confidence, hope and the joy of life
will also disappear: no truly beautiful life can be lived without religion.
The great masses of people, when religion wanes, are left with nothing to
replace it.[15] Accordingly the tendency to suicide has its roots in the
absence of a religious spirit in his times.[16]

Masaryk then sought to trace historically whether, as nations changed
in religious commitment over the course of time, there had been an increase or decline in the ratio of suicides, stating again his two basic assum-
tions: that suicide was a social mass phenomenon; and that the tendency
to suicide had in all times had identical causes.[17] Two extremes were
compared: primitive peoples with virtually no tendency to suicide and
the highly civilized nations where suicide abounded. To him this morbid
tendency had developed gradually; it was a product of progress and
civilization.[18]

The two spiritual powers behind modern society, science and religion,
were so much in conflict that neither could provide really effective
guidance. In the absence of a unitary world outlook intellectual and
moral chaos was bound to ensue. In this sense suicide was a consequence
of the "break-down of a uniform world outlook which had been consistently enforced by Christianity amongst the masses in all civilized
countries." The struggle of free thought against positive religion led to a
religious void among the masses that meant intellectual and moral
anarchy—and death.[19]

Although Masaryk believed that man "as much needs religion to live
as he needs air to breathe,"[20] he developed the thesis that in the course
of history mankind had gone through successive cycles of faith and the

lack of it; on this generalization he conferred the status of an empirical law of history and sociology.[21] For example, after a period of lack of religious faith in antiquity, Christianity had appeared with its doctrine of monotheism and the immortality of the soul. As interpreted by him, Christianity sanctified the relation of man to God; perfect unselfishness was elevated to the status of a moral rule and became a new life-principle for every believer. Christianity raised believers above nonbelievers; a non-philosophical Christian stood above a philosophical heathen, even if he were a Marcus Aurelius.[22]

In Christianity itself Masaryk distinguished two fundamental systems of thought, based on opposing principles of authority. The first was the medieval authoritarian faith that wholly captured men's thought and will. The uniform world outlook of the Middle Ages radiated peace and contentment; there was no tendency to suicide. Human society was organized in a homogeneous way; each individual had a fixed place. Through the influence of the medieval church, the minds of men remained fully satisfied, and over a long period men felt themselves spiritually secure. Religion suffused a spiritual atmosphere over all mundane affairs, accustomed men to a single spiritual leadership and offered strong support under the dreary vicissitudes of medieval life.[23]

The systematic order and organization of medieval society was, however, only external, resting as it did primarily on authority. A uniform world outlook, Masaryk believed, could be established either through authority more or less external (for example, papal infallibility) or by an authority originating within man himself, an organic process of free persuasion leading to an internal certainty (as in Protestantism).

Moreover, such a perspective might to varying degrees be false; since there was only one truth, only one *Weltanschauung* could be the true one. Catholicism, with an infallible Pope at its head, had organized society in this spirit and with the best intentions, but it could not establish a permanent state of harmony. Masaryk thought it obvious that mankind strives to reach a spontaneous, voluntary and conscious unity without interference from an external authority; in principle, he wanted mankind to arrive at unity through freedom. Of these two methods of social integration—an external authority as in Catholicism or the free inquiry of Protestantism—because the former case was easier to adopt, a strong and united Catholicism arose that was superior to "splintered" Protestantism.[24]

Protestantism, nevertheless was a natural development from Catholicism.[25] To identify Protestantism with freedom of conscience and tolerance was correct only insofar as Protestantism was used in a general sense; many of the confessions that actually existed permitted little freedom and were in fact intolerant of it. Masaryk conceived of Protestantism and Catholicism as antithetical historical principles, the former representing "religio-ethical individualism." He added that since the sixteenth century the real struggle had been between belief and lack of belief, and this was of course to be attributed to science.[26]

Thus Masaryk made a fundamental distinction between a world outlook imposed from without and one adopted voluntarily. In the second, another criterion was involved: the scientific tenability of the system. Could not an imposed doctrine be true, or a voluntarily adopted one—unscientific? Masaryk seems to have considered the possibility of such combinations when he admitted that sometimes external authority might be of help in the imposition of a scientifically valid system. While medieval or Catholic Christianity had been characterized by the rule of an individual and the application of external authority, this did not guarantee that the ideology thus enforced would be in accordance with modern science, thereby leaving the ground open for intellectual dissent and revolt. On the other hand, the prospects for the adoption of a religion of the Protestant variety, which would have to prevail spontaneously and without direction from above, were minimal.

Masaryk was cautious about committing himself to any definite forecast about the future shape of religion, but in 1877 he wrote to Zdeňka Šembera that in his view Christianity had fulfilled its cultural role and was on the wane. Whether Christianity would vanish completely and be replaced by a new popular religion or continue in a new form to provide satisfaction for men's souls was a question he was not prepared to answer.[27] He appeared to be more willing to disclose his thoughts in the concluding pages of *Suicide*: he mused that his time seemed made for a new religion.

> Often I think ... that it could, exactly like medieval Catholicism, inaugurate a new, better Middle Ages, after which a new period of free thought would begin, and so on, until through alternating periods of faith and lack of faith finally one flock and one shepherd would come into being.[28]

But, whatever the future might hold, Masaryk the old admirer of Plato looked upon one possibility with particular sympathy:

> Were it possible to guide the masses, systematically and logi-
> cally, step by step, from the simple to the complex, from the
> easy to the difficult, from error to truth, there would be no
> struggle of conflicting views, no superficiality; every new achieve-
> ment would develop naturally from the earlier stages of culture.[29]

Here he stressed again, as he had in the article on Plato, his ideal relation-ship between the masses and their educated leaders. This problem of leadership and popular allegiance was to remain one of his most central and constant preoccupations.[30]

Masaryk assumed that men have the freedom not only to choose their own ideals but also to command their own motives and direct their own actions. When he called suicides immoral he repudiated his own argument: if they found themselves under a greater pressure than they could with-stand, one could not condemn their actions. Elsewhere in *Suicide* Masaryk wrote: "Knowledge gives us the power to intervene in the re-lations of cause and effect; we can set up certain goals as our ideals and choose appropriate means." Insofar as we are able to analyze the reasons why we act as we do, we are able to distinguish the influences of particular factors and so direct our lives toward the realization of our ethical goals. We do not always pursue the strongest motive; other motives affect us as well. Before making a decision we reflect and make a choice, we look for those means that will best serve our aim. The choice we make depends on character; and that is something we form ourselves. If a life-or-death decision depends ultimately on the man who is free to choose his goals and direct his actions, suicide is not inevitable. It was Masaryk's conclu-sion that a society need not remain static; if it resolves to change, it can do so, and in such a manner that suicide will be unknown.[31]

As the contemporary tendency to suicide had been caused by increas-ing withdrawal from religion, so the malady could be completely healed when irreligion and the superficiality that accompanies it have been set aside. But what can one do, Masaryk asked, if the tendency to suicide and irreligiosity is a periodic occurrence?[32] Indeed, the law implied inevitable passing from one stage to the other; it could therefore be assumed that the present stage of disbelief would be succeeded by an era of faith. Masaryk did not expect that the course of events alone would again make men hunger for religion; nor was he prepared to admit (as might have been expected from his theory of historical stages) that in some periods men could live without religion while at other times they could not.

Giambattista Vico was particularly close to Masaryk in his interpretation of history;[33] Masaryk himself used to mention Vico's name in his writings, and he considered him the first great sociologist.[34] Vico had a somewhat different assessment of the importance of religion. While Masaryk had come to the conclusion that men always feel a need for religion and sink into a state of crisis when deprived of it but are entirely free to recover their lost faith at any time, Vico thought that religious declines and revivals depended on the overall conditions prevailing in a society in any given age.[35] In surveying the sociological ambiance that he felt was conducive to suicide, Masaryk considered of first importance those conditions that related directly to man's intellect and emotions and to the formation of his character in response to his individual view of the world around him. Suicide had its source in the whole character of man.

We should note in passing Masaryk's concepts of determinism, indeterminism and fatalism, and his contention that freedom was possible only in a determinist world.[36] But there was surely a sharp conflict between his belief in universal determinism and the existence of social laws on the one hand and his belief in free will on the other. This conflict remained unresolved: it was evident, for example, in his later attempt to build a world view based on a classification of the sciences, and again in his critique of Marxism.[37]

An analysis of the views of any political and social thinker should seek to elucidate his concept of human nature. Unlike those who consider human nature a product of historical evolution, and therefore capable of change, Masaryk saw it as constant and unchanging. "Men are what they have always been,"[38] was a characteristic phrase. He assumed, as has emerged from this discussion so far, that man is a free and responsible moral agent, but he did not grant equally to all men a capacity to make correct decisions, especially in the domain of public affairs. All men were morally free, but some were destined to be leaders and others were fit only to be followers. Let us continue then our discussion of Masaryk's view of human nature, which so far has led us to the conclusion that he did not resolve the question of determinism versus free will (other than to postulate the operative validity of the latter), and turn to his position on leadership, political and intellectual, and the masses. In *Concrete Logic* he maintained that man is more practical than theoretical, made more for work than for reflection, and tends to rely more on traditional authority than on judgment.[39] Forty years later Masaryk's view of man was essentially the same. In his account of World War I and his own role in it, Masaryk stated: ". . . men are wont to make their earthly and heavenly gods in their own image . . . . Politically and religiously they fashion their ideal of the future after their own capacities . . . . Parliaments represent parties, coteries, and strong and influential . . . personalities, rather than the nation, the people, the masses."[40]

It is a fair conclusion from this and other statements that Masaryk held a basically low estimate of the "masses." His evident lack of regard for their political wisdom or historical importance prompted Emil Ludwig, a prominent political writer of the 1930s, to comment in a conversation with Masaryk: "You have mentioned all the factors that make up a democracy except the masses. It seems that you did not come very much into touch with them before the war." Masaryk did not react directly. He discoursed on his school years, and on his interest in socialism and in Marx, and concluded: "The Masses—a word which just like the Nation, People, Church, State, is understood properly by few people and misapplied by many. All collective units [groups] are organized and will be led. Were Marx, Engels . . . Masses?"[41] It was on the activity of critical and thinking individuals that the progress of society would depend, and one may infer that it was in this light that Masaryk regarded his own scholarly activity.

Masaryk first presented his political ideas, and his reflections on leadership, intellectual and political, in particular, in the essay on "Plato as a Patriot." He applauded Plato's dictum that the good society should be led by philosophers. Their right to rule was a function of their mental superiority, and their rule would bring forth harmony within the state. Wisdom would spread to all the people who would be happy to obey superiors who governed in the best possible way. Everyone would take care of his own duties, the idealistic young Masaryk wrote, for "injustice grows only when man interferes with someone else's affairs . . . ."[42]

Since the welfare of the state depended on good government, rulers should be properly prepared; statesmen adept in sociology would be required.[43] In his very first article, "Theory and Practice," Masaryk gave the following description of this new science of sociology: "If politics is to be a science, it must have a subject with which it, as a science, is concerned . . . . As medicine has to care about the healing of diseases and prevention of diseases, so sociology must have . . . human society as its subject, sociology must care about the *welfare* of this society."[44]

The young Masaryk had already decided that politics was a domain to be best controlled by experts, by the scientists of government and society, doing what was good for the people, not simply what the people wished. Just as the patient is not himself allowed to select the method of treatment, so implicitly the populace was to benefit from, although not qualified to determine, the policies pursued by its leaders. There is a certain similarity between Masaryk's position as formulated in the 1870s (and reaffirmed later), and certain arguments advanced by John Stuart Mill, whose works he knew and often admired. Mill saw politics, as Graeme Duncan points out, as a cognitive science, "satisfying the needs rather than demands of the people, and seeking the popular good rather than the popular will." Yet Mill retained doubts as to the integrity and reliability even of wise leaders. Although he was willing to grant extensive powers to the experts, he wanted them subject to election (although not necessarily by a popular, mass electorate).[45] Masaryk, like Mill, wanted to improve all men, but he did not express any fears about the leaders' integrity— by no means regarding it as necessary to investigate their actions by legal means—and at least in the early years he did not concern himself with subjecting the men of wisdom to an electoral challenge. Masaryk took firm exception to any who accused Plato of lacking concern for the people:

> . . . . it is [not] because of a negligence on the part of Plato that he speaks so little in his State about people; and by no means shall we allow anyone to think that Plato did so because of enmity towards democracy . . . . It is self-evident that when there is the right ruler and the right government no wrong can be done to any part . . . .[46]

Masaryk, quite aware that Plato's insistence on the rule of philosophers had been subjected to criticism, hastened to point out that Plato's philosophy, based as it was not only on theory but on practice was quite different from academic philosophy. True, he could not see the philosophers of his day giving direction to men's lives; they spoke of practical philosophy without knowing what it meant. Plato, on the other hand, advocated a state wholly governed by philosophy,[47] where any discrepancy between theory and practice would be abolished. This fusion of theory and practice could be realized only under suitable political conditions, and Masaryk well realized this. He considered Plato's world outlook and his advocacy of enlightened absolutism admirable:[48] "Plato knew very well . . . that government based on laws is better than the lawless rule of an ignoble man; but it is not so good as government without laws when a noble man is in power." Masaryk agreed absolutely. Absence of laws would have, Masaryk thought, another advantage: statesmen would no longer be judged by isolated successes but by their total contribution to the state.[49]

Plato did not live to see his state become a reality; and indeed in his old age he abandoned his prescription that rulers be philosophers, emphasizing only that rulers be moral and just. He came to recognize the importance of religion, and Masaryk compared him in this respect to the French philosopher Auguste Comte. Both Plato and Comte turned toward religion: Plato to mythology; Comte to Catholicism. While Masaryk felt that modern statesmen and philosophers, ignorant of the true nature of religion and its relation to the state, might learn from Plato and Comte, he made it clear he did not mean that philosophers of his own time should become rulers. All he recommended, he said, was that those who participated in government have a knowledge of sociology.[50]

Several years later, in 1881, when Masaryk was writing about his own time, he did not entirely renounce his earlier convictions as to the ideal form of government; he still advocated a religious revival, condemning in strong terms all the politics of his day—whether parliamentary, reformist or revolutionary. He rejected political action in the first place because he found it ineffective: if the crisis of civilization was indeed brought about by the decline of religious faith, one could scarcely expect to resolve it by political means.[51] Political and economic conditions were only external manifestations of the inner spiritual life.[52] If this were so, it

followed that revolutionary tendencies and movements were symptoms
of spiritual illness. Later, in his critique of Marxism, Masaryk returned
to this concept: "Modern man does not fall into despair simply because
of want and poverty, nor does he, on the other hand, become angry
simply because of poverty. This mood has another source: in the head
and in the heart; in philosophy."[53]

It is clear from these statements, which span a number of years, that
Masaryk did not think of society as made up of diverse groups in conflict and competition, whether in the legal political arena, e.g., in parliament, or resorting to extralegal, revolutionary methods. The struggle
for material rewards or for power, he thought, was a pathological sym-
ptom, which required treatment in a nonpolitical sphere—in philosophy
and religion—not a fact of life in a normally functioning polity. When
one reads such statements as those just cited, or to which we shall turn
presently, one is inclined to agree with Zdeněk Nejedlý, Masaryk's heretic
disciple (Nejedlý became a Communist, and in the 1950s was a member
of the government and president of the Czechoslovak Academy of
Sciences), who in the 1920s maintained that Masaryk was not really a
sociologist. Masaryk, Nejedlý wrote in 1925, drew attention to those
questions with which sociology was concerned, but he approached them
not sociologically, through a study of society, but through the study of
the individual. What Masaryk called sociology was really practical philosophy which tried to answer the question: "What should man do?"[54]

Masaryk's comments on the nineteenth-century Russian intellectual
and political movements seem to furnish support to the Nejedlý thesis.
He saw the great mass of the Russian people, with their ignorance and
lack of education as strongly church-oriented, and the clergy as equally
without education, with more superstition than sound theological knowledge. Accordingly conflict arose between the deeply religious ordinary
Russian people and the intelligentsia, whom he blamed for having
accepted as their own the antireligious elements of Western civilization:
the educated Russians trod "the ideals of their childhood, the ideals of
the people underfoot." In their opposition to the tsarist regime, Masaryk
commented, "Voltaire, Byron and Schopenhauer have become a new
Gospel for the Russians: dissatisfied with themselves and with all social
institutions, modern Russian youth turn their anger against themselves
and against the restraining authority of the Church and State . . . ."[55]

Masaryk's criticism of modern civilization came out not only as a critique of violence and revolution but also as an indictment of freedom under political systems more liberal than that of Russia. He tended to express this position either in the form of personal statements or of quotations from other writers. "We find the tendency towards suicide amongst nations with various forms of government. It is, however, greater on the whole in free, smaller in unfree, states;" "Haushofer complains of unbridled freedom."[56] A republic was the worst form of government: suicide was more frequent where there was universal equality, while under despotism everyone remained in his assigned place.[57] Present-day nations, he felt, arrange social conditions according to the will of the people—to their detriment. While past societies developed more spontaneously, with accelerating economic progress men's ambitions and aspirations have risen. But their aspirations are misguided if they forget that the economic world is only the external expression of inner spiritual development.[58]

As we have said, the first reason for Masaryk's aversion to politics was that he found political action ineffectual—one wants to say irrelevant; the second that man needs authority.[59] Yet he felt strongly that modern political theories made men seek to throw off the burden of authority and try to escape from the positions into which they were placed by birth—to feel an urge to leave their stations, to aspire to a higher social level. When the excitement of the masses is nourished by ideas of emancipation, he said, passions of all sorts are released. Nations become drunk with emotion, with the value of the individual, with ever-new impressions: suicides increase as delusions exert their influence over the souls of men. How different are the Arabs and the Indians with their primordial usages, with their belief in immutability (*Unveränderlichkeit*) that still prevails in Asia.[60]

Many years later, still pondering the same problem, Masaryk wrote that man must be very objective if he is to overcome the tendency to suicide; Kant had said long ago that introspection was dangerous, leading to conflict. It would seem that the ultimate reason for Masaryk's detestation of politics was that it tended to exalt men's subjective judgments. In other words, he wanted to free man from taking upon his shoulders the whole burden of life.[61] Politics, by enticing man to believe he was more powerful than he really was, caused particular damage. Masaryk undoubtedly felt himself justified in holding unbridled freedom responsible for the fatal diseases of modern civilization.

What should be done? In opposition to what Masaryk considered the morbid and godless dreams of the revolutionists and the illusions of the parliamentary reformers, he constructed his own model for alleviating the dismal conflict of man and evicting the evils inherent in society. Predictably, this was again a call for the intensification of religious feeling. He compared the Roman world in the time of Christ to the society of his day:

> . . . then, as now, a morbid tendency to suicide prevailed; men were dissatisfied and unhappy. . . . in that time of political and social agitation Christ abstained from all politics; how easy it would have been for him to win over hearts through political and socialist [sic] inflammatory agitation. . . . But Christ asked for improvement of character. . . . He wanted men to be good because he knew that only thus they would find rest for their souls.[62]

This was Masaryk's view of world problems in his Vienna years, but he was never to become a preacher or religious reformer. He moved to Prague to become a philosophy professor instead. In Prague his views changed and evolved under the impact of a new environment and in reaction to new challenges. In *The Foundations of Concrete Logic* (1885), Masaryk proposed an alternative to his earlier solution, a new religion that was to replace traditional religion by a philosophical outlook that would abolish all antagonism between religion and science. The feeling of piety, Masaryk wrote, might as easily spring up in response to a theoretico-philosophical religion; it could prevail exactly as had the theological one and could replace it.[63] At this time he was still envisioning a conflict between science and religion. Still later, however, in the German edition of *Concrete Logic* (1887), he declared that there need be no antagonism between the two outlooks—one might simply choose between a theological and a scientific religion.[64] Of these two possible world views, Masaryk, in contrast to his earlier choice in *Suicide,* now chose the latter, on the grounds that truth was always superior to myth and that it was more rewarding to prefer it. Therefore the unified world outlook was to be

established though the work of properly educated scholars. The importance of religion for society had been stressed in *Suicide,* but now Masaryk
expected the scientific point of view to be an inspiring substitute for
the religion that had failed to satisfy the spiritual needs of modern man.
It would teach him to live a whole life.[65] Men could be induced through
indoctrination to accept a scientific rather than a theological way of
life; in other words, the common man could indeed be led to the acceptance of beliefs that to Masaryk were the "right" ones.

But Masaryk never really coordinated his voluminous and sometimes
contradictory discussions of religion, despite the fact that all his writings
were devoted to or touched upon the subject.[66] It held for him an endless
fascination; he said of the religious question: "it has always existed and it
will always exist . . . . All my life experience and study have confirmed
me in this conviction again and again . . . ."[67] Even as late as 1925,
Masaryk was still faithful to the same principles. He said then that a new
philosophy, "the true philosophy and science," would demand "that
men should think, that they should gather wide experience, observing
and comparing the present and the past, and verifying their deducations
from experience." But such a happy state had yet to be achieved.[68]

In the 1880s Masaryk attacked the task of unifying the sciences as a
backdrop for his new scientific religion. A new system providing men
with a "logical orientation" was indispensable; homogeneity of belief
was essential both for the individual and society. Insofar as the social
mechanism depended for its existence on ideas, a uniform world view
would preserve society and direct its progress; Masaryk always clung
to the hope that unanimity among men was an attainable goal. First
the philosophers and scientists had to be united, for any discord or insecurity within the community of scholars would be reflected in dis-
harmony within the populace.[69] Masaryk stressed the importance of
this point of view, saying that if Aristotle had constructed his Logic
as a essential law of philosophy, so might he "with an even greater right"
regard *Concrete Logic* as an essential law of scientific philosophy.

Masaryk divided the sciences into discrete categories beginning with
a division between the theoritical and practical sciences. Theoretical
sciences were subdivided into abstract and concrete sciences. The abstract sciences were: mathematics, mechanics, physics, chemistry, biology,
psychology, and sociology, the latter two belonging alos to the hierarchy

of spiritual sciences, the others belonging to the hierarchies of mathematics and natural sciences. Linguistics, esthetics, and logic were not included. Abstract sciences served as the foundation for concrete ones, e.g., sociology was the foundation of such concrete sciences as ethnology, political science (*Staatswissenschaften*), political economy, statistics and history.[70] This classification reflected Masaryk's hierarchy of human knowledge, to him always inferior to God's knowledge. Abstract sciences were the structures through which the human spirit was guided to the proper objects of its knowledge. But man, who relies more on memory than on reason, cannot recognize them directly, as God does. Only by means of art does man to some extent attain a true direct knowledge.[71]

Sociology, having appeared as an abstract science, was also the basis of two of the practical sciences, politics and ethics, the latter described by Masaryk as "the science of the perfect life." He underlined the importance of practical ethics, feeling that it taught man to formulate his relationship to the universe and to his fellow men. But practical ethics had to be integrated with theoretical science if the result was to be a harmonious life based on a philosophically unified attitude.[72] Masaryk's classification was completed by a set of "artificially constituted sciences", classical philology and theology. It was precisely the task of concrete logic to delimit the spheres of men's intellectual achievement and to construct a single system of total knowledge.[73] Only philosophy had been omitted, and to it Masaryk devoted the last part of his treatise. Philosophy had been reserved for special treatment because he believed it to be the most comprehensive science, embracing indeed total human knowledge, a unified scheme for looking out upon the world.[74]

Since concrete logic was to determine how particular sciences were to be made into an organic whole, logic was a fundamental discipline. But if logic constituted formal science, metaphysics still lay above it as the real science. While concrete logic might organize science in a logical manner, metaphysics was directed toward the substantial issues in scientific work.[75] A uniform outlook would have to be based on all the sciences. Since the abstract sciences were so far the most developed ones, to put them to full use remained a task for the future,[76] and Masaryk was unwilling to predict philosophy's future course. As he put it: "It cannot be demonstrated here, nor is it necessary to do so, exactly how a modern philosophy or metaphysics should be organized so that it would really correspond to the modern sciences; practice will teach us about it, while logic says only how one could go about it. In general it is easier to talk than to act."[77]

Masaryk believed that the task of philosophy was to cultivate the study of nature and man and to blend its conclusions into one harmonious whole through the study of the human spirit. Since a philosopher was apt to be a specialist in another discipline initially, he would reflect the influence of his particular scientific discipline; thus various individual philosophical currents might exist side by side within a broadly unified system. Descartes's thought reflected a physico-mathematical influence, and Comte's a sociological orientation. Since this was so, Masaryk raised the question of whether any one of the sciences might have a superior claim to shaping the others into a uniform whole. To him, psychology was that science. "Since every kind of cognition is simultaneously a psychological phenomenon. . . . we possess materially the best philosophical integrating medium in psychological inquiry."[78] Masaryk rejected Comte's bias for the preeminence of sociology as well as his dynamic viewpoint, declaring himself on the side of one more static. This was consistent with Masaryk's conception of human nature as constant ("men are what they have always been"), rather than as subject to major changes throughout the course of history.

Would not the admission that diverse philosophical outlooks obtained defy Masaryk's purpose? What if scientists in general refused to recognize the leading role of psychology? Or if several schools were to develop within psychology? In either case there would be little hope of establishing a uniform *Weltanschauung* for the masses that would replace religion as such. Masaryk appears to have been more in favor of a deliberate indoctrination than of a reliance on natural evolution to produce the desired institutional union of thought. A corporation of scholars, representing all fields of human knowledge, could agree on a certain philosophical interpretation and, with the help of Masaryk's concrete logic, elaborate it into the highest possible outlook on life.[79]

It would be the psychologists' task, presumably, to give a unified touch to the whole, while the details could be left to, say, an Academy of Sciences. In fact there would be little constructive work to be done by such an academy, since concrete logic would already have provided for the classification and hierarchy of the sciences; what remained would be only to incorporate individual opinions within the system. Here Masaryk probably envisioned departmental divisions within his hypothetical Academy. He decided that the representatives of a single discipline (psychology) would be given leading roles in decisions outside the jurisdiction of any one discipline; the Academy would reach its decisions, one supposes, by means of a majority vote. Masaryk did not explain who, or to what extent, would be permitted to disagree with these decisions. Since his purpose was to eliminate conflicting judgments, any discord among the Academicians would not be widely advertised, although presumably they would enjoy freedom of research in their respective branches of knowledge.

Masaryk's proposals, needless to say, were not even in his eyes immediately practicable. Rather, they represented his utopian hopes and were to bestow a higher meaning upon his various activities and initiatives in Prague, to which we shall turn briefly in the following chapter. We conclude here by noting that in *Concrete Logic* Masaryk established a direct link between his ideal of a new faith—scientific religion—and an institutional arrangement to uphold and formulate it. His concept of leadership was becoming more down to earth, more realistic; from Platonic philosophers Masaryk had moved to modern philosophers and academicians as those to whom he was ready to entrust spiritual leadership. In the following chapter we shall examine the evolution of Masaryk's thought on leadership, beginning with a brief summary of his life in Prague against the background of the social and political setting in which he lived and worked after his move from Vienna. It is reasonable to treat even such seemingly abstract works as *Concrete Logic* in a social context and to view his activities as an expression or amplification of certain facets of his thought.

CHAPTER III

LEADERSHIP: DEMOCRACY VERSUS THEOCRACY

As can be seen from our preceding discussion, Masaryk recommended the rule of philosophers to replace the declining authority of established religion. In the 1880s, in Prague, he proposed to replace traditional religion with a new scientific outlook and to give a leading role in society to philosophers, by which term he meant men of science broadly defined. All this was theory, bearing little relation to reality, but Masaryk was increasingly to be involved in public affairs, real issues and problems of the day. What was the relation of his utopia to the real world? Let us begin with certain basic facts and observations. What kind of society was it that Masaryk joined in 1882? What authority did it recognize and follow?[1]

At the time of Masaryk's arrival in Prague organized Czech nationalism was politically divided into two parties. One, the National party (later called the Old Czechs), had emerged in the early 1860s, when the constitutional system was established in the monarchy. Following the example of the Hungarians, the Czechs withdrew from the Reichsrat in 1863, demanding that the historic identity and rights of Bohemia should be recognized. The program the Czechs upheld in their fight for a self-governing Bohemia was presented in the form of so-called "historic rights." The recognized leader of this national movement was František Palacký, the "Father of the Nation," who died in 1876, leaving the leadership to his son-in-law, František Rieger. The old Czechs suffered a political defeat in the mid-1860s, when the dynasty achieved a compromise with

Hungary while Czech national aspirations remained unfulfilled. They were to be defeated again in 1871, when the Emperor retreated from his promise to recognize a special status of the lands of the Bohemian Crown within the framework of the monarchy and to be crowned as King of Bohemia in Prague.

In the aftermath of the defeat of 1871, the National party split and in 1874 a new party, the National Liberal party, or the Young Czechs, emerged. (As a recognizable wing or faction within the old party the Young Czechs had been formed in the later 1860s.) In 1879, the Czechs (Old and Young) returned to Vienna and established a cooperative relationship with the government of Eduard Taaffe. The new government coalition, which they joined, the so-called "Iron Ring of the Right," rewarded the Czechs with various linguistic and cultural concessions, among them a Czech university in Prague. A majority of the professors in Prague took the option of joining—or remaining at—the already existing German university so that many vacancies obtained in the new Czech institution. Masaryk was one of those appointed to the Czech university.

Thus, at the moment of Masaryk's entry into the Czech national community, the Czech nation had achieved a major victory: only one other non-German nationality in Austria, the Poles, could claim a university of its own. (The Poles in fact controlled two universities, Kraków and Lviv, although the latter recognized to some extent the Ukrainian language in teaching.) In many other ways as well the Czechs were a successful and highly advanced society. In addition to the Society of Sciences and the National Museum, they maintained a network of educational, literary, and musical societies and organizations; they had a well-developed system of schools, including an impressive number of secondary and vocational schools, and, most important of all, a Technical University in Prague, founded in 1869. They had a strong and dynamic middle class, and their intelligentsia—lawyers, engineers, doctors, civil servants, teachers—was growing rapidly. Last but not least, the industrial working class was not only increasing in numbers—Bohemia was one of the most advanced areas of the monarchy—but was becoming politically aware and active through the Social Democratic party. That party was still an all-Austrian one, but in the Czech lands it identified itself increasingly with Czech national aims.

Meanwhile both the Old and the Young Czechs had a pronounced national character. Although there were some differences between them, these two parties were similar in structure and in the electoral base from which they drew their support. It should be noted that, although Austria had had a constitutional system from the 1860s, its representative body, the Reichsrat, was elected by a narrow electorate, organized in several colleges (great landed property owners, chambers of commerce, certain categories of urban property owners, the more well-to-do peasants). Until the franchise was ex tended, which took place gradually in the 1880s and 1890s, the Czech parties relied on a small constituency of supporters, consisting of men of property and education.

There is no doubt that Masaryk had entered a relatively complex and highly organized society, in which several elite structures, to some extent overlapping, existed. One was the old cultural establishment, in control of the national institutions such as the National Museum or the Czech Foundation. The other was the political leadership, headed by parliamentary deputies to the Reichsrat and the land assemblies of Bohemia and Moravia. It controlled the political press, just as the cultural elite was responsible for academic and literary publications. There was an elite of wealth, which controlled banks and savings associations and was politically integrated with parliamentary circles. Finally, outside the pale of recognized national leadership, were the leaders of the working class movement which would join the national elite only in a later generation.

But the Czechs of course were not an independent nation. The power in the state belonged to the monarch, who did not have to govern with parliamentary support and whose extensive prerogatives included the conduct of foreign affairs and control over armed forces. The monarch was served by a bureaucratic machine centrally run from Vienna. Socially the monarchy was allied with the landed nobility, who owned extensive holdings in Bohemia and Moravia and politically were represented—via a very restricted system of suffrage—in the provincial diets, in the Reichsrat, and in the upper chamber, which was composed of hereditary and appointed members only. Economically the Czech bourgeoisie was in a relatively weak position compared to the big-business interests of Vienna. Spiritual authority in the state was in the hands of the Catholic church, even though in the 1850s the Emperor had renounced a Concordat with Rome. All schools except universities were required to provide religious instruction to their students; non-Catholics were instructed in their respective religions and were not forced to study the articles of Catholic faith. Historically, the Catholic church acted as a close ally of the dynasty; socially, its upper ranks were drawn from the aristocracy. Finally there was the world of academic learning, held together by the German language, and led in Austria by the University of Vienna. Masaryk was, like many of his elders and peers, a product of that world.

In the Czech context, where Czech nationalism was struggling to assert itself against German domination, all these forces—the dynasty, the bureaucracy, the nobility, the church, big business, the universities— were perceived as German or pro-German. The Czechs were asserting themselves in a conscious confrontation with Germany but at the same time lived under a pervasive Germanic influence.

We can easily imagine that Masaryk did not hold in high regard— by way of understatement—the world of established religion and monarchical authority. He did not speak directly about economic or social issues, but from what he did say, for example in *Suicide,* we may safely conclude that he was not prepared to support the claim of the nobility or the bourgeoisie to lead society. Similarly, he did not take socialism seriously as a program of economic and social transformation, which means that he did not consider socialist theorists and leaders to be suitable guides of the people. In Prague, the traditional leadership of the nation derived its claim to rule not from political, economic or social power nor from established religion; rather, it derived its authority from its claim to be the best representative of the national character of the Czech nation. Speaking anachronistically, in late twentieth-century American terms, we might say that the Czech elites had first argued that "Czech is beautiful"—this was an assertion of the originality and individuality of Czech national culture—and then, even in Masaryk's time, had moved on to demand "Czech Power." Although the Czechs had become a socially and economically diversified society, it was the cultural elite, not the businessmen or politicians, who were the nation's recognized spiritual leaders. In practical terms this meant that politics and economic activity were legitimized ideologically by reference to service to the nation—nation being defined culturally or linguistically. Ethnic nationalism likewise did not command Masaryk's allegiance at the moment of his entry into Prague. He did not use this concept in his analysis of the world or in his prescriptions for rescuing modern man. Sooner or later, he would of course have to take a stand on this issue as well.

So let us begin by looking at Masaryk's actions when he came to the historic capital of Bohemia. The basic facts are simple enough. Within weeks after his arrival in Prague (16 October), Masaryk found himself in a public controversy with a senior colleague on the University faculty, one Josef Durdík. The occasion was quite trivial: Durdík, spoke to an undergraduate philosophical society and apparently gave an (intentionally) not quite serious talk on "The Five Most Significant Names in the Literature of the Nineteenth Century." The story is scarcely worth recalling except that Masaryk—who was never accused by anyone of an exaggerated sense of humor—chose to attack the speaker in a rather stern manner, lecturing him, it appears, on such matters as the difference between Comte and Kant. What interests us here is that Masaryk publicly challenged a senior colleague in a setting that was bound to be thought by his target particularly unsuitable for such an exercise. Durdík, who may have been a limited man in any case, did not like to be criticized and never forgave Masaryk for this attack. But this was only a modest beginning. In 1883, Masaryk and several other members of the faculty organized a periodical, *Athenaeum,* which was to review and report on the progress of all branches of knowledge at home and abroad. The funds were provided by Masaryk. A student of his from Vienna, who had been greatly impressed by Masaryk's teachings on suicide and the crisis of modern civilization, followed him to Prague, and, after having committed suicide in 1883, left all his money to Masaryk. The will was challenged by the family but in a settlement Masaryk received the very substantial sum of money that made the *Athenaeum* possible.[2]

Although the *Athenaeum* had an editorial board, with individual members responsible for their special areas of expertise, more than once Masaryk bypassed them to publish material to which they could be expected to object. Moreover Masaryk did not limit his own contributions to those fields in which he could reasonably claim to be expert. He reviewed books dealing not only with philosophy, logic, psychology, statistics, ethics, religion, anthropology, politics, ethnography, and history, but also those devoted to philology, health and hygiene, law and geometry. Simon R. Green, who has examined Masaryk's work on the *Athenaeum* in detail and with care, comments about those early years in Prague: "Masaryk's relationships with his colleagues showed both his sense of superiority and his anti-authoritarian stance (at least so long as he was not the one in authority)." "What should strike us, though not surprise us, is his audacity . . . . [in] assuming a role of leadership."[3]

In 1886, the *Athenaeum* and Masaryk became involved in the celebrated "Manuscript Battle." The Manuscripts were the supposedly medieval, indeed early medieval, Czech texts "discovered" (but in reality forged) in the early nineteenth century by the Czech patriot and scholar, Václav Hanka. Encouraged by his initial success–the texts were accepted as primary sources by no less an authority than František Palacký, to whom they provided evidence of the antiquity and the high level of Czech culture–Hanka went on producing his discoveries, but his later products did not win scholarly acceptance. In the 1850s, even the earlier forgeries began to be questioned–it so happened that the first to do so was a German journal in Prague. As time passed, and as the Czechs were gaining in national self-esteem and confidence, Czech scholars were becoming increasingly uncomfortable with those national "treasures." In 1885, a professor from Prague and Masaryk's colleague and collaborator on the *Athenaeum,* Jan Gebauer, published a critical article on the Manuscripts in a German encyclopedia. Gebauer questioned the authenticity of the documents and demanded a new chemical and paleographic analysis of them. The publication of his article caused an uproar among the Prague academic establishment and Gebauer was attacked in the daily paper *Národní listy*. Gebauer sought to publish a rebuttal in a professional journal, but its editor suggested that he should submit it instead to the *Athenaeum.* The publication in the *Athenaeum* inaugurated the "Manuscript Battle" in which Masaryk took prominent part as editor, as the author of an editorial which accompanied the Gebauer polemic and as a later participant. (He wrote among other things a "sociological" analysis of the forgeries.) At least one of the journal's editors, Albín Bráf, thought that while Gebauer's article was a serious piece, Masaryk's statement–which he printed without the knowledge of his editorial board–was both unnecessary and tactless.[4]

It is customary for writers on Masaryk to present the Manuscript controversy as an illustration of his determination to fight against all lies, however flattering or convenient those lies might be. This may have been so, but one might look at the affair also from another angle. In a letter to Edward Albert, professor at the University of Vienna, written several years after the Battle, Masaryk said that what really had been at stake in the controversy was "the organization of spiritual authority." "Speaking more concretely," he explained, "the battle was waged by the younger generation of scholars and journalists; speaking of persons, Grégr (*Národní listy*) and later Rieger fought against Masaryk." He ended his long letter by repeating:

> Thus, Herr Professor, the Manuscript Battle is really a battle over the organization of spiritual authority in our nation, because after Palacký's death the older authorities—the Museum, the Sciences Society—are dead and a new one is only slowly constituting itself. Naturally, this battle is a battle of the press and of the philosophical faculty which to a large extent are concerned with those studies that directly and indirectly affect the life of society.[5]

Thus Masaryk admitted (even if only in a private letter) that he and his associates had challenged the Czech establishment as represented by the National Museum, the Society of Sciences, and similar bodies on the ground that they were unscientific. Against those who derived their authority from their alleged expertise in the traditional national disciplines—history, language, literature—Masaryk and his supporters invoked the authority of science and philosophy. This was the meaning of Masaryk's comment about the difference between a university and those other older institutions. One might say that he presented an argument for giving recognition to the "other" culture—a typical conflict between two cultures, one traditional and humanistic, the other modern and scientific.

We may appreciate in this light the various proposals that Masaryk advanced for the improvement of intellectual life in Bohemia. He recommended the founding of an academy of sciences, a second Czech university, a scientific review in one of the international languages, a new encyclopedia, and so on. He also spoke up strongly in favor of publishing foreign works in Czech translation.[6]

The Manuscript Battle ended in a victory for the critics and did not lead to their isolation from the Czech national community. In fact the Realists, as they were called, were coopted into the establishment. By 1890 their leaders, Masaryk, Josef Kaizl, and Karel Kramář, became members of the Young Czech party, while another leader, Albín Bráf, had been politically active even earlier. In 1891, they were elected to parliament as Young Czech deputies. Before joining the Young Czechs they negotiated the conditions of their entry into the Old Czech party—which suggests, first, that the dividing lines in Czech politics were not yet sharply drawn, and second, that the pool of political talent in those days was still rather limited. We might add, as a third point, that until 1897 suffrage was also still very limited in the monarchy and that therefore all political forces were based on relatively restricted and homogeneous social groups. Eventually, Kramář became leader of the Young Czech party, and Kaizl and Bráf advanced to ministerial appointments in Vienna.

Masaryk did not follow this path. In 1893 he broke with the Young Czechs and withdrew from conventional politics for a number of years. Only in 1900 did he form his own political party, the Czech People's party, or Realists. But he did not retreat from public life altogether. In fact he was very active in the 1890s, when his political thought took a new turn, and this phase will be discussed in the following chapter.

Although Masaryk had joined the national community of the Czechs, he was not a nationalist. As we saw, he challenged the authority of those who represented the *ethnos*; and he did so in the name of nonnational values, by claiming to represent the forces of a modern advanced science. A bit pretentiously, we might say that against the *ethnos* Masaryk asserted the rights of the *logos,* which he also wanted to make the masses accept as an element of faith. He recognized no claim to leadership accruing to those who possessed wealth, whether inherited or earned, social privilege, traditional political power, or those who might invoke popular support (who were in fact only beginning to emerge on the political scene). He invoked his right to leadership by virtue of his intellectual preeminence. But there was a question that remained to be answered: what was the constituency over which those intellectuals were to exercise their leadership? In the natural course of events, Masaryk as a Czech professor who taught and increasingly wrote in Czech, addressed his message to the Czech national community. But why should it be so in terms of the world view that Masaryk had developed in his pre-Prague years and reformulated, in *Concrete Logic,* in the 1880s?

In 1886 the fortnightly *Čas,* a periodical more openly political than the *Athenaeum,* was founded. Although it was commonly believed to have been inspired by Masaryk, his friend and disciple, Jan Herben, was the editor. The opening issue contained an article entitled "Our Two Problems" on its front page. The author, signed "H.G.," raised the question of whether the preservation of a separate Czech nation was worth fighting for. Would it not be better culturally, he asked, to join an advanced, powerful and civilized nation instead? Masaryk disowned this article and claimed that he had known nothing about it until it was published. But his denial was discounted. He and his friends were known from then on for many years as "national nihilists."[7] Albín Bráf, in his memoirs published posthumously after 1918, recalled that before the *Čas* article appeared, sometime in 1886 he, Masaryk and a mutual friend had had a long discussion centered around the question that Masaryk had raised. The question was whether it was worthwhile for the Czechs to expend so much effort simply to maintain a separate identity. Would it not be more reasonable to join a larger civilized nation already in existence and use the energies so released to attain certain positive cultural and political goals? Bráf argued that this could not be done, that the masses would not become assimilated. Zeman, who recounts this incident in his book on the Masaryks, observes that Bráf "used rational arguments, though he knew that Masaryk was questioning the very existence of a movement which the Czechs had cherished over the decades."[8]

It is on this issue that we may notice the principal difference between Masaryk and his contemporaries, including those who shared so many of his views. They accepted the fact that the Czech nation existed; to them this was no longer a question *sub judice.* If the existence of a Czech nation had ever been in doubt, they would have argued, this would have been in the late eighteenth or early nineteenth centuries. In the 1880s the question was pointless. The Czech nation was a fact of life to them. Being more practical and less philosophical than Masaryk, they were no more inclined to question the purpose of its existence than they were to question the purpose of life. With Doctor Zhivago, they might have answered that the purpose of life is life. Masaryk did not accept such answers. He answered to his satisfaction the question of the meaning of the Czech nation in the 1890s. His answer then aroused another public controversy which involved among others his friend from the 1880s, Kaizl. It is appropriate to note here, in advance of our theme in the next chapter, that participants in that polemic spoke on completely different levels. To quote Garver on this, even though his concerns are different from ours, and even though he completely passes over the Nihilist Affair: "In marked contrast to Masaryk's work, *Česká otázka*, which aimed at nothing less than justifying the existence and future advancement of the Czech nation, *České myšlenky* [by Kaizl] sought primarily to justify the principles and policies of the Young Czech party."[9]

Masaryk's search for authority, as these comments indicate, would eventually result in his discovery of the nation as the bearer of a religious and philosophical meaning, in a synthesis of the universal elements of his ideology with the nation. But the problem of leadership and its justification was not resolved for Masaryk by simply vesting it it a *national* leadership. A legitimate national leadership had to be justified intellectually too. Masaryk was enough of a realist to understand that there was little chance for anyone to assert the rights of an intellectual leadership in the actual context of politics in the monarchy. He realized that the main lines of conflict were drawn between those who represented the traditional world—the monarchy, the established church, the aristocracy—and the new forces of democracy, socialism, the masses. Although he formed his own party, it was more like an intellectual club than a Leninist avant-garde party, or any of the elitist nationalist movements.[10] He joined the democratic camp broadly defined, and he began himself to speak of democracy as a desirable goal. Indeed, he preferred it as an alternative to the existing regime.

In the 1890s, and even more so in the 1900s, he began to speak approvingly of political reforms and a democratic system of government in general. Given his earlier opinions, it may be asked precisely what his political and ideological position was. A reading of his works leads to the conclusion that Masaryk used the term "democracy" in two senses. In one, he supported democracy, as it was then understood, in practical politics and in opposition to the monarchist, Catholic (he included under this term also what he called the Eastern version of Catholicism, Russian Orthodoxy) and feudal-absolutist state. However, democracy so understood, we believe, had no more than a negative claim to his allegiance: in his criticism of Austria and in his critical study of Russia, Masaryk did not hesitate to favor democracy as an alternative to, or a program for the reform of, the existing regimes.

We will argue in this chapter that Masaryk continued to uphold his earlier understanding of "the good state," even in those statements which were ostensibly made in defense of democracy . We will try to reconstruct this concept of democracy by following up his thoughts, which were never fully expressed because of unpropitious circumstances. It is perhaps not unjust to argue that historical events, rather than a change in his basic ideology, were the reasons he never developed his Platonic ideas of good government more openly in those later years. Neither in the Habsburg monarchy, where his principal opponents were the aristocratic and bureaucratic state and the established Church, nor in Czechoslovakia did conditions encourage him to develop the themes of his youth. Until 1918 Masaryk was a critic of the reactionary monarchy, and this critical thrust in his activities was not conducive to a full and free statement of a position of basic mistrust of popular government. Later, in an independent Czechoslovakia whose President he was, the conditions were likewise unfavorable for a statement of a Platonist political program. And yet, this chapter argues that Masaryk did indeed remain faithful to his old credo, and in Chapters VI and VII we will provide additional evidence in support of this interpretation.

When Masaryk discussed democracy, he was apt to start from one of two premises. At times, he reflected on the need for modern man to live a moral life, in which he included both its social and political aspects; Masaryk called democracy a political system that would best promote life in accord with ethical values. His other point of departure was historical: contrasting theocracy and democracy, he saw the latter as a product of the historical evolution of mankind, one destined to succeed theocracy. Masaryk tended to stress one theme or the other—moral or historical—in his ensuing reflections on democracy. Thus, at the close of the nineteenth century and the beginning of the twentieth, he often spoke of democracy as an ethical system, which, for example, he opposed to Marxism with its belief in inevitable material progress and the primary importance of the material components of human life. After the Russian revolution of 1905, on the other hand, Masaryk regarded the evident growth of democracy in Europe in the light of his notion that democracy was a product of the struggle of science against myth; in other words, as a scientific form of government that had evolved (inevitably?) from autocracy and theocracy, which he labeled mythical, reactionary, and superstitious. Democracy seemed to him, then, in the ethical conception, an application to the political arena of universally valid moral rules, rooted in the preeminence of humanity as such, while in the scientific or evolutionary conception, democracy was an application of the scientific method to the organization of society.

The revolution in Russia made a powerful impression on Masaryk, stimulating him to a thorough revision of his political views. Not only did he conclude that tsarism was historically doomed, but he came to look at the Habsburg monarchy with a more critical eye. His criticisms of tsarism in *Russia and Europe* (1913)—especially because Russian autocracy was so intimately tied to religion—could be applied to the Habsburg monarchy as well. Austria too, in the person of the monarch, stood for the combination of secular power and established religion. Nothing in Masaryk's system of values would require him to be loyal to the Habsburgs once he had despaired of their desire or capability to institute fundamental reforms.

This did not mean, however, that Masaryk identified himself ideologically with the contemporary political opposition to the autocratic state. He still took his stand on concrete issues in terms of that broad philosophical position he had formulated in the earlier nonpolitical phase of his life. A close study of Masaryk's statements on democracy offers an illuminating insight into the permanent and transient elements of his political philosophy. In them we can perceive an outlook uniquely his own, one that made him a spiritual stranger in all the major political camps of the day—whether left, right or center.

Masaryk could see that Austria and Russia were the states most deeply torn by internal conflicts. In his search for the explanation he did not go far: their religions were theocratic and unscientific. Masaryk's basic assumptions remained unchanged; ". . . religion constitutes the central and centralizing mental force in the life of the individual and of society . . . . The content of history is the peculiar struggle . . . between critical and scientific thought on the one hand and mythology on the other." Yet, he did not identify all religion with mythology. He insisted that "the crowning of the present" was to create a religion and a religious organization of society that would be compatible with "the critical understanding," and he denied, in opposition to the view of those "liberals, socialists, and anarchists who are hostile to religion," that a nonreligious stage of human development had come to succeed a lower religious stage.[11]

In this lay also the gravest error of the Russian philosophers of history and religion: they confused myth—uncritical credulity and mysticism, theocratic religion—with religion itself. Nevertheless Masaryk, as had ever been his custom, did not say precisely what religion should be. He simply noted that ever since the reforms introduced by Peter the Great, the struggle between rationalist enlightenment and the philosophy and practice of the church had formed "the substance of Russian writing, both philosophical and literary," and that it had intensified from the moment Kant's influence began to be felt. In *The Spirit of Russia,* he wrote: " . . . the main problem [is] that of revelation and tradition versus experience and science."[12] Thus the Russian revolution was for him the problem of God and revealed religion; and in this regard Russia constituted for Masaryk merely another case illustrating universal evolution. Russia, after having remained in "a state of spiritual arrest" for centuries, was only now about to progress beyond a stage that Europe had passed through long ago. The struggle between myth and science was not only philosophical and theological; it was also a political struggle between absolute monarchy and democracy. "Belief in divine revelation, belief in God, has ever been, and is of necessity, belief in mediators between God and man, belief in priests. This belief, this faith, created the church, created theocracy."[13] The functions of priest and ruler were in the past not differentiated; later priests were the intellectual leaders while the ruler relied on his military prowess and became the arbiter of economic and social conditions. A ruler, nevertheless, like a priest, based "his right and his power upon the will of God."[14]

While Masaryk presumably did not believe that the Deity literally sanctioned theocratic rule, he does seem to have decided that it was the particular type of religious faith that determined the form of government; not for him, clearly, was the position of those who argued that religion served to legitimize the power relationships that owed their origins to secular temporal factors, such as superior force. Thus in his treatise on Russia he argued, to the amusement of Trotsky, that tsarism was a tool of Orthodoxy; it was quite obvious to Trotsky that Orthodoxy was a tool of tsarism.[15] It is worth noting that *Russia and Europe* was originally conceived as a study of Dostoyevsky: "but I lacked the literary skill requisite for the interweaving of all I wanted to say into an account of that author." These two large volumes, amounting to more than a thousand pages, were in their author's judgment merely the first part of his work on Dostoyevsky. In creating such a grand design, Masaryk apparently remained faithful to his conviction that the study of outstanding persons of any era was the key to an understanding of history: "The work will afford proof that an analysis of Dostoyevsky is a sound method of studying Russia . . . ."[16] What Masaryk certainly demonstrated, though, was that in order to write about Dostoyevsky as a key to Russia one had to write a thousand pages about Russia as a key to Dostoyevsky first.[17]

As late as 1913 he was convinced of the critical importance of a question that had perplexed him in 1880: "Can the scientific and critical thinker, can the philosopher, have a religion: and if so, what religion?"[18] He answered it by treating the emergence of Protestantism as more conducive to democracy than "essentially aristocratic Catholicism." His interpretation of Protestantism was a personal one, as we have seen, in that he saw it as having developed from within in contrast to Catholicism, which had remained static.[19] One is reminded here of a distinction he made in *Suicide,* a reversal of this estimate: in 1880 Masaryk had called Protestantism the more dangerous because it stimulated the tendency to suicide. From this new point of view, Masaryk found it significant that "It is where Catholicism is still enthroned that the movement for disestablishment has become anti-religious as well as anti-clerical; . . . Protestantism . . . though anti-ecclesiastical is on the whole friendly to religion." This antithesis had its roots in the very nature of the two:

> This peculiar contrast . . . can be discerned in the two greatest French philosophers of the revolution. Voltaire, the Catholic, is the revolutionary negation of the church; Rousseau, the Calvinist, endeavors to sustain democracy by means of a civil religion.[22]

Scholars of Rousseau do not quote his ideas on civil religion when they speak of the democratic elements in his thought, but civil religion would sustain solidarity, that consensus of opinion that Masaryk praised in the German nation, and he may have attributed this too to Protestantism.[21] It is not unusual for specialists in German history to point to the political docility of the German nation, and some scholars attribute this, at least in part, to German Protestantism.[22] Was this docility of the German character the same quality that Masaryk so admired and recommended to his Czech compatriots as a "consensus of opinion"?[23] Rousseau's civil religion might also be thought of, depending on one's point of view, as one producing docility or a consensus of opinion among its adherents.

Masaryk believed that Protestantism as a *Weltanschauung* did not encourage "nihilistic and extremist negation" but could even serve as a foundation for a new higher religion. Regardless of how the reader may feel about his judgments of Protestantism, Masaryk may have been not entirely wrong, at least with respect to Germany—the country which, next to Austria, was the one he knew best.

In *The Spirit of Russia* Masaryk contrasted Germany, which "with its Prussian junkerdom is being steadily democratized," with England, which "nominally a monarchy is actually subject to an aristocratic oligarchy." Germany, he continued, had "the most progressive and strongest social democracy in Europe; in Germany, Bismarck, the most efficient and most stalwart champion of monarchy, was opposed to the absolutist and theocratic pretensions of the Emperor, and was in effect a rebel."[24] Masaryk was not making an explicit judgment here on Bismarck's policies, but since he spoke of Germany approvingly and saw Bismarck as an opponent of the pretensions of the ruler, his estimate of him was favorable; he called Bismarck an expert politician who knew his job, opposed to an ambitious but ignorant and theocratic Emperor. He even felt that in Russia, Orthodoxy was being replaced by German Protestantism.[25]

Masaryk also emphasized in *The Spirit of Russia* his belief that democracy could be regarded as the heir of theocracy, and he took the Russians to task for their failure to understand this. He suggested that to promote the attainment of desirable aims by a process of organic development, the Russians would have to abandon their extreme nihilism and their rejection of Russian traditions. The social and political system that Masaryk labeled theocracy, represented in varying degrees in all countries, would inevitably be succeeded by democracy: "The philosopher of history can already regard democracy as an attainable ideal, as the predestined heir of theocracy."[26] Masaryk found the basic difference between theocracy and democracy in their conceptions of authority; aristocracy derived its authority from revealed religion, democracy from the people and a progressive historical development.[27] Democracy was anthropocentric, by which he meant antitheocratic.[28] Masaryk found, logically from his assumptions, that the evils inherent in theocracy had to come from belief (admittedly based on "revelation") in God, and in such evils as inequality, domination, and subordination of a majority of subjects by a ruling minority. Aristocracy in the political sphere was intimately connected with an ecclesiastical social organization that exerted power over its workers. Myth again played a part: theocracy was devoid of science, promoting only esoteric mysteries and prophecies.[29] To inequality under aristocratic rule, Masaryk counterposed the ideal of equality and voluntary cooperation in a democracy. Everyone would work; any disinclination to perform assigned tasks would be overcome by a sense of duty. By its very nature, democracy would espouse science and philosophy instead of theology and scholasticism.[30]

From the significance that Masaryk attached to the fact that reactionary governments claimed divine sanction, it may be inferred that he presupposed otherwise the existence of a basic and natural harmony within society: oppressive rule was a product of certain beliefs, not of profound and irreconcilable conflicts within the society itself. In Masaryk's view nothing but belief in God—or rather, an *unscientific* kind of belief—led men to seek power and privilege at the expense of others. He did not seem to think that different, and sometimes conflicting, interests and aspirations resulted in an imposition of rule by some men over others, sometimes over a majority of their fellow citizens. Masaryk's assumption that human interests and aims are ultimately reconcilable and so in truth in harmony explains what he meant when he said that the purpose of democracy is to abolish all government. The abolition of theocratic religion would be followed by a withering away of politics; what remained would be only the functional and technical problems of administration. In practice this would presumably mean that *all* problems would have to be regarded as administrative ones and left to the discretion of administrators with appropriate—scientific—qualifications. A system of majority rule was therefore impossible, and Masaryk produced only one alternative: "As aristocratic monarchy was always an oligarchy, so also is democracy in actual working an oligarchy,"[31] brought about by the mechanics and techniques of social coexistence.[32]

Still, Masaryk wrote of democratic equality as possible of achievement, providing all forms of labor were directed to the good of the community.[33] The opposition between aristocratic inequality and democratic equality lay in the fact that under theocracy, aristocrats did not work. Thus democracy meant to him the diversion of deposed rulers to useful work—and not, as one might expect, the rule of the people. Masaryk implied that democratic oligarchs, since they would be workers imbued with knowledge, competence, and efficiency, would presumably exercise a power far greater than the theocrats (who were lazy and ignorant) had ever been able to wield.

If theocracy had its foundation in God, what was the foundation of democracy? Masaryk acknowledged that democracy appealed to the authority of the people, but he thought that this authority itself required a foundation.[34] Rousseau had sought to define the genuine will of the people, which he considered infallible and absolute. Masaryk held that "every relective person who abandons myth, and who with Kant explains all knowledge as derivable from the natural faculties of man," would face the same problem. But the questions Masaryk asked were philosophical: what does the critical, scientific thinker recognize as supreme? What authority is for him vested in the people, in humanity, in the parliamentary majority? And the characteristic answer was that the critical thinker could be guided only by inner authority.

Masaryk did not try to analyze the categorical imperative when he spoke of the difficulty to which its acceptance led.[35] All that need be said, he felt sure, was that the democratic principle of authority is purely ethical. The sovereignty of the people does not correspond to a monarch's absolute sovereignty and indeed does not rest solely on preponderant opinion.[36] It was not that he was concerned with protecting individuals against the curtailment of their rights by a democratic but oppressive majority; he had a rather different rationale in mind when he defined democracy as something other than merely the rule of the majority. What Masaryk seems to have wanted to justify was to call minority rule democratic, free from responsibility to, or control by, the whole body of citizens.

Thus Masaryk opposed God to man, myth to science, theocracy to democracy, and assumed a natural harmony between men. He conceived of democratic government as administration, that is, as a field of activity subject to management by technicians, by professionals. If such a democracy were to function properly, it presupposed by its very nature that administration would be undertaken by the most knowledgeable men of the community. Nevertheless there was a strong possibility that the masses would remain largely under the influence of myth.[37] He arrived at this conclusion by reasoning that if democracy involved the right of all to make policy decisions, it might then fail to listen to those who knew the "truth," and so be transformed into a mythic theocracy. What mattered was not who or how many decided, or by what method; the essential thing was what they decided and whether the decision was right or wrong. And this did not depend on numbers.

Aware of these dangers, Masaryk insisted again that democracy was something other than merely the rule of all the persons in it and that it ought not to be equated with a prevalent opinion, however universal. To him the point was vital, since democracy had not only to decide questions of administration but had to establish the goals to which the work of all was to be directed. Scientific method and judgment could be applied to decision-making as well as to the carrying out of decisions: ". . . scientific history and the philosophy of history reveal to the modern politician, through the idea of progress, a direction; it gives him guidance, and shows the life of society in historical perspective." This meant, Masaryk concluded, that men should practice politics only after intensive preparation. "Democracy is a *Weltanschauung* and a way of life"; it is the political consequence of modern humanitarian ethics.[38] The science based on this principle was modern philosophy, directed to the discovery of the new morality and "the new democratic political and administrative system." This new political system was to be built on sociology and other abstract sciences and based upon morality. For, as Masaryk had repeatedly said, it is the function of politics to realize ethical principles for society and within it.[39]

Naturally the realities of political life did not yet fully conform to the ideal. The influence of the old theocratic outlook made itself felt in parliaments that paid no heed to the voices of apolitical experts. The need for talented leaders led Masaryk to remark nostalgically, "Democracy

. . . [means] a definite Life and World-Outlook . . . . In essence we always come back to Plato and his dilemma about kings and philosophers."[40]

These considerations were given due emphasis in Masaryk's critique of Marxism: against the deterministic and amoral doctrine of historical materialism, he put forward his own ethical conception. He declared his sympathy for the plight of the working people but appealed to them to renounce their utopianism, their hopes of carrying out a total transformation of society. Materialism should give way to educational, cultural, and economic improvement. "This means to carry on all work, not only political, from a unitary point of view and to subordinate it to higher aims." The political side of the new democratic way of life was to be subordinated to its more crucial aspect as an ethical system that was above circumstances and institutions.[41] Such a political system was to rest, through its ethical principles, on the authority of God, basing its precepts on human nature. It was not enough to argue that a social ideal was deduced from ethics: such an admission led to questions about the meaning of history and ultimately to questions about the meaning of the world and of life itself.[42]

Materialism had no answer to questions pertaining to the meaning of history, evolution, and progress.[43] Obviously Marx's humanitarian ideal was too intellectual, too one-sidedly positivist, emphasizing that there can be no valid humanitarian or social ideal without a religious one. "Man is not just a body but also a soul. An immortal soul!"[44] Masaryk called his own view "synergism," by which he apparently meant the joint action of man and God, and believed it to be free from the shortcomings of Marxism; its theistic determinism made his system a truly metaphysical one.[45] In his philosophical structure, Masaryk related synergism to the problem of man's freedom in a history dominated by determinism.[46]

As he had done for so long, Masaryk regarded suicide as a vital social problem. Granted that the material conditions of the working class needed to be upgraded he was still more personally concerned with subjective pessimism, the "trend toward suicide and psychosis."

> Consider: in civilized countries . . . some sixty thousand suicides take place annually . . . is that not a terrifying number? What are wars by comparison! . . . Even more terrifying is the fact that annually some two thousand minors, frequently actually children,

seek death. There is an uproar when several men are killed in
open combat somewhere in Cuba or the Philippines, and yet,
what is that compared to a single case when a child already
despairs![47]

Masaryk justified his conception of ethics (and so of politics) on
empirical grounds that, he felt, needed no scientific proof. He contended
that there were two aspects of the problem: formal and material. The
formal principle of ethics was concerned with "ethical sanction," while
the material dealt with "the content of the ethical commandment."
Moral philosophers of all persuasions, Masaryk said, agree that conscience
is a fact no less real than material phenomena. It is conscience that makes
man shrink from inhumanity and rejoice in humanity. All philosophers,
even materialists like Feuerbach and Mill, recognize the binding force of
the ethical principle, which is an integral part of man's character. Otherwise mankind would not have been able to attain the moral level that it
has. The inner voices of humanity created their own sanction.[48]

As for the moral principle, Masaryk declared that it was the humanitarian ideal that comprised its content. The humanitarian ideal had been
developing over the course of history and its content augmented by the
contributions of moral philosophers—in the nineteenth century, for
example, by Kant, Beneke, Feuerbach, Schopenhauer, Nietzsche, Mill,
and Spencer.[49] Nations had identified this ideal in diverse ways: "How
differently is the humanitarian ideal formulated by Kant, Comte, and
Mill! How much Herder, Kant, Feuerbach, Kireyevsky and Kollar,
Dostoyevsky and Nietzsche differ! And yet all of them have Man and
Humaneness as their ethical and social ideal." [50]

Masaryk's increasing tendency to recognize ethics as the basis of
political behavior was also expressed in a change in the hierarchical classification of sciences he had drawn up in *Concrete Logic* in the 1880s.
At that time, politics had its place along with ethics, but it was not subordinated ot it. In the late 1890s, when he was criticizing Marxist
determinism, Masaryk elevated ethics from the rank of a mere practical
science to a position as a constituent part of philosophy, along with logic
and metaphysics.[51] Politics was an area of human activity where the precepts of ethics ruled because ethics defined the aims of life, whether
social, political, or economic. The ends to which human action were

directed brought in teleology, a branch of politics; specific economic concerns were likewise determined by an appropriate branch of politics.[52] Thus, all human action was subject to ethical rules. Masaryk argued against the Marxist view of ethics, emphasizing that, although certain actions were dependent on present or future events, there was also the question of one's moral choice, which could be considered in terms of the individual's responsibility before his conscience.

Simultaneously, as we have noted, Masaryk made the domain of politics subject to scientific direction, for ethics was one of the sciences. We may ask therefore whether there was not a contradiction between his emphasis on moral responsibility as bound up with choice and his recognition of ethics as a scientific discipline? What if an individual's decision to act in accord with conscience, his personal sense of what was right, was contrary to the science of ethics in its philosophical interpretation? We remember that politics, including politics based on ethics, was a science, and Masaryk believed in the existence of a distinct political talent as a factor that could not be denied. He went on to say that it was obvious that a parliamentarian unacquainted with education or taxes could not make decisions in these areas. But politics as he defined it was something greater than education, school taxes, railways, and so on.[53] Masaryk also rejected the Communist doctrine that crucial decisions should express the judgment and will of the people, for this implied that all men were capable of decision-making. The scientific and expert nature of politics in which Masaryk placed his faith would always keep it a closed domain for the majority of men; the growth of mass knowledge could never keep up with the march of science. Politics was a discipline like other disciplines, and it required of its practitioners special inborn talents, and special education open to those with a talent for politics. With such specifications, only a few could hope to acquire a mastery of politics.

It was precisely because of the scientific character of politics that Masaryk insisted that equality was an impossible dream. No improvement in mass education would make a community capable of rendering decisions about its own welfare. Therefore he did not welcome any extension of the franchise without regard for quality; if neither birth nor a restricted franchise could ensure political acumen, a wide or universal franchise would not do so.[54] No will of the community as a whole could ever guarantee scientific certainty. Psychology, logic and epistemology, all departments of science and philosophy, called out against absolute equality as postulated by Marx and Engels. Masaryk rejected their view because he believed so firmly that it was the outstanding individual who had always exercised a decisive influence in every field, including politics.[55] Social inequality plainly originated in the natural inequality of men's minds, feelings, and wills, their talents and needs, and their positions in nature and society.[56] It was this very inequality that led to a society hierarchically structured. Politicians were proved unequal by the fact that some of them sought power while others preferred subordinate positions, so that there were psychological restrictions to equality.[57] Indifference and passivity, in addition to intellectual and educational inequality, contributed to the growth of oligarchies.[58] Masaryk had no wish to deny that social organization had never been perfect, that it had often resulted in oppression, but for him it followed that oppression had to be wiped out. Instead, what Marx and Engels did ("as usual") was to throw the baby away with the bathwater.

The masses would always have considerable power, but Masaryk could not see how that power could be combined organically with logic and knowledge.[59] As for universal suffrage, he admitted that a larger population would probably produce more men who thought politically; the problem was to be sure that these men had a lasting, rather than an accidental and temporary, social and political influence. His concern was still to establish politics as a practical science and as a practical art founded on science; to guarantee the social influence of political experts.[60]

Masaryk was convinced that the Marxist leaders had given little thought to scientific and philosophical politics. Marxism had in practice recognized a constitutional parliamentarianism that Engels sought to use as a road to political power, while his successors thought about improving it. But Marxism had found an obstacle to its efforts in its own politics. "Their uncritical, inarticulate, anthropomorphist concept of 'the mass' leads them to democratic superstition."[61] Masaryk claimed no share in this sort of superstition—not because of a leaning towards aristocracy but because he saw true greatness elsewhere. ". . . the numerous socialist, democratic, popular—and aristocratic—demagogues are to me quite repulsive," he wrote. One might learn much from the workers, yet not set them up as all-important. He posed another question that seemed to him of great moment: how could one guarantee that the educated expert would indeed influence the opinions of the masses, particularly in the sphere of politics?

But Masaryk was never to explain how his plan for scientific politics might be implemented. Modern parliamentarianism seemed to be in the ascendant, and his nearest approach to a practical suggestion was his recommendation that measures be introduced to ensure that the rights of minorities, including expert individuals, would always be taken into account.[62] Since Masaryk's conclusions could not be implemented in practice, his statements tend to sound simply like a moralist's ineffectual appeal, calling on men to be just, good and honest, not only at home but at the office and in the parliamentary chamber.[63] But when these statements are seen in the context of some of his later activities, they appear in a different light.

In 1908 Masaryk had asked in his parliamentary constituency: "What does progress consist of in the sphere of politics? What is a progressive program?" He had answered: "To put in one word the political program of everybody who believes in progress: equality .... Another word is liberty .... I could say that our program is democracy, literally the rule of the people."[64] It has been said, Masaryk continued, that absolutism is possible only when society was organized around an aristocracy. Every worker knew that the American and French republics were not more pleasant for the general population than were the monarchies of Germany, Austria, and elsewhere. The source of evil lay in the fact that aristocracy prevailed everywhere. "I am an aristocrat myself," Masaryk confessed, meaning that he was a professor, as none of his listeners was. There were aristocrats in the context of property or language or religion. To extend education to the masses would be to eradicate any aristocratic distinction between the educated and the uneducated and would be to promote democracy.[65]

As time passed, Masaryk spoke about equality with less and less constraint, on one occasion saying that modern democracy "proclaimed not merely political but also economic, social, moral, religious, spiritual and intellectual equality .... "[66] In the speech of 1908 quoted above he defined practical equality as "that inequality which is bearable ...." At the same time his assessment of democracy became more concrete: "Now, what does it mean to be a democrat, politically, socially, economically, in public life? It means to work." We will have democracy when all men "become industrious, become true workers and labor with conviction and conscientiously."[67]

Masaryk conceived of liberty in much the same way. He had once quoted Anasthasius Grün with approbation: "Liberty is not enjoyment but work, incessant work in the interest of the great cultural tasks of the modern state."[68] For this education was necessary; and it is significant that, although Masaryk discussed democracy in terms of the actual working of its institutions, he constantly examined the problem of educating wise and good leaders and citizens in general.[69] It seems quite correct to summarize Masaryk's position as follows: "Liberty is work. Democracy is knowledge."[70]

One of Masaryk's most criticized aphorisms was "Jesus not Caesar—this is the meaning of our history and of democracy."[71] It was pointed out with some justification that Jesus had never been a statesman at all, much less the ideal statesman. It was also asked whether he who said "render therefore unto Caesar the things which are Caesar's and unto God the things that are God's" could really be called a democrat.[72] Misgivings were also felt at Masaryk's "antithesis between Beethoven and Bismarck," with Beethoven as the representative of democracy in Germany.[73] These examples suggest that Masaryk was inclined to call a government democratic if the rulers felt sympathy and love toward the governed, if they directed their rule to the promotion of the good or even if they merely advanced the public welfare.[74] Nor did he think that their actions necessarily had to accord with popular opinion, particularly if it were the wrong opinion.[75] Rádl's comments on Masaryk's democracy of humanity, though they refer primarily to the status of the German minority in Czechoslovakia, might be applied more generally:

> It is the characteristic feature of humanitarian democracy in Masaryk's interpretation that it speaks from the point of view of a statesman who possesses sovereign power and limits it out of his sympathy for other men. Thus it does not see democracy as defective when the authority of the state legislative and administrative apparatus has practically no limitations. This democracy seeks those limitations only in the free will of the legislator who from moral conviction sets out to treat his fellow-man humanely.[76]

The only aspects of political liberty about which Masaryk wrote were freedom of conscience and freedom of speech. He defended them against the Catholic Church and against the state that supported it, but, as F. Fajfr noted, he shifted the emphasis from "right" to "duty," and treated freedom of conscience and speech as prerequisites in a successful struggle of science against myth.[77] Fajfr traced this feature of Masaryk's political thought to the influence of Comte;[78] but it may also have been due to the strong religious element in his world view and perhaps to a residuum of the Platonic idea of the philosopher-kings who were to be unfettered by the ties of law.

Democracy, Masaryk said in his later years, was "a complete view of the world which strives for fraternity, not only in the getting of daily bread, but also in the laws, in science and education, in morals and religion."[79] This expresses in large part a central idea of his ideal "good society." Fraternity did not necessarily imply liberty or equality; it meant only that society was to be supported by a sense of duty and solidarity among its members. As Masaryk told K. Čapek, he based his idea of democracy "on love and the justice that is the mathematics of love, and on the conviction that we should help towards the realization of the rule of God, towards synergism with the divine will."[80] Masaryk was thus harking back to his themes of 1898, and even of 1876, except that he did not speak of government by the best and wisest, the other element of his original structure, as an alternative to democracy. He therefore gave the impression that he was more oriented toward religion than was actually the case. No wonder that many of this contemporaries regarded him simply as a romanticist or political mystic.

However, as Masaryk's actions after 1914 demonstrated, he was in fact a practical politician. His politics after the outbreak of the war implemented and developed his theoretical propositions on scientific leadership, as well as his stand on the relation between nation and state. Masaryk's theory and practice were united.

CHAPTER IV

RELIGION AS NATIONALISM

Whatever doubts he may have had in the 1880s, during the "nihilist" affair, Masaryk accepted the existence of the Czech nation and his subsequent political and scholarly activities took place within a national framework. In 1891-1893, he was a parliamentary deputy as a Young Czech, and although he withdrew from active party and parliamentary politics in 1893, when he clashed with his party associates, he did not renounce involvement in Czech national life.[1] He founded a new periodical, *Naše Doba,* and he began to publish a series of works which mark a new, the nationalist, phase in his developing thought.

While Masaryk retained his old position regarding the crisis of modern civilization and its causes, his grasp of social realities was enriched by the realization that mankind is not made up of individuals in the abstract. He discovered that the reality of ethnicity was a factor that had to be taken into account in any analysis of human society: universal man did not exist. In between the individual and the human race stood the nations: people were Czech or German, Polish or Russian, or any one of a vast number of other nationalities. If any measures were to be effective in solving social or cultural problems, the particular conditions of individual nations had to be identified. To arrive at the right solution in general terms was not enough. Yet concentration on a single society meant knowing less about the specifics of other societies, an inevitable consequence if one were to link one's ideas with an ethnic group who would accept these ideas as its own. Masaryk became a Czech scholar, a Czech writer, a Czech politician, and his primary, though never exclusive, audience was the Czech nation.

Once he had decided to take nationality seriously, it had to be assigned a place in his total conception of man, history and the world: Masaryk continued to think that everything should be viewed *sub specie aeternitatis.* Therefore Masaryk sought to bring about a synthesis between his convictions and the historical and cultural realities of the Czech nation. His message remained essentially the same, but now it was presented in a national costume. His program, Masaryk said, was based on a study of Czech history and articulated its deep inner meaning.

While his previous interpretations had contrasted a prescientific, authoritarian and dogmatic past with the scientific, free, rational outlook of modern man, Masaryk now created a synthesis of past and present. In other words, he endowed the past with the features he now hoped to promote, and presented this reinterpretation of the past to the people of Bohemia. Not only was he not a "national nihilist," as he could tell his opponents (and did), but was on the contrary better attuned to the spirit of Czech history than they could ever be. Yet, as we have suggested, Masaryk had not had a change of heart; his *national* philosophy of history merely served as another source of support for his original doctrine. Masaryk gave his program a "dual legitimation": it was universal and scientific, but it also was national and historical. The Czech nation became for Masaryk the bearer of a new and true religion of humanity, and the nation thus acquired a moral significance. The Czechs became a "secular 'chosen people.' "[2]

This chapter argues that when Masaryk abandoned his concern with universal authority—the subject he had sought to explore and resolve in his earlier writings—his outlook underwent a very profound change, even though he himself did not seem to realize it. Masaryk claimed to have detected a universal humanitarian content in the "Czech idea," but he now treated the universal problem of religion—he continued to regard the religious question as the central one—within the frame of a community defined in *ethnic* terms. It is essential, therefore, in any discussion of his thought to pay serious attention to what Masaryk said he regarded as important—even if his ideas appear odd, "mystical," "unrealistic," or incompatible with our preconceptions of "what Masaryk really meant."

In examining Masaryk's nationalist writings, this study takes a course that differs from those followed by two recent works. Professor Bruce M. Garver, in his comprehensive study of the Young Czech Party and the emergence of a multiparty system in Bohemia, treats Masaryk's writings on the Czech problem in relation to the concrete and specific issues and problems of the 1890s. Although he notices an affinity between Masaryk's political ideology and Polish messianism, he treats the former as a program of practical work in conformity with "enduring moral principles like 'humanity,' 'democracy,' and 'work.'"[3] He is not concerned with treating Masaryk's nationalist ideology in a broader framework of the development of his political thought or philosophy. Antonie van den Beld, on the other hand, views Masaryk's nationalism in the light of what he considers Masaryk's fundamental (and basically unchanging) concept of humanity. In van den Beld's interpretation, Masaryk applied the universal principle of humanity to the specific problems and concerns of the Czechs. He grants that "Masaryk comes dangerously close— in spite of himself—to a form of nationalism (the idea of a chosen nation) whenever he acknowledges the special and peculiar national character, as well as the vocation of the Slavs in general and the Czechs in particular:"[4] but he does not explore the implications of this admission. According to van den Beld, Masaryk became a political nationalist only in the World War—and did so for opportunistic reasons.

In *Concrete Logic* Masaryk had spoken of Providence as leading men though time from myth to science;[5] now that he recognized nations as the basic units of history, he saw them as the instruments through which Providence was able to carry out her grand design. Since he was a Czech, his primary concern was to discover the particular role of the Czech nation; once he had grasped the significance of Czech history and of the Czech national character, he would be able to give guidance to his compatriots. Just as Marx claimed that he and Engels had transformed socialism from a utopia into a science, so Masaryk, though he was a latecomer to the nationalist cause, offered the Czechs a "scientific" nationalism.

Masaryk presented his own interpretation of Czech history in a series of articles and books, the most important of which was *Česká otázka (The Czech Question).*[6] The nation needed a philosophy deeper than could be arrived at through common sense; a national policy had to be preceded by a national philosophy.[7] Only a firm philosophical foundation could give practical activity meaning.[8]

Masaryk claimed Karel Havlíček (1821-56) and František Palacký (1798-1876) as his principal sources of inspiration. In Havlíček, he found that "he had already written almost everything that [he] wanted to say politically," while "in the writings of Palacký [he] found the reasoned philosophical justification of his political program . . . ." The agreement between Palacký and Havlíček proved to Masaryk that he was on the right path. They confirmed his own feeling that he had to be in touch not only with his immediate predecessors but with all of history.[9]

The ideas to be included in a unified view might change at times; what Masaryk never doubted as the indispensability of the unified view, and again it was Havlíček who insisted on the close connection between politics and philosophy. Havlíček had demonstrated not only that the principles of practical politics had to rest on a philosophy deeper than common sense, but also that there can be no national policy without a national philosophy.[10] Such a national philosophy had actually been worked out by those in the past who were striving for an independent and original culture, and it had to have been based on a sure and firm philosophical foundation. "It doesn't matter what foundation," he said, "every thinking individual must have one."[11] The choice of that philosophy was of utmost importance to Masaryk. He believed with Jan Kollár that no nation's history was accidental but was rather a definite plan of Providence. Therefore philosophers and historians of every nation should fully comprehend this plan, find their own place therein and act accordingly, politically and otherwise.[12]

It was Kollár who made Providence's design known to the Czechs: Kollár had learned from his German masters, and mainly from Johann Gottfried Herder, to look upon mankind as an organized whole, whose evolution served the grandiose plans of Providence. Herder, Luden and others had taught Kollár that nations, not individuals, execute the cosmic designs. "Mankind in a given era expresses itself in particular nations; particular nations lead mankind."[13]

To grasp the meaning of history and of the Czech's national mission it was not necessary to delve deeply into the past. "History indeed is *magistra vitae*," Masaryk acknowledged, adding however that the main teacher of life should be present-day life itself, supplemented by the study of history. "It is not the evolution of things but the things themselves that are of first importance for the spirit."[14] The student should not dwell on historical change, for the "essence of things" remained always the same. Here again is the theme that man remains what he has always been. Masaryk's own statements made it plain that the direction and meaning of these studies were entirely his; he relied on Palacký and Havlíček only for a "clear confirmation" of his own development.[15]

The national awakening of the Czechs, he wrote, dated from the time of the European upheaval that had produced the French Revolution and also profoundly influenced the Slav peoples. The first ones to awaken national consciousness—such as Kollár[16]—had had to create and develop an independent and original Czech culture and a language that would make it suitable for literary work. They found the *Weltanschauung* they needed for such a national program in German philosophy. "A strange destiny," he commented, if German philosophy is to give a philosophical foundation to anti-German nationalism.[17]

German philosophers tended to regard nations as "natural organs" of the human race. Kollár accepted this view and so did Masaryk, who said that, though humanity may express itself differently in particular nations and languages, each nation is essentially a special "organ of Mankind." He stressed that the national awakening of the Czechs had been inspired by cultural and libertarian trends that were not in themselves consciously national, and this was quite understandable, since nationality and language were not at that time clear cultural concepts in Bohemia. All Czech history had pointed to the great era of the Czech Reformation in the fourteenth century and thus to freedom of conscience. Until that time languages and nationality had constituted only a means of civilization and education, and only in the course of a later evolution would the preservation and development of language and nationality become the primary aims of political nationalism. Masaryk strongly proclaimed that natural right did not permit one nation to rule another; nor was there anything in natural law to bar a nation from following its own course of development.[18]

Masaryk said that the lofty ideals of Herder and Jacob Friedrich Fries that Kollár accepted and forged into a Czech national philosophy were merely the repayment to the Czechs of a historical debt by German philosophy: the Czech reform movement of the fourteenth century had first fertilized German soil with new ideas; indeed Masaryk claimed that the eighteenth-century Enlightenment in Germany, France and England had been only a "continuation of . . . the main ideas of the Czech Reformation." Thus, when at the end of the eighteenth century the Czech nation returned to the true philosophy assigned to it by Providence, the Germans were merely a tool or medium through which the transfer was made.[19] "Humanity in the ethical aspect, culture in the intellectual, became the national ideal for Kollár," said Masaryk. Thus Slav nationalism (which Masaryk called "The Slav Idea") contained the universal ideals of mankind applied to the Slavs. It manifested itself in Bohemia, in Poland and in Russia through the persons of Kollár, Adam Mickiewicz and Ivan Kireyevsky and took the forms of Czechoslovak Mutuality (by which he meant solidarity), Polish Messianism, and Russian Slavophilism. The doctrines of all three of these Slav thinkers were concerned with the problem of "the historical destiny of mankind," with the question of how the future of all nations, of all mankind, were to be settled. Masaryk commented that the Czech relied on science and philosophy, the Pole and the Russian on religion, but each in his own way.[20]

It appears that Masaryk accepted the idea of a Czech nation because he felt that it had been conferred upon the Czechs by Providence and so of course was unavoidable, but he would have also accepted it had Providence given him a choice. Pekař argued[21] that Masaryk had repudiated his earlier stand when he wrote in his book, *Jan Hus,* that the Czech problem was always a question of religion:

> most people . . . think that religion is possible only in historically institutionalized forms as if religion itself was not changing and developing. Just as a nation develops economically, socially, politically, intellectually and artistically, so it develops [morally] . . . . Public attention is turned towards national and social problems, but . . . there too the main question is moral and therefore also religious.[22]

This quotation demonstrates not that Masaryk had changed his fundamental point of view but rather that he chose to emphasize now what he thought was the most important element in the Czech problem. When Pekar quoted from "The Czech Question" in order to show that Masaryk did not consider religion an essential aspect of Czech ideals (even while he was claiming that religion was essential for the Poles and the Russians), he did not realize that Masaryk made a distinction between positive religion—e.g., he felt that both Poles and Russians relied on "positive" religion—and religion properly so called. On the other hand, reason and ethics, allegedly characteristics of Czech thought, were compatible with (and to some extent synonymous with) what Masaryk thought to be true religion. As he wrote in his book on Palacký: "The guiding idea of our renascence is the idea of our reformation." He went on to say that the idea of religion had constituted the main content of Czech history and had instilled *meaning* into the past. He denied that it was possible for the Czech nation in modern times to deviate from its real nature: a nation could not have "two souls" at the same time.[23]

It seemed inconceivable to Masaryk that a nation might change its nature in the course of time and acquire a second "soul." If nations were natural units of mankind, not merely collections of individuals; if nations had certain tasks assigned to them by Providence within a great design; and if nations each had a distinct character suited to the performance of these tasks, then this soul would be permanent and incapable of change. Masaryk applied this general truth to the Czech nation, and he regarded it as self-evident. But although he felt sure that he knew what the true Czech nature was, it did not mean that the Czechs knew it; even fewer of them lived in accord with it. Indeed, to a man who, like Masaryk, believed he had the only right understanding, Czech history displayed a picture with sharply contrasting colors: in Masaryk's description it was a tale of fall and redemption; inspired enthusiasm and ignoble vacillation and weakness; loyalty and betrayal; divine wrath and punishment. He told the Czechs that they had betrayed the commands of humanity in 1487, when their nobility enslaved their own people, and that they were punished accordingly in 1620, when Imperial forces crushed the Czechs at White Mountain. "Could the Czechs have been more cruelly humiliated by Providence than by that ultimate fall . . . ?"[24] Masaryk noted also that a dual nature obtained in Czech character itself. Critics implied that a military tradition also held a legitimate place in Czech national history, and to this Masaryk agreed.[25]

Masaryk returned to the problem of national character in a lecture delivered in 1898 and published under the title, *The Ideals of Humanity and How to Work.* He appealed to his listeners and to his compatriots on behalf of a new, modern attitude toward work. He deplored the Czechs' predilection for martyrdom, saying: "Self-sacrifice has been our ethical ideal since Wenceslas, St. Ludmila, John of Nepomuk, Hus, and the Unitas Fratrum, through the Counter-Reformation and up to the most recent times. Every politician prates of it. This is a great danger, for the idea of martyrdom will become a commonplace to the nation which toys with it constantly." But how easy it was to swing to the other extreme: "I am convinced, however, that the very man who exults in it, may yet exult in agressive strength . . . ." Thus it was not "that at one time we were softer, at another harder; it is that we lack unity on a higher plane." The chief task for the Czechs, as he saw it, was "to work against this division, to reconcile the two opposites." This weakness of the Czech character was not unknown to other Slavs, said Masaryk, so that "it is perhaps legitimate to conclude that by nature the Slav has within himself a conflict, a contradiction."[26] Thus Masaryk meant more than "work" in the ordinary or practical sense when he implored his compatriots to action: he also meant work toward the developing of an integrated national character.

While Masaryk certainly advocated a national philosophy, he opposed "exaggerated" nationalism and, in a later book on Marxism, made it plain that he did not accept a nationalism that subordinated all other social forces to it.[27] Yet it might be asked whether Masaryk's basic assumptions and principles, which had little to do with nationality originally, remained unchanged once he had accepted the idea of nationalism. Here it is illuminating to examine the relationship between his ideas of nationalism and religion, including the ideals of humanity, in his writings.

Masaryk criticized those who were one-sidedly nationalistic and ignorant not only of Czech history but also of the Czech aims and methods then current. Masaryk was still sure that: "Our glory, our struggles, . . . have a *religious,* not a national meaning." Although nationalism might be a new idea for his country, he did want its history reinterpreted from that point of view.[28] Masaryk's denial of the existence of Czech nationalist sentiment before the eighteenth century has been contested by many, the most notable of whom was Josef Pekař. Pekař argued that nationalist feelings were expressed, in varying degrees, throughout the course of Czech history along with religious and other (e.g., monarchical) loyalties: thus, he said, the Hussite wars were not only religious in character, as would follow from Masaryk's statements, but contained national and social elements as well.

If we are to understand Masaryk's view of nationalism, his statements quoted above should be considered only in close connection with other statements he made on the subject. It should be remembered that he declared that nations were an organic part of humanity, invested with historical assignments bestowed on them by Providence. In this sense nations, and the Czech nation among them, had certainly existed much longer than could be inferred from his writings on the appearance of nationalism. The nationalist revival at the end of the eighteenth century was merely a national *awakening,* an act of self-recognition and self-awareness,[29] that is, in it the nation was recovering a knowledge of its true nature and mission. Before the awakening, in Palacký's words which Masaryk quoted, ". . . during the two preceding centuries we vegetated bodily while our soul remained hidden."[30] Thus nationality gained in Masaryk's philosophy of history a distinguished place in its own right, for to him the nation was not merely a group of men speaking a common language. For Masaryk history was primarily the history of religion; the humanitarian ideal that he saw as a religious principle became the cornerstone of Masaryk's social analysis of his country.

One theme with which the "Czech Question" had to deal was the so-called Cyrillo-Methodian concept. Its followers argued that Saints Cyril and Methodius, apostles of the Slavs, had been of Eastern Orthodox persuasion and that therefore the Czechs should renounce the Latin of their Catholic churches for the Czech language and the Eastern Orthodox Church. It was another, a pro-Russian, interpretation, and Masaryk set out to show how little historical foundation there was for such a proposal, accusing its proponents in fact of being indifferent to religion altogether, and of being dishonest as well as mistaken. Religion was a vitally important matter for the Czechs; and again it was Masaryk who felt he knew which religion this should be.[31]

He tried to convince his compatriots that they should accept the "humanitarian ideal" because he believed so strongly that it was the *Czech* ideal. Yet he ought to have realized that such localized support was not necessary if his real concern was with humanity. In *Our Crisis Today* he said: "I wasn't engaged in 'The Czech Question' in supplying philosophical proofs that the humanitarian ideal was the only legitimate one. I simply accept the teachings of Christ."[32] Certainly acceptance or nonacceptance of the teachings of Christ could in no sense depend on, or be influenced by, the nationality one belonged to. But Masaryk had not only decided on this somewhat irrelevant line of argument; he "reconciled" his previous ideas (from *Suicide)* about religion and its historical manifestations with his present preoccupation with nations as historical instruments of Providence. The procedure was not complicated. Masaryk recalled what he had said about Catholicism and Protestantism as the two historical principles of religious world outlook. Men as individuals were either Catholics or Protestants, but he now argued that nations themselves could also be so divided:

> As each individual settles his choice of the form which is suited to his subjective needs, so do nations as a whole strive to find their religious satisfaction in either of those forms. The Czech nation, as Palacký tells us over and over again in his 'History,' is by nature particularly pious, as is, indeed, all the Slav nation; at the same time it is, by nature, more peaceful than its Western neighbors, it is in its national character humane .... In its reformation the Czech nation produced a Christian church which has been the purest so far: The Brotherhood, which for this reason constitutes the central point of historical evolution of mankind.[33]

Palacký, one of the greatest leaders of Czech national revival, was known to have been influenced by Kant's philosophy: in fact, Masaryk said, Palacký found in Kantian philosophy the continuation of the efforts of the Bohemian Brethren, who "laid stress on life, not on dogma." And even when he discussed Kant's personal contributions to philosophy, Palacký sought to interpret them in relation to the Czechs.[34]

Masaryk did not devote so much time to writing about humanity and its relation to nationalism as he had to religion. By the term "humanity" (Czech: *humanita)* he meant all that the modern man might, according to him, designate as his hopes and aspirations, and which medieval man had summed up in the word "Christian." He found the humanitarian ideal the foundation of all the hopes of his time and, in particular, of national hopes. Masaryk hoped to convey two meanings by his term, the "ideal of humanity": first, proper manhood; and second, consideration for all mankind. It appears that Masaryk believed that humanity in either of the two meanings could apply to nations as well as to men; the meaning of what it was to be a man differed according to national boundaries. And indeed the actual content of "ideal of humanity" varies with periods and peoples: the English, French, Russians, Poles and Czechs each had an interpretation of the humanitarian idea peculiar to themselves.[35]

Again, as in the case of religious divisions, this did not mean that all the members of a nation accepted its ideal; but if not, they were that much less nationalistic. It certainly meant also that a given philosopher's system corresponded, in some not very precisely definable way, to his own nation's character: "And philosophy of nations has its character! . . . Herder for the Germans, Comte for the French, Spenser for the English are the representatives of the national character."[36] Masaryk added that a Czech historian would not only interpret Czech history with greater empathy, but his nationalism would be expressed in the way in which he looked at his nation's history and his interpretation of the events within it. As to the second meaning of the "ideal," Masaryk wrote:

> We are beginning to realize today that the idea of humanity is not opposed to that of nationality—but that nationality, like the individual man, both ought to be and can be human, humanitarian. Humanity is no abstraction enthroned somewhere above real men in the sphere of thought. Nations are, as Herder said, natural organs of humanity. It is in this sense that Kollár and Palacký based nationality upon the concept of humanity.[37]

But love of humanity has tended to become abstract, to exist more in fantasy than in reality. What that love required was to be concentrated on specific objects, for no one could love all men equally. Masaryk made the perceptive declaration that "People often take the hatred of another nation to be love of one's own," and went on to say that he would not argue that anyone can love a foreign nation as much as one's own. To do so would be unnatural. What was required was "to love our own nation, our own family, our own party," without an afterthought of hate.[38] And yet Masaryk never succeeded in proving that a positive love of one's own nation would not in certain circumstances generate enmity against some other nation. He agreed with Kollár that love for nationality was always a necessary step toward love of humanity. But Kollár who had been a warm defender of the humanitarian aspirations of German writers— Lessing, Schiller, Goethe and others[39]—was the same Kollár who wrote *Daughter of Slava,* a passionate attack on the enemies of the Slavs throughout history; and the foremost place among them Kollár assigned to the Germans.

Masaryk admitted that the Czech national revival had been by its very nature directed against the Germans. His observation that German philosophy had been used as a means to fight the Germans has been noted earlier. Masaryk made other statements of this kind; for example, he recognized that the Czech national revival included opposition to "German culture and German influences in general."[40] While the Czechs believed that in their developing nationalism they were working for humanity, development of a Czech culture carried with it a sharp struggle against another culture, even though that German culture was humanitarian and was also a highly advanced one. Why should men of Slav origin not have joined the already existing, highly developed national culture of the Germans, instead of building an alternative culture? One had to resort to another argument in addition to an abstract humanitarianism to justify the national emancipation of heretofore "unawakened" nations.

While Masaryk was an opponent of blind national fanaticism, he could not avoid certain situations when it seemed that a choice had to be made between nationalism and what would appear to have been the best interests of humanity. Thus, for instance, he wrote: "Today, surely every educated person knows German . . . . The evil of a universal acquaintance with German is assuredly a threat to us." "Our goal must be to rid ourselves of it all along the line." The matter was not only an intellectual one but was primarily a moral one: ". . . Anti-German violence will not mend matters when combined with a subservience to the German language."[41] He did recommend that German books be made available in a Czech translation, thus restricting the knowledge of German to a small group.

What Masaryk proposed was certainly compatible with the interests of the Czech nation. If its separate identity and character were to be

preserved; if one of the most important features of the nation was its
language; and if a thorough knowledge of German might induce the
Czechs to prefer German to their own language and bring them within
the sphere of German culture at the price of their neglect of Czech culture;
then, of course, a knowledge of German among the Czech people had
better be discouraged. On the other hand, one had to concede that this
also meant that the Czechs, taken individually, would not be so well-
educated and would in a sense be isolated from direct contact with an
admittedly advanced culture. What was good for the nation, it seems,
entailed a certain loss for its members—who were also members of mankind.

We have already spoken of Masaryk's judgments on the past: too many
sins had been committed against true Czech ideals; they had to be re-
pented of and undone. The Czech national character itself needed to be
raised higher in a new synthesis which, Masaryk hoped, would come in
the future. As a consequence of the split within Czech character, Czech
history (at least from the Awakening), as described by Masaryk, depicted
an internal struggle between Czech and non-Czech ideas. The latter usually
came from outside the country, but not infrequently they found a favorable reception on Czech soil; even those who had taken part in the
national Awakening succumbed occasionally to alien ideological influences. Perhaps the gravest danger of all came from liberalism,[42] which
tended to weaken "the principal idea of our revival, that is . . . the idea
of humanity which originated with our Brotherhood." He went on to say
that the Czech Brotherhood was quite different from that of the French
revolution, being founded on religious sentiment while the French revolutionary brotherhood denied religion and was a purely political group.
Liberalism in Bohemia had exerted a fatal moral and social influence.[43]
This alien liberalism had found an advocate even in Kollár, whom Masaryk
accused of transforming "our Czech humanitarian ideals" into an alien
Renaissance humanism.[44]

While "indifferent liberalism" was one danger, clericalism was another.
Masaryk condemned the Catholic movement for seeking to "subvert
the reformation ideal of our people . . . . Here compromise is not possible
. . . the Czech nation, because of its past, simply cannot accept clericalism."[45] Conditions in morals, the arts, and letters were very unsatisfactory
too. He saw the younger generation of Czechs falling under the influence

of Stirner and Nietzsche, and of various anarchist trends, particularly the doctrines put forth by Tolstoy and Ibsen. "Anarchism, call it by whatever name you like, is not Czech."[46]

From his philosophy of history Masaryk drew practical lessons for his own times. Conditions that had prevailed in the days of Havlíck and Palacký had now changed, Czech political practice had departed from the principles and directives formulated in past decades. In this departure and in the presence of various, and often conflicting, political, philosophical and religious tendencies in Czech life, Masaryk saw the root of what he called uncertainty or insecurity (*nejístota*). Obviously his country's program needed new "formulations in many important points," if it were to conform to the progressive spirit of the age. Since his concern was with the national program as a whole, he left many contemporary questions unanswered, in order to concentrate on what he deemed most pressing. It was not easy to discover a sound and appropriate formula for an all-embracing national program that was supposed to incorporate so many elements: concern for humanity and nationality, the restoration of Bohemia's constitution (*státoprávnost*), social reforms, cultural and educational policies.[47] He attempted to do all things in his writing; the Realist party's program also offered some answers.

In an attempt to relate his philosophical concerns to practical realities Masaryk declared that the Czech problem was a social one. It was the special task of the Czechs to make education, culture and economic progress accessible to the great masses of people. Social responsibility had become crucial in politics, literature and art, in science and philosophy, as a result of the national evolution.

To undo the events of 1487 (when the Bohemian nobility imposed serfdom on the peasants) was the national aim; it involved granting freedom of conscience and equality before the law to all citizens, so that all men might lead moral lives and fulfill the ideals of the Czech reformation, while working consistently for humanitarian ideals. The social problem was not merely one of labor, any more than it had been confined to the question of the peasants in 1487. "It is the question of morality or immorality .... of violence or active humanity .... What matters is that all of us should be brothers." Practically, Masaryk said, it meant extending the right of suffrage to all, including all Czechs in national politics. Havlíček had stood for this, although Palacký, to be sure, had opposed it, and in this he was wrong.[48]

Masaryk criticized the two large middle-class parties, the Old-Czechs and the Young-Czechs, because they overemphasized a narrow nationalism, reminiscent to him of the French revolution and the revolution of 1848, and failed to see that the working classes, as constituent elements of the nation, should also be included culturally and politically in the nation. Both parties lacked a truly Czech understanding of social problems.[49] Although Masaryk was no adherent of Marx and the social democrats, he regarded as only just the workers' demands for better living conditions. "Criticisms raised by Marx and socialist theorists are justified and, by and large, accurate . . . . I have no authority or right to oppose the demands for justice and equal rights." At the same time Masaryk, reiterating that for him the social question was primarily a moral one, appealed for a moral renewal. If they had a proper example, the working classes and social democrats would not cling to materialism: yet philosophical and theological adversaries of materialism were often as individuals no better, and often worse, than materialists.[50]

Masaryk's philosophy of Czech history did not find many adherents; indeed he never intended to carry out his program through political action, but he did hope that he would be able gradually to introduce among the Czechs a *tacitus consensus* on important matters so that national life might become more sound. Masaryk hoped that a properly organized program of national education might provide the people with the kind of knowledge that could not be found in their existing government-controlled schools. This national program was to achieve "a general education unified by a single point of approach, a philosophical, complete outlook on the world."[51]

It was not correct to say that the Czechs lacked a "national consensus" in fundamental matters such as their relations with the Vienna government or their position within the Empire: but Masaryk was thinking of a consensus that went far beyond these issues. Many years later, in his conversations with Čapek, Masaryk recalled:

> I should so much have liked not to have had to publish books;
> I never polished and perfected them enough. When I published
> them it was only because I felt that they had a topical impor-
> tance. If folk (sic) had left me alone—and I them—I daresay I
> should never have published a single volume . . . . I hurt people,

it is true, but I got more than I gave. I often overlooked people; and I used to be vain. But my chief fault was impatience. I felt that people should accept truth at once and act on it.[52]

This recollection appears to have been accurate. Neither Masaryk nor his followers showed much patience with their critics nor much tolerance of opposing points of view. Masaryk's distinguished polemicist Josef Pekař observed in 1912:

I would say that he both loves and hates to the same degree.
With what a contempt he speaks about liberalism . . . ,
with what mercilessness he passes moral verdicts . . . .
Were Masaryk to write a Czech history from *his* point of
view, his work would be a burnt offering to *his* God. The
blood of the offenders against *his* view of love and truth would
be flowing down from sacrificial altars . . . .

Referring to Jan Herben, one of Masaryk's disciples, who alleged that this antagonism between Masaryk and the historians was a "matter of conscience," Pekař added: "And it seems to me that this fanaticism of 'humanity,' had it only the power, would start criminal proceedings against us for the crime of heresy."[53]

Other Austrian nationalities such as the Ukrainians or South Slavs lived under a political regime where Masaryk's humanitarian message could be interpreted differently. "It would have been impossible to publish a translation of these [Havlíček's] poems in Galicia twenty years ago," Ivan Franko wrote in 1901, dedicating his translation of Havlíček's poems to Masaryk. The oppressive rule of censorship had lasted until almost that date. Franko was inspired in Masaryk's writings by the view that a nation's advancement was measured by the growth of political liberty within it and by its intellectual progress; national oppression, whatever lofty ideals it might invoke, meant a denial of progress.[54] On the other hand, Ernest Denis, perhaps because he lived in Paris, not in Lviv, confessed he did not understand exactly what Masaryk meant by "*humanita.*" He considered the "romanticist" Masaryk "little capable of drafting a parliamentary bill, but he can design an excellent program; programs have often the greater effect the less clearly they are worded."[55]

There were many valuable practical postulates in Masaryk's program. Also his intentions, insofar as one of them was a desire to calm down extreme nationalist passions, may be thought commendable. But the remedy he introduced, the *Weltanschauung* he called "Czech National Philosophy," was unacceptable to his contemporaries for many reasons. His polemical temper and zeal contributed additionally to Masaryk's remaining a lonely fighter in Czech society right up until the outbreak of World War I and his departure for abroad in 1914. Even his former associates, who had worked with him in academic, literary, journalistic and political spheres when "realism" stood for a program of rational and critical work, broke with him when they saw their old fellow-fighter and leader succumbing to myth-making and mysticism. One of the most distinguished critics of Masaryk's writing was his former friend, Josef Kaizl, who wrote a critique of Masaryk's history in *České myšlenky*.[56] Ernest Denis, a sympathetic, though not uncritical, observer of the Czech scene and a noted historian of Bohemia, praised Masaryk for connecting the situation in Bohemia to its past history and to general evolution of the Slavs, but considered many of his interpretations mystical and disconcerting. To see in Dobrovský and Havlíček direct successors of the Brethren or precursors of Tolstoy was a fantasy that proved the power of Masaryk's imagination. Masaryk was a prophet whose "mysticism" was unacceptable to Denis, but he recognized his merits as a moral leader and a writer.[57] A small group remained faithful to Masaryk, and revered him as the disciples of Comte had looked up to the founder of the Religion of Humanity fifty years earlier. Some of this attitude was carried over into American historical scholarship. S. Harrison Thomson felt that Pekař had entirely misunderstood or misconstrued Masaryk's position, and that the logic of history lay with Masaryk and his defenders. Thomson agreed with Masaryk and with his view of Czech historiography that: "Czech history was a spiritual pilgrimage in very essence sui generis; . . . the Slavic kernel of Czech development was so distinctly humanitarian and religious that any suppositious German influence was minor and superficial . . . . The principal credit for this radical change in the Czech concept of their own history is without doubt to be given to Masaryk himself. It would be difficult to find a clearer proof of any thesis than the actualization of this view in the free Czechoslovak Republic of Masaryk and Beneš."[58]

In his introduction to a recent English edition of Masaryk's national writings, René Wellek has remarked that if Masaryk's books amount to a political program, "they certainly go about it in an unusual way."[59] Indeed, did a modern political and cultural program have to be supported by references to the Czech national Awakening at the end of the eighteenth century, a discussion of all those early scholars and poets, not to mention going as far back into the past as the age of Hus? Wellek, unlike some earlier admirers of Masaryk, clearly states that Masaryk was not writing objective scholarly history in those national works—or even philosophy or theory of history. "Masaryk was not and did not pretend to be a professional historian doing research in archives. Admittedly he did not know or did not care about the exact nature of the theological disputes that brought about the death of Hus and the Hussite wars." Indeed Wellek felt Masaryk cared for the past only as he could use it to influence his contemporaries. Thus "the creation of a tradition that would become a force in the present and future seems an overriding duty to Masaryk."[60] In Masaryk's interpretation (as Wellek points out) the Czech national revival was not only a rebirth of language and national consciousness (we might add: not simply a process in the sphere of social change, a modernization or development), "but also a rebirth of what to him is the specific glory of Czech history: its Protestantism, which Masaryk interprets. . .as an assertion of intellectual freedom, of the right for the search for truth against any authority, and even more importantly, as an assertion of common humanity of man, the truly Christian practice of brotherhood, and the love of one's neighbor." Democracy meant to him that "every man should be able to strive for perfection." In Hus, likewise, Masaryk admired his zeal more than the content of his arguments. Like Palacký, he exalted "the Hussites who. . .defended Bohemia against the crusades sent for decades to bring them to submission."[61] Wellek reminds us that the Czechs themselves were at a loss when Masaryk first presented his ideas. Professional historians, such as Pekař, and politicians like Kaizl, were puzzled by Masaryk's message. For, as Wellek explains, Masaryk's view of Czech history—its "meaning"—was "a call to action, an appeal to his nation, which he wanted to become free in terms other than those claimed by nineteenth-century nationalist ideology." Masaryk wanted to give his people a national, and at the same time, a universal code of ethics.[62] While Professor Wellek's favorable evaluation of Masaryk's aim is very clearly stated, one cannot but note that the idiom and mode of Masaryk's argument was in no sense modern; did many Czechs view their social problems in terms of what went wrong in 1487 and who was punished for what in 1620?

What does come through from a reading of Masaryk's national writings is the earnestness and sincerity of his approach: if Masaryk had been any ordinary political entrepreneur, he would have been most unlikely to resort to the language that he did. Clearly, religion *was* the basic conceptual frame of his thought, and however one may be tempted to explain away the "real" meaning of Masaryk's message (for example, by arguing that he was in fact a modern, secular, realistic and practical politician), the evidence does not support this interpretation. Religion was vital to Masaryk, and he did not see any other way of coping with the problems of the modern world except in broad ideological, that is, religious terms.

Since Masaryk wanted to influence his contemporaries in a certain way, let us conclude this discussion by noting the practical, political implications of his national-religious doctrine. It has to be borne in mind that the dreamer of 1894 would play an enormous role in Czech politics after 1914. What were, then, those implications?

One relevant fact is that Masaryk's ideological concept allowed him to define nationality in two ways. In one sense, the Czech nation was composed of all those persons who, according to the usual criteria (i.e., language, race, birth or national consciousness), were called Czechs. The second meaning referred to certain specific religious, political and cultural ideas and values, which for Masaryk were either truly Czech, that is conforming to his own view of the Czech national character or soul, or "non-Czech" insofar as they did not conform. Such ideas were non-Czech even if they were present in the thought and action of certain living Czechs. In Masaryk's interpretation, national values and ideas existed independently of the actual national consciousness of the individuals who made up a nation: when members of a given nation were ignorant of its true character and direction, this meant that the nation "slept" or "lived only a physical life." There also existed, he conceded, a national consciousness that did not correspond to the true national spirit—a false national consciousness, so to speak. Masaryk's point of view and the Marxist concept of the ideology of the proletariat have certain common features. For example, what Marx wrote in reference to the consciousness of the workers could as well be applied to Masaryk's concept of the Czech nation:

> The question is not what this or that proletarian, or even the whole of the proletariat at the moment *considers* as its aim. The question is *what the proletariat is,* and what, consequent on that *being,* it will be compelled to do. Its aim and historical action is irrevocably and obviously demonstrated in its own life situation as well as in the whole organization of bourgeois society today.[63]

It had been Masaryk's purpose in his writings on the meaning of Czech history and its ideology to justify, on the ground of conformity with the true Czech character, a program for the future that was to become common for all Czechs. Advancing his own theories as the only ones that were truly Czech and fighting for the ideological purity of the Czech nation, Masaryk simply labeled those who disagreed with him "non-Czech."

While only those who accepted Masaryk's interpretation of history and his Realism as the program for the present day were truly Czech, not all who applauded his humanitarian ideals qualified thereby as Czechs. One first had to be an ethnic Czech, i.e., by virtue of the Czech language, culture, traditions, and political aspirations. Masaryk's national philosophy, while it upheld universal religious and humanitarian ideals and might thus appear nonnationalistic, was in fact a doctrine addressed solely to members of the ethnic Czech nation. It was not sufficient to recognize his principles in order to be admitted to Masaryk's "Brotherhood." Czech ideals might have been espoused by some Germans when no Czech entertained them, but no German could become a Czech (not even a "spiritual" one) just because of this. As nations were for Masaryk instruments of Providence and were defined by language and culture, so their existence as distinct ethnic entities was a prerequisite to their creation of national humanitarian ideals and religion. In effect, Masaryk provided a justification for Czech nationalism (as well as for nationalism in general) that even many a radical nationalist might not have dared (or cared) to invoke. In his view everything ultimately and surely depended on, corresponded to or was guided by, nationality: morals, religion, politics, art and literature.

To work for one's nation in accord with its nature and spirit was to obey historical necessity and man's moral duty. Such a position, rigidly follow-ed, would tend to make the solution of interethnic conflicts (for example, within a multinational state dominated by one nation) more, rather than less, unmanageable. The implications of Masaryk's national philosophy became clear when it was accepted as the official "philosophy of Czecho-slovakia." Because of its national Czech character it estranged Slovaks, Hungarians and Germans, while its "Hussite" flavor made it no more sympathetic to those Czechs who remained loyal Catholics.

On the other hand, we must also conclude that the refusal of an over-whelming majority of the Czechs to follow Masaryk's philosophical message was evidence of their political and cultural maturity, rather than of their failure to heed the voice of a prophet. The Czechs in the 1890s (and even more so in the 1920s) were too far advanced, too mod-ern, too rational, too educated, to believe that their problems could be solved by a mass conversion to Masaryk's religious philosophy. This growing maturity of the Czech nation was attested to in many ways—among others by the emergence of a network of modern political parties, which represented different soical groups and upheld different political ideals. (Masaryk himself had helped to modernize his nation through his teaching, publishing projects, involvement in public controversies, etc.) In other words, the Czechs had managed by then to face the crisis of modernization without feeling they had to seek salvation in messian-istic ideologies that held out the promise of solving all their problems at once.

Eventually Masaryk seems to have recognized this fact himself. Begin-ning in the 1900s, he concentrated his attention on concrete, specific issues that could be presented without reference to any cosmic structure. This does not mean he abandoned his basic beliefs, however: a careful reading of his public utterances strongly suggests that he continued to view the world *sub specie aeternitatis.*

CHAPTER V

NATION AND STATE

We have followed Masaryk's evolution from philosophical and religious cosmopolitanism to a nationalism grounded in history and language. Once he had abandoned his concern with universal authority, symbolically represented by *Suicide* and *Concrete Logic,* and turned his attention to the *Czech Question,* his world view changed substantially: he placed the problem of religion and authority within the framework of a national community. The consequences were not immediately evident; Masaryk claimed to have discovered a universal humanitarian content and meaning in the Czech national past. His emphasis gradually shifted, however, from the question, "What spiritual authority should man accept in order to lead a good life?" to "What political authority should the Czechs obey if their nation is to live freely?"

We noted briefly certain political implications of his cultural nationalism, both with regard to the relations between those Czechs who subscribed to Masaryk's program and the rest of the Czech nation and with regard to the relations between the Czech nation, the German population of Bohemia and the Austrian state. Now is the time to examine Masaryk's position on those questions more thoroughly, even though the history of the nationality problems in the Habsburg Monarchy and the reforms introduced during the last years of its existence—or the question of Czech autonomy itself, that most notorious and possibly most significant part of the entire nationality problem in Austria—is not a major concern of this study. How did Masaryk interpret the German-Czech conflict, how did he propose to solve it, and how were his proposals for its resolution related to his philosophical and political stance?

In the *Czech Question*, he had tried to tell his compatriots what their responsibilities should be if they were to attain their national ideals and thus preserve and develop their own nation. This material was addressed to, and of concern to, the Czechs alone. He went on to pose questions that had presented themselves to many Czechs long before Masaryk voiced them in 1900: "Can our nation . . . become politically independent? To what degree? And through what policy?"[1]

To recognize this new emphasis on politics and political independence is not to suggest that before 1900 Masaryk had ignored the problem. However, in earlier times he had defined his position on Czech self-rule in the language of "State Rights." As we recall, the program adopted by the Czech politicians in the 1860s and still regarded, at least in theory, as the foundation of Czech national aspirations, was based on the Historic State Rights of the Lands of the Crown of St. Wenceslas. These historic rights had been adopted to provide a constitutional foundation for the autonomy of the Bohemian lands (Bohemia, Moravia and Silesia) within the Habsburg Empire. The Czechs here were consciously imitating the concept of the Holy Crown of St. Stephen, the basis of Hungarian independence. Modern Czech nationalism thus justified its demands for autonomy and national unity in Bohemia, Moravia and Silesia by claiming to be the only legitimate heir of the old Kingdom.

Gradually, especially after the collapse of the constitutional reform of 1871, the historic rights ceased to be treated as a realistic political concept and became a slogan. Czech political endeavors became concentrated on specific issues, such as the right to use the Czech language in administrative service, expansion of Czech education, and in other areas.

During his first term as a Reichsrat deputy (1891-93), Masaryk upheld the validity of historic rights. However, even then, unlike his Czech parliamentary colleagues, he usually based his arguments on the achievements of the Czech nation in modern times rather than on the legalistic or constitutional arguments employed to prove the validity of the Czech cause.[2] The Czechs' accomplishments in the cultural and economic fields, according to Masaryk, justified their demand for political independence and the right of self-determination for the Bohemian nation.[3]

The political independence hoped for by the Young Czechs was to be granted to the three provinces as a unit, while the "Bohemian nation" was to consist of both the Czechs and Germans living within them. The concept of a political Bohemian nation corresponded to the theory on which the claim to self-rule was based: "State Rights" referred only to the historic, and not to the ethnic, Kingdom of Bohemia. Masaryk, like other Czechs, spoke of a "Bohemian nation (*Volk*) of Czech and German nationality," and of "Bohemians of both nationalities."[4] The Bohemian State so conceived would remain under the rule of the Habsburgs and maintain a close union with the other parts of the Empire, although details were not clearly defined. In 1890 Masaryk wrote:

> . . . our main aim is independence (*samostátnost*) within the Austrian framework. Our Slav program is not directed against our German compatriots. . . . If the Germans, having an identity of language, religion and culture [with the Germans in the Reich] can be good Austrians, why could not the Czechs, with their Slavic sentiment, [but] who are separated from the majority of Slav peoples not only by language but also in culture and religion, be [Austrians] too.[5]

As a member of parliament, Masaryk distinguished himself from the other Young Czechs by his loyal pro-Austrian attitude; the above lines suggest that he believed in Czech-German cooperation even within the narrow boundary of Bohemia. But it should be mentioned that he expected the Germans of Bohemia to make a double sacrifice: that is, not only to renounce a national unity with their co-nationals in Germany but also to accept separation from their fellow Germans in Austria. Such a separation would have been an inevitable consequence of making Bohemia a distinct political entity.

Any difficulties in relations between the two nations within Bohemia were to be solved by local conclaves of the Germans and Czechs: "Autonomy, not mechanical dismemberment of the land, will bring us together." But again the implication was that the Germans would be in a less favorable position than the Czechs. In 1890, referring to the agreement between the government and the Old-Czech Conservatives that had given certain concessions to the Czechs in Bohemia but not in Moravia or Silesia, Masaryk asked the House: "Do you not understand that our State Right rests on that ethnic basis for which we fight now?"[6] National unity, which he and most Czechs would have liked to see renounced by the Germans, nevertheless remained a basic aim for the Czechs themselves.

It would be incorrect to overemphasize the political side of Masaryk's orientation at this time, but he did support two basic points: first, the continued existence of the Empire as in principle compatible with freedom and "self-realization" of all its nationalities including the Czechs— though reforms to resolve certain conflicts would be essential; and, second, the confinement of Czech nationalism to cultural matters. "When we speak of. . .local self-government, autonomy and political independence, we mean first of all that we may educate and teach our nation in its own spirit."[7] Underlying this was Masaryk's relative lack of concern for and appreciation of politics in general, which were plain to be seen in his virtual equating of such concepts as autonomy, local government and independence. Thus his acceptance of Austria and his lack of interest in the strictly political side of the Czech question combined to isolate Masaryk from the politically active Czechs. He withdrew at that time from public affairs and addressed the nation in the series of articles and books on the historical and moral meaning of the Czech question which were examined in the preceding chapter.

By 1900 the Czechs and Germans were engaged in a protracted and bitter struggle that preoccupied their respective national adherents in the Bohemian lands; in many cases, it led to the breaking off of personal relations between Czechs and Germans. Time and again projects and schemes were devised and drafted that promised a solution of the ethnic conflict in Austria and elsewhere. But, as Robert A. Kann was to observe much later, while such proposals were often sound in themselves, they were for the most part directed to symptoms rather than to the disease: they were "only symbols concealing the real issue, federalization or centralism, even reorganization or dissolution of the empire."[8]

The Czechs had made considerable progress, but gradual concessions and reforms were not enough to resolve the basic issue of Czech-German relations. For the Czechs, reforms were but steps leading to the desired goal of the unification of all three lands under some form of common authority in Prague, in a political structure where the Czechs would constitute a majority. The Germans, on the other hand, increasingly clamored for a *de facto* administrative division of Bohemia into Czech and German districts, hoping to facilitate in this way eventual political and constitutional partition of the crownland.[9] The two goals were incompatible. Count Karl Stürgkh, the Austrian Prime Minister, declared in 1914 that the Czechs and Germans were separated by a wall "the thickness only of a piece of paper." But, as A.J.P. Taylor has pointed out, Stürgkh "did not see that this piece of paper was of impenetrable thickness: it was a literary idea, the conflict of two historical claims which had separated them all along."[10]

Before we embark on a discussion of Masaryk's position on the Czech-German conflict in the 1900s, let us note that theoretically three solutions were possible: first, Germans could dominate the Czechs in the Habsburg Monarchy or perhaps in a united Greater Germany that would include the historic lands of St. Wenceslas; second, there could be a partition along ethnic lines, preventing domination of one nationality by another; and third, a Czech state could be formed, either within a reformed monarchy or as an independent country, which would include also those areas of the historic kingdom that were predominantly German in population. If such a Czech state were "national" in the sense this designation acquired in the nineteenth and twentieth centuries, its German citizens would have to be considered a national minority within it. Finally, going beyond nationalist solutions, various nonnational or supranational solutions could be contemplated—although they were not generally throught practicable. Where did Masaryk stand on these issues?

Although he had initially equated national identity with a spiritual and cultural force, he now had to grapple with political reform; he realized that the State could no longer be excluded from nationalist considerations. The State controlled the life of its population, but on the other hand ethnic groups aspired to establish their own states and to promote their own causes. In the Czech situation, it was necessary to take into account the so-called historic rights that all the Czech nationalists strongly supported and all the Germans bitterly opposed. When Masaryk returned to practical politics in 1900, after a break of seven years, he announced that he no longer recognized the validity of the historic state rights. Although he would repudiate this point of view in 1914-1918, he believed at this point that a better solution to the Czech-German conflict could be reached by renouncing the state rights.

First, he denied the legal continuity of the Crown of St. Wenceslas, which the advocates of State Rights were using as a basis for claims to independence. The changes in the constitution that had gradually deprived the Bohemian Crown of its independence had been introduced not by arbitrary acts of the monarchs but with the consent of the legitimate representatives of the Bohemian estates, if not through their direct action. This meant that the Bohemian State no longer existed legally. Second, Masaryk pointed out that the Czech national leaders had recognized the revolutionary changes of 1848 that overthrew the old constitution based on the estates (nobility, clergy, the burghers). The Czechs had taken part in the Reichstag of Kroměříž, which had been convened on the basis of a centralist constitution; they had also recognized the latter constitutions. Not until after the Hungarian Compromise of 1867 did the Czechs begin to claim a status for Bohemia equal to that enjoyed by Hungary. But the Hungarians, Masaryk pointed out, had been behaving in quite a different manner: they did not send their representatives to governing bodies of the Empire, and moreover until 1848 their Diet was exercising rights that Bohemia had lost long ago.[11] Thus, whatever the question of pre-1848 constitutions, the Czechs' actions after 1848 had deprived them of any possible right to invoke a law now superseded by a new one that they had themselves recognized.

Third, even had the historic rights remained in force, they would have carried a meaning unlike that attributed to them by some of their advocates when they referred to the old constitution of the Crown as a sufficient basis for a Czech national state. Masaryk accused such people of ignoring the historic rights of both Czechs and Germans in Bohemia: "The historic right, conceived only territorially, is a right of the Czechs and Germans and it cannot be [used as] a miraculous device for bringing about our national independence."[12]

Against historic rights Masaryk put forward "natural right," that is the right of a nation, defined by common language and culture, to live its own free life. On this principle Masaryk and his party, the Realists, based their plan for a Czech-German compromise that was to satisfy the national ambitions of both peoples.[13] They proposed to preserve the three historic crownlands of Moravia, Bohemia and Silesia and to divide each of them into a number of autonomous and nationally homogeneous districts (Czech, German, or Polish). In exceptional cases, mixed districts would be formed. In their dealings with citizens all public offices and agencies were to employ the language of the citizen concerned. While lower-level officials might know only one language, employees of central offices were to be bilingual, able to conduct business in the language of any of the lower units. The language of the majority of the people in a province would determine the particular language used in its provincial offices, which meant Czech in Bohemia and Moravia.[14] Correspondence between the lands (Bohemia, Moravia, Silesia) and Vienna was to be carried on in the language of the land: central offices of the Empire would be obliged to deal with Czech matters in Czech; Czech was to be introduced as the language of the Supreme Court in Vienna when the case before it had originated in Bohemia. The governing bodies of the lands—their Diets—would be elected in nationally homogeneous constituencies and would sit in separate political divisions called *curiae*. The program did not indicate whether the *curiae* would possess equal powers or whether the *curia* representing a majority nationality would prevail.

This program rested on two basic principles: equality of the nationalities and languages that made up Austria, particularly of those nations living in Czech lands; and primacy of the natural right over the historic rights that Masaryk claimed to have "reconciled." According to him, Czech political demands had vacillated between a political claim, i.e., the demand for equal political rights for the Czech lands within the Monarchy (which were ethnically mixed), and a cultural, mainly linguistic, claim for the equality of the Czech nation among other nations. He argued that this vacillation had been present even in Palacký's earlier program, when he recommended a federation of lands on some occasions and a federation of nationalities on others.[15]

However, Masaryk's interpretation of Palacký's intentions was not entirely correct, for Palacký had not wavered between self-government for the lands and one for the nationalities; rather, the alternative that Palacký proposed was a federalism of nationally mixed historic lands and a federalism of nationally homogeneous lands that had yet to be created. To implement the latter option it would have been necessary to partition Bohemia and Moravia into separate areas, German and Czech. For a time Palacký acceped this, but he later returned to his former position and upheld the integrity of the lands of the Bohemian Crown. Thus the choice for Palacký was in both cases territorial, involving either bilingual or linguistically homogeneous territorial units. In other words, a nation would exercise its rights over certain defined areas through the population of those areas.

While Masaryk invoked Palacký's authority when he made a distinction between "political" and "national" independence, he was not if fact reviving Palacký's program. The alternatives suggested by Masaryk allowed for the whole State's being organized internally as a group of provinces and/or an association of nonterritorial nations, speaking a single language and enjoying a measure of self-government. In the latter case, a citizen would be entitled to participate in his nation's affairs regardless of his place of residence.[16]

Which option did Masaryk prefer? As we recall, he had asked, "Can our nation be politically independent?" Political independence of a nationality presumably meant an ethnically independent unit; in the Czech case, an independent state might include the purely or predominantly Czech parts of Bohemia, Moravia and Silesia. Insofar as the Realist party made any concrete suggestions for reform, it is evident that it envisioned neither a national nonterritorial autonomy, like Karl Renner's plan, nor the creation of a single Czech national state within the Monarchy. This was a disappointing answer to the question regarding the feasibility of Czech independence. Masaryk replied to one of his critics that if the Czechs aspired to form an independent national state covering all the Bohemian lands, the same right could not be denied to the Germans. He and his party accordingly proclaimed the equality of all the nationalities within Austria, including those of the Bohemian lands.[17] What did this equality amount to in practice?

The Realist program guaranteed the right of citizens to speak German in their dealings with public offices of any rank and in any place in Bohemia, Moravia or Silesia. In this respect the language rights of German citizens were equal to those those the citizens of Czech nationality would possess. This equality, however, did not extend to the officials of central provincial agencies: there, in internal official use, only Czech was to be employed. More importantly, having repudiated the historic rights and their dogma of indivisibility of the lands, Masaryk did not exclude the Germans from a nationally mixed land. Here he was not so much obeying a principle of equality as recognizing the fact that the Czechs were not strong enough to impose their will on the Germans, who made up more than a third of the total population of Bohemia.

In practice, Masaryk failed to recognize the equality of the German and Czech nations as entities comparable, in the words of the Realist program, to individuals. Masaryk was prepared to grant this equality only in the sphere of education: in that field every nation in the State was to make its own plans, excluding all outside authority, and each nation would have its own School Board, related to the ministry of public instruction under special regulation.[18] By retaining ethnically mixed provinces, the possibility was left open for the majority population to exercise a predominant influence in legislation; separate national councils were proposed, but no one of them was given the right of veto power over the decisions of any of the others. Thus the equality of nations (as distinct from equal linguistic rights of individuals) remained problematic.

While such an arrangement would give the Czechs a clear majority and thus the opportunity to outvote the Germans (the two nations would vote separately to elect a fixed number of deputies allocated to them), the program was disappointing to the Czechs too. It was not enough for them to have a majority in two or three separate provinces: nationalists, including the Czechs, have always regarded a unified nation under one central authority as essential. The Realists had fulfilled this demand only in the field of education. Moreover the Czechs, with the exception of the Socialists, refused even to contemplate an administrative subdivision of their lands into districts according to ethnic composition. They saw in it a first step toward a political partition of the historic lands along ethnic lines.[19]

Since Masaryk rejected historic rights in favor of the natural right of nations to political independence, to be consistent he should have proposed a partition of Bohemia into Czech and German areas. Instead, he introduced into his argument the alternatives of a political independence of nationally heterogeneous states on the one hand and a national *nonterritorial* independence on the other.

His real reasons for the rejection of historic rights were based not so much on the dubious legal standing of the concept as on his pragmatic belief that the goal it was designed to achieve was, under existing conditions, unattainable: the Germans were too strong to permit the Czechs to organize a state opposed by a third of the population. He rejected historic rights also because reliance on them would deprecate the need for contemporary political action; therefore, Masaryk proposed "to invoke first of all the so-called natural right, and with it we give content to the historic right."[20] While he denied the legal thrust of historic right, he recognized the expediency of accepting it with qualifications. "Real law," Masaryk explained, was not created by the earlier law, but it originated in the moral and political aspirations and actions of a conscious nation. He did not wish to slight the "state rights" consciousness of the Czech people, he said, but he conceived the historic right "mainly nationally and economically." This meant that all political activities would have the political independence of the Czech nation as their ultimate goal.[21]

Masaryk's program was so formulated as to support not only a Czech national independence but also to justify the retention of all historic lands within the future Czech state. Unlike the traditional "historicists," who defined the nation of Bohemia as composed of Czechs and Germans, i.e., in a territorial sense, though they hoped that the Czechs would predominate, Masaryk sought to keep the best of the two principles: the right of an ethnic nation to political independence and the preservation of the whole of the historic kingdom as well.

His reconciliation of these two mutually exclusive principles was logically questionable. We do not know whether Masaryk was aware of his dubious logic; certainly he knew what he wished to accomplish with its help: an independent Czech state. The Realists openly admitted that prevailing political conditions, as well as "the small number of the Czechs, their geographic position, and the fact that Czech lands are inhabitated also by Germans and Poles," had forced them into an association with other nations.[22] Yet the small likelihood of attaining independence in the foreseeable future did not necessarily mean that more favorable conditions might not subsequently arise for Czech aspirations. By 1905 Masaryk had recognized unequivocally that every nation seeks to establish its political independence.[23] He described the "national ideal" as a full cultural program, reflected in the economic sphere and the national character, in labor, in the sciences and philosophy, and in art, morals and law.[24] In private, he had expressed an anti-Austrian sentiment even earlier. Thus in 1899 he wrote to Karel Kramář: "The main thing: you worry about Austria! I don't. Palacký said: We were before Austria and we will be after it. But while for him this was only a catchword—I want it to become a fact. (Such facts do happen too.)"[25]

There is little doubt that Masaryk had accepted the principle of nation as superior to that of the state (rather than vice versa, as he had done in the 1870s) long before 1914. In 1907, in a letter to the *Neue Freie Presse* he expressed his conviction that the national movement in Austria had not reached its culmination: "The government must be prepared for nationalism to grow extensively (politically) and also intensively (culturally). . . . Austria must at last carry a positive nationalist policy."[26]

Considering his other statements about political independence as an ultimate national goal and his insistence on the indivisibility of Bohemia in defiance of German opposition, it is difficult to understand what a "positive" Austrian policy could have meant to Masaryk except the surrender of the Bohemian Germans to residence in a state that would have a Czech national character.

The movement from a cultural toward a political nationalism was but one facet of Masaryk's evolving world view. There was another, a countervailing tendency. This tendency reflected his perception of the nature and direction of social evolution toward universal "autonomization" or "socialization" of states and societies.

In his youth, Masaryk had witnessed the decay and gradual dissolution of a rural, patriarchal and traditionalist society and the rise of an urban and industrial civilization. He was appalled by the consequences of this great transformation, and he sought refuge in a new religion. By 1910, or even by 1900, the world had changed for the world he had known and interpreted earlier. Society did not disintegrate under the impact of secularization and modernization. Initially an overwhelmingly rural people, the Czechs had made a successful transition to urban life and become a dominant element in Prague, relegating its German-speakers to a minority position.[27]

While traditional religion was losing its former power, new social and moral bonds were holding society together—despite the absence of that new religion Masaryk had so warmly espoused. National consciousness and class consciousness were gradually spreading among the masses, awakening in them an ethnic sense and integrating them effectively enough for them to pursue common political and economic goals. One indication of this process of gradual integration of the Czech nation was the "nationalization" of socialism in Bohemia: what had begun as an internationalist, German-led force was transformed over the years into an element of the Czech nation. By 1914 independent Czech trade unions were formed.[28]

Tensions and conflicts generated by the social and economic transformation found an outlet in mass organizations like trade unions and mass actions such as strikes, as well as in the press and the political arena. By 1900 the Czechs had developed a multiparty system characteristic of a socially differentiated, economically advanced society.[29] The electoral reforms of 1897, which extended suffrage to urban masses, and the reform of 1907, which established universal male suffrage in Austria (but not in Hungary), were milestone events.

These developments encouraged reliance on piecemeal reforms; gradual change, as opposed to violent revolution, was widely believed to be the dominant tendency of the modern age. If conditions were not satisfactory yet, then wider suffrage (or better use of existing suffrage), stronger unions, more effective local government, more popular education, were all seen as the proper means for bringing about the desired goals. Even if the nationality conflict was increasingly perceived as potentially disruptive, its resolution through peaceful reform was generally proclaimed as a possible and desirable course. In international affairs, pacifist movements worked for the elimination of war from the civilized world. There were of course the dissonant voices that foretold the coming of the twentieth century as the inauguration of an age of social and national upheaval, but they were clearly in the minority.

Masaryk was an eloquent preacher for reform and against revolution. It was quite in accord with his turn of mind to approach contemporary issues from a historical and philosophical point of view. He claimed to have detected the direction of the evolutionary process of change in modern Europe and argued that commonly held notions of political science, including the international relations and domestic affairs of various states, ought to be brought into conformity with this overall evolutionary trend. As he wrote in 1896 in a Viennese journal: "The decline of absolutism is certainly connected with the continental and global organization preceding it; obviously one has to define State independence and sovereignty quite differently from the way one did before 1848."[30]

This new trend prevailed not only in relations between states but also within them: "The older cosmopolitanism as liberalism has formulated it is giving place today to a more adequate development—an uncoerced international organization of independent cultural groups."[31] Thus Masaryk's conclusions on the historical meaning of the Czech question now seemed to him to have been brought into accord with the general direction of the modern world: the weakening of the old centralized states and the emergence of autonomous cultural groups, or nations.

Autonomization, Masaryk declared, was as necessary as centralization, or integration, for modern society and state. A certain degree of local autonomy was indispensable if the State were to function properly; self-government was desirable "not merely in the economic sphere but also in the political, national, ecclesiastical." Masaryk acknowledged the influence that the English Fabians, whose writings he had read in the original and in German translations, had had on his position, and he included them in the bibliography of his *Grundlagen des Marxismus.* He spoke approvingly of the work being done in England, remarking that English Socialists took enthusiastically to local self-government and that municipal socialism had become a very opportune and fortunate part of English self-government.[32] In this spirit Masaryk, when he spoke at the founding congress of his party, the Czech People's Party (*Česká strana lidová*), in 1900, said, "we want autonomy and self-government not only political, but also economic, social, linguistic, national and cultural."[33]

At this time, Masaryk was not writing systematically about the State and had little theoretical interest in social groups, but he often spoke about society and social forces, by which he meant to include the State. Let us see then what his view of contemporary affairs was—especially his concept of the State and society—in the context of European evolution. In his book on Marxism, Masaryk enumerated the basic categories in which, he said, the "collective life of men and all the content of history" were contained. They were: religion and the Church (morals and customs); art, science and philosophy (culture, education, intellectual pursuits); State (including the military) and law; nationality and language; economy and social organization; and biological organization of the population (the last presumably referring to health care).[34] Of course the basic categories could be further subdivided. He refrained from ranking the categories in the order to their importance as he saw it, but he attributed a key role to religion and the Church.[35]

Masaryk believed that the State and its political ramifications mattered less than some people thought, doubtless because of his assessment that the processes leading to autonomy and world centralization were the two principal causes of the weakening of powerful states in modern times.

This point of view was also in accord with his belief that religion and the Church have have been the strongest social factors throughout history while the political factor is merely one among many social and cultural forces. In other words, the State, as the political sphere of action, is intimately connected with all its cultural spheres: it reflects and corresponds to the state of church and religion, and to the level achieved by literature, science, economy and trade.[36] The state, Masaryk continued, has always served cultural, religious and moral ideals, even in the absolutist era. Now that the State was weaker than the other forces of society, cultural life was in the ascendant in nations and society. Masaryk distrusted, and had little respect for, academic philosophers and political thinkers who dealt with question of the State, authority, sovereignty, and so on, in the abstract. Although he made no claims to resolve these questions himself, fearing perhaps that he too might succumb to "the scholastic method," at times he made broad statements on his concept of politics:

> . . .we have to make an attempt to comprehend every collectivity, such as the State, church, nation, people, etc., in its fullness in a given time. Therefore not the State in the abstract, but so and so many soldiers, etc.; in a word: to have a view of the State that is full, definite, not . . .hazy or abstract.[37]

To this concept Masaryk opposed the older view of the State as independent, outside or above society: "we should not look at the State in the *mythical* way, i.e., we ought not to see and idolize it as a demigod or even god . . .to a large majority . . .the State is a huge entity which stands above society and the individual; a wise and all-wise being, good for some, evil for others."

Masaryk rejected the aristocratic flavor of that older view in which the State served only as a political organization for the upper classes, insisting that the people were the State. The reactionary concept of the State as merely an unwielding abstraction and an embodiement of law was a relic of medieval scholasticism. Thus he strongly opposed what he called the liberal view that the State was omnipotent as one deriving from absolutism and reaction. Not surprisingly, in light of his general views, he added that while the State should serve the needs of all classes, a government with universal suffrage would not in itself answer this requirement.[38]

A well-known Liberal and former associate of Masaryk, Josef Kaizl, observed that Masaryk made no distinction between the view of the State as it actually was and the view of what one thought the State *should* be. Kaizl wrote: ". . .here in Austria. . .one sees in the State the political organization of the richer classes, above all the aristocracy . . .there is no "older view" in such an allegation . . .merely a simple truth."[39]

Masaryk attributed to the Liberals a faith in police power and the position that the State was omnipotent.[40] Although it was true that they were not primarily concerned with the social, economic and political conditions of the people, as Masaryk had been since the 1890s, the Liberals were not quite guilty of the charges that he aimed at them.[41] Admittedly they argued that the State was too strong and that its power was capable of abuse, but Masaryk took this to signify that if the Liberals had not believed in the omnipotence of the State and the police, they would not have continued to demand legal reforms to be enacted by the State. He charged them with a "negative" faith, as it were, in the State: they expected miracles to ensue from political reform. Masaryk, on the other hand, thought that conditions would improve if the people could be persuaded that the condition of the existing State was really not so bad, and in any case no worse than that of religion or of the people themselves. Politics was quite secondary and did not merit the concern the Liberals gave to it.

For similar reasons Masaryk also disagreed with some of the opponents of the Liberals, seeing State power to be less substantial than they did. Thus he said that he was in accord with the Church's conviction, whether represented by Catholic, Orthodox or Protestant politicians, that by its nature political power is inferior to spiritual.[42] Masaryk saw proofs of the spiritual and moral character of the State in its peculiar relationship with the Church. The State had had a cultural and ethical role from the very beginning, through the Middle Ages and into modern times. The fact that the struggle between Church and State had so long endured implied that the State, like the Church, had an ethical and rational dimension. But in modern times the State had been usurping the intellectual and ethical leadership of the Church.[43]

Though Masaryk laid so much stress on the moral and religious factors in society, he never fully developed the idea that the State should be the institution for the promotion of morality, perhaps because the religion and ethics of the Habsburg Monarchy directly contradicted his own values.

After the Russian Revolution of 1905, when politics became his overriding interest, Masaryk was still extolling the virtues of moral and religious perfection outside the framework of the State and within autonomous bodies free from State interference. Only after World War I, in an independent Czechoslovakia, when a national Czechoslovak Church was established (which, as President, he enthusiastically supported), did Masaryk rediscover the "higher meaning" of the State. In Prague in 1928, he said: "The State has a spiritual meaning, a moral meaning."[44] It was at the time of his Presidency also that Masaryk spoke of law as the means by which the State gradually extended "the injunction of love to all the practical relations of social life" and, if necessary, enforced compliance with it. "In practice," he said, "the State approaches the ethical maximum —the ideal—through the ethical minimum—the law."[45] This Hegelian statement may be seen as more idealistic than practical—but it might also be perceived as placing the State and its officials above the level and judgment of ordinary politics.

Before the war Masaryk was not in a position to influence Czech or Austrian politics directly; his impact was that of an outsider who might bring certain issues to the attention of the public and thus create a climate favorable to certain recommendations, but he was himself not participating in the decisionmaking process. Zeman did not exaggerate when he said that in the last years before the war there seemed to be two Masaryks: "the Masaryk in Prague, an outsider, who had come from a remote part of the country, was educated in Vienna, married a foreigner and upset his compatriots many times," and the Masaryk who "made his mark abroad."[46]

This duality is a point to remember as we consider Masaryk's proposals for the solution of the Czech-German conflict within the monarchy. The proposals are interesting as illustrations of his thinking, but they had little if any influence on formation of the policies that bore directly on the problem. They are also worthy of note because a time would come when Masaryk would be in power: accordingly we will be able to compare Masaryk the prophet unarmed with Masaryk the prophet armed, to borrow Machiavelli's phrase that was popularized in Deutscher's biography of Trotsky. Much more revealing as to what Masaryk actually did before 1914 are his reflections on autonomization as the direction in which modern politics—not just in Austria but in the civilized countries of the world—was moving. The Masaryk who had once decried all reforms as pointless and revolution as a self-destructive act of rebellion against God now recognized the necessity for social and economic reforms. He became a fighter against popular superstition, the intolerance of the Church, the abuses of state authority, and militarism. He supported the rights of the individual and the cause of industrial labor; in the Austrian parliament he spoke for oppressed nationalities; and he advocated political reforms. As our account will show, it was in this area that Masaryk "made his mark" not only abroad but also at home—even though he did not win thereby recognition as a national leader.

Continuing the theme of *Suicide*, Masaryk published in 1896-1898 a series of articles that dealt with philosophical, artistic and literary questions in the light of his religious ideals; their joint title was *Modern Man and Religion*. Connected thematically with that series were his university extension lectures, published in 1901 as *Ideals of Humanity*. In 1900 he again advocated a religious faith that would be distinct from, but compatible with, science. He revised his system of sciences by elevating ethics to the rank of a philosophical discipline; in *Concrete Logic* it had been treated as a practical application of sociology.[47] He even recognized theology as a science, having treated it before as an expression of mythological thinking. It does not seem likely that Masaryk revised his system for scientific reasons; rather he may have realized that his proposed institutional solutions were impractical and therefore decided to stress the validity of ethics and religion. The more he engaged in the practical, social and political problems of his time, the less attention he paid to the creation of grand designs for a total reform from above. Nevertheless he did not give up his conviction that the practical questions of the time should be set within the framework of a comprehensive and integrated scheme that would embrace both the world of action and the world of thought.

As early as the 1890s Masaryk began to take an active interest in social questions. He went to the workers and, when there were strikes in Prague and Kladno, he gave talks to the strikers. He hoped to divert their thoughts from hunger and poverty and ended by being labeled a Socialist, a term that "was like a red rag to a bull to the middle classes and intelligentsia." He supported the demand for an eight-hour working day and insisted that the professional and academic education of workers should be promoted. He opposed Socialism as a doctrine, finding himself a Socialist simply in his "love of one's neighbor, humanity."[48] In 1898 he published

in Czech, and in 1899 in German, *The Social Question,* a voluminous critique of the philosophical and sociological foundations of Marxism. The
book exercised a considerable influence on the Czech reading public;
outside the country its critics included Kautsky, Cunow, Labriola, Van-
dervelde, Bernstein and Plekhanov.

Masaryk understood that the social question and the nationality conflict were closely connected. Specifically, the social conflict in Austria
had a pronounced ethnic facet because Czech industrial workers con-
fronted German industrialists. But the social conflict also divided the
Czech nation into two: the bourgeoisie against the workers. As he said
in his lectures at the University of Chicago (1902): "Our nation is therefore actually divided into two, and as long as it is divided . . . one cannot
speak about a complete rebirth of the nation. In order for the [national]
revival to be complete this question must be solved."[49] Among those
particular aspects of the social question which Masaryk considered especially acute and demanding solution was the women's question, by which
he meant that in Austria and Bohemia women had to work not only in
the family but also for wages outside the family. The women in those
countries were therefore more oppressed than were the women in England or America, where a much smaller proportion of women had outside jobs. Thus, the Czech national revival still remained "incomplete
and imperfect." Not only did the Czechs lack political independence,
but they still had to solve their social questions; for the national revival
was not simply a "national" but also a "moral and social process."[50]

Around the turn of the century Masaryk also became practically involved in ethnic and indeed racial controversies connected with Jewish-
Christian and German-Czech relations.

In 1899 nineteen-year-old Anežka Hruzová was found dead near the
town of Polna, in Moravia, and Leopold Hilsner, a local Jew, was soon
thereafter charged with murder. Although the authorities launched what
appears to have been a normal kind of investigation, the case was quickly
transformed by the public and by the press into a "ritual murder" case.
Especially active in giving this direction to the investigation was Dr. Karel
Baxa, a Czech politician (and the mayor of Prague, 1918, in independent
Czechoslovakia). Baxa represented the family of the deceased, and in
this capacity was a private prosecutor. At the trial, Hilsner was found
guilty of (ritual) murder, and was sentenced to death. It was only then
that Masaryk became involved in the case, after a former student of his

from Vienna had asked him to take a stand on the matter. Masaryk responded and published, among other statements on the Hilsner case, a brochure arguing that the case should be retried. He did not question Hilsner's involvement in the murder, that matter having been, in his opinion, a proper subject of investigation; what he objected to most firmly was the charge of ritual murder, which, to his dismay, was widely believed in the Monarchy, including the Czech lands. Because of Masaryk's stand, the Czech University in Prague became the scene of hostile demonstrations. Masaryk was publicly accused of having sold himself to "the Jews" and to "Vienna." His classes were suspended for two weeks. Only two professors publicly condemned those demonstrations: the others, including Masaryk's friends on the faculty, chose to remain silent.[51]

The Hilsner affair was a dramatic event in the Habsburg monarchy and in the Czech lands, and it became a matter of deepest concern to the Jews not only in central Europe but all over the world, including America. It uncovered not only German anti-Semitism, but also the power of anti-Semitism among the Czechs, including the educated strata. Baxa, a leading anti-Semite in 1899, made a career as a Czech politician; and during the Dreyfus affair almost all Czech newspapers were anti-Dreyfus.[52] It has been noted that in tsarist Russia in 1912 in the ritual-murder trial of Beilis, the defendant was found innocent and the ritual-murder legend refuted, while in the Hilsner case the defendant was sentenced to death on the same charge.[53] Whatever the broad historical significance of these events, it would seem that in a study of Masaryk's thought two points need to be stressed. First, the Hilsner case, if it influenced Masaryk's thought at all (and we tend to suppose that it did), reinforced his skepticism about the natural wisdom and goodness of the masses; after all, Hilsner was condemned by public opinion, and it was the Emperor's mercy, not the people's will, that changed his death sentence to life imprisonment. Second, it must have brought to Masaryk's mind once again the critical importance of the intellectual and moral education of the populace especially now that they were participating in government and serving on juries in cases like Hilsner's. Masaryk's Platonism, however disagreeable it may appear to a dedicated democrat, has to be seen in the context of his time. Masaryk knew, or thought he knew, "the people." Politically, the Hilsner affair moved Masaryk to the left: the Social Democrats fought anti-Semitism and accordingly were his principal allies, even though philosophically he opposed them.

When one speaks about the German-Czech confrontation in the Habsburg monarchy or in Czechoslovakia one does not always recognize that the confrontation had a pronounced Jewish dimension or aspect. Linguistically and culturally, in virtue of their predominantly urban habitat and occupation, the Jews of Bohemia belonged to the German world, especially before 1848. Later in the course of the nineteenth century increasing numbers of Jews adopted Czech and began to consider themselves a part of the Czech nation, even though in the capital, Prague, they remained overwhelmingly German in orientation.[54] We have already reviewed Masaryk's stand on the German problem. What was his position on the Jews? His support for Hilsner was a question of human rights, so to speak, and it implied no political stand per se.

As early as 1883 Masaryk was speaking of the Jews as a distinct nation, not merely a religious community, and demanding that they be recognized as such.[55] A Zionist leader from Bohemia, Felix Weltsch, commented in 1931 that Masaryk's statement had preceded by fourteen years Theodor Herzl's similar declaration, and that it sounded like "a prelude to Zionism."[56] In the 1890s Masaryk criticized Marx for his simplistic, economically-oriented treatment of the Jewish problem. He argued that the Jews were a nation even though they had lost their original language and referred to Zionism as a movement that would promote their moral regeneration.[57]

Masaryk's view that the Jews were a nation in virtue of their religious beliefs and historical traditions accorded with his position on the spiritual and religious nature of Czech nationhood. He did not think that emigration of Jews to their historic homeland was a precondition of their enjoying the rights of a nation, feeling that mass emigration posed a number of practical problems, but he certainly supported granting them recognition as a national group in those countries, such as Austria, where they lived. He did not favor allowing Jews to be designated as Czechs (or Germans) by nationality if they retained a Jewish religious affiliation. Masaryk's identification of Czech nationality with the legacy of the Czech Reformation obviously made it impossible for someone to be Czech (that is Christian) and a religious Jew at the same time. He did not exclude, although he did not promote, religious conversion. In his stand Masaryk was faithful to a tradition going back to Karel Havlíček who as early as 1846 had declared himself against the inclusion of the Jews in the

Czech nationality. According to Masaryk, the Jews of Bohemia, who found themselves in the middle of the German-Czech conflict, should choose to be neither German nor Czech but to declare their Jewish nationality instead. He had little sympathy for the so-called "Czech-Jewish movement." In this regard his stand was not shared by his own Realist party, which in 1912 declared itself in favor of the "Czech-Jewish" solution, by which one could remain a Jew by religion and be a Czech by nationality.[58]

It goes without saying that Masaryk opposed all discrimination, whether for reasons of religion or of ethnic or racial origins. His own party had Jewish members and sympathizers. He favored granting the Jews full rights and he fought anti-Semitism and other forms of prejudice, both before 1914 and later, in an independent Czechoslovakia. At the same time he believed that *national* unity ought to rest on a community of spirit, which to him was a community of religion or at least one based on a common religious tradition. Understandably, the emerging Jewish national movement in the Habsburg monarchy found a supporter in Masaryk and some of its adherents drew inspiration and encouragement from his ideas. The young Zionists in Prague, organized in the *Bar Kochba* society, admired Masaryk not only for his courageous fight in Hilsner's defense, or for his earlier campaign against the national forgeries of Hanka, but also because he argued that politics ought to be guided by the principles of morality and insisted that nationalism is not a goal in itself but a means to promote the welfare of mankind.[59]

We can now see more clearly why Masaryk made Liberalism a frequent target in his nationalist writings of the 1890s. It would seem that he disapproved of the legalistic and political, therefore "abstract," approach of liberals to the question of citizenship: for them it was a matter of the law, the constitution, of a general principle that disregarded the spiritual content of the nation. A political community, Masaryk held, ought to be based on the stronger foundation of a spiritual community embodied in the nation. We might say that for Masaryk citizenship in the state pertained to what Ferdinand Toennies called *Gesellschaft* or "society," while nation was a *Gemeinschaft,* or "community," a deeper and more enduring form of human association.[60]

In 1900 Masaryk's political party, the Czech People's Party or Realists, was founded; its program was adopted at a convention in Prague where

Masaryk made the principal speech. Masaryk would have preferred to call his party "Czech Unity of Brethen," but he was persuaded to abandon this idea.[61] The program proclaimed Clericalism as its main philosophical enemy. With renewed energy Masaryk defied the Church's rule over the souls of men, and preached a new humanitarian religion "free from myth and revelation" and based, as he said, on belief in a personal God and the immortality of the soul. Clericalism, said the Realists, abuses religion; while they opposed this, the Realists declared themselves in opposition also to the Liberals and in favor of "genuine" religion.[62] When in 1906 a Catholic priest denounced a schoolteacher to the authorities for holding unorthodox opinions, Masaryk, in a speech of protest, said: "A catechist of this kind is no guardian of religion but an informer paid by the Government."[63] A libel action was brought against Masaryk by 308 "catechists," and then, charging him with an offense against religion, criminal proceedings were instigated. The catechists lost their case, and Masaryk was acquitted by the court.

By this time he was an internationally known personality; his name had become familiar to a wide European and American public during the Hilsner affair. He attended international temperance congresses in Vienna and Danzig; in 1907 he was present at the Boston International Congress of Religious Liberals. He had visited America also in 1902, exploring religious conditions there and the life of Czech immigrants. A year later Masaryk sprang to the defense of a professor from Innsbruck who had been attacked by the Clericals, making a celebrated speech in the Reichsrat against a "Church-restricted" *Weltanschauung* in favor of a free scientific outlook.[64]

Just as atheists, "indifferent liberals," and free-thinkers, even though Masaryk was not one of them, became his fellow fighters on many concrete issues, so in politics he became allied with the Socialists. Masaryk could be seen marching in the First of May parades, and in 1905 he was one of the speakers at a huge demonstration for electoral reform, organized by the Socialists.

In 1907, in the first election based on universal male suffrage, Masaryk was returned to the Reichsrat. Running as a Realist, he contested a Moravian constituency with a Socialist and a Clerical; he won on the second ballot, after the Socialist had withdrawn in his favor.[65] It is worth noting that the Realists polled less than one percent of the Czech vote countrywide. In the Reichsrat, Masaryk took part in the parliamentary debates on the Czech-German question, spoke about conditions of the Slovaks in Hungary, Polish-Ukrainian strife in Galicia, and on the Jewish question—all internal issues that the multinational Habsburg monarchy faced before 1914. Masaryk consistently argued that major structural reforms, giving all peoples of Austria their due, were necessary if the state was to survive. In his speech in the debate on the Polish-Ukrainian conflict in Galicia (a debate occasioned by the assassination of Count Potocki, governor of Galicia, by a Ukrainian student), Masaryk condemned this particular act of political anarchism, but conceded that even Catholic and Protestant theologians had in the past approved of anarchistic acts of the so-called "Monarchomachs" (i.e., regicides). He was thus letting it be known that under certain political conditions Christian ethics could sanction a recourse to violence.[66]

He also devoted a good deal to attention to Austria's foreign policies, especially the monarchy's relations with Serbia. This was an issue inseparably tied to the state's internal nationality problem as well, since after the annexation of Bosnia (1908) the South Slav population of the of the state had sharply increased. Two celebrated incidents—the so-called Agram Treason Trial, at which a group of South Slav politicians (all Austrian citizens) stood trial as Serbian agents, and the related "Friedjung Case," which involved a Viennese professor who believed himself in possession of documents compromising the South Slavs (in fact these were forgeries)—gave Masaryk an opportunity to raise the entire South Slav problem at the parliamentary forum. He attacked the foreign minister, Aethrenthal, and demanded a full parliamentary investigation of the affair.[67] He suspected that the authorities, including foreign service officials, had actually fabricated the treason case in order to foster anti-Serb sentiment. Masaryk returned to the South Slav question in 1912-1913, when he traveled to Belgrade and then to Vienna where he talked to the foreign minister in a vain attempt to bring about a rapprochement between the two capitals. He was profoundly offended to discover that the Viennese foreign minister suspected him of seeking a monetary reward for his trouble.

Because of these concerns, travels and polemics, Masaryk's name appeared often in the European press. In 1913-1914, he began to be mentioned as a candidate for the Nobel peace prize, presumably because of his efforts in Belgrade and Vienna. These press rumors were taken quite seriously in Vienna, and the military chancellery of the heir-apparent of the monarchy, Francis Ferdinand, sent inquiries to Austrian ministers in Stockholm and Copenhagen urging them to make sure that the prize was not in fact awarded to Masaryk. Vienna was informed that Christiania (Oslo) was the seat of the committee for the peace prize (still a novelty in those days) and that Colonel Straub, the Austrian military attaché in Stockholm, would travel to the Norwegian capital to intervene personally. The Austrians breathed a sigh of relief when they learned there was no likelihood of Masaryk's receiving a Nobel prize.[68]

Active as he was in domestic and international politics, Masaryk did not neglect his academic pursuits. As an earnest of his life-long fascination with Russia, two large volumes on *Russia and Europe* were published in German in 1913. The work was not only a scholarly achievement but was incidentally a revealing statement of Masaryk's political orientation, which he presented in the guise of a historical and philosophical comparison of Russia and the West.

Masaryk had long argued publicly that a reform of the Habsburg monarchy was desirable and necessary. It is impossible to identify the precise moment when he finally despaired of the possibility of peaceful change and decided that the Czechs could fulfill themselves as a nation only in an independent state of their own. A study of Masaryk's writings indicates that by 1900 he had come to believe, at least theoretically, that a self-governing state was the most desirable goal for any nation.

Thus, before the outbreak of World War I, Masaryk had reached a turning point in his political evolution. There was a potential conflict between his pleas for autonomization and decentralization of the State, on the one hand, and his tendency to view the State as an instrument of national self-assertion on the other hand. There was also a discrepancy between Masaryk's advocacy of a pluralistic program, his support of various autonomous social organizations, and his increasing preoccupation with nationality as having a value superior to other social and cultural values. Perhaps it was in relation to Vienna and the still centralized State existing there that Masaryk was a "pluralist" and "autonomist;" by weakening the State, he may have thought it would be easier to strengthen national unity outside the political framework, through cultural and educational work within the nation alone.

Masaryk followed the convictions he had formed perhaps as early as 1900, when in 1914 he openly challenged the legitimacy of the Habsburg monarchy. He proclaimed a revolutionary authority in the name of the

Czech nation and himself as its leader. The reactionary and multinational monarchy had by then lost all justification, and the established leaders of the Czech parties had failed to act. To understand Masaryk's actions in 1914, his changing position on the question of leadership must be taken into account. For Masaryk was not condemning Austria simply because it was not a national state of the Czechs. He categorized the Habsburg monarchy and its established religion, Roman Catholicism, as survivals of a prescientific, theocratic order that would inevitably be succeeded by an "anthropocratic democracy." He believed himself to be a leader of a new kind, just as he viewed Vienna (and tsarist Russia) as regimes led by incompetent, therefore illegitimate, oligarchies. Masaryk's resort to revolution was predicated on a broader conception of a conflict between theocracy and democracy. This interpretation of Masaryk's attitude toward the Habsburg monarchy is different from that of a number of writers on Masaryk. For example, in a recent study, Antonie van den Beld writes: "He spared Austria none of his criticism; though he remained loyal to the idea of the Empire . . . it cannot be said that the idea of national identity is an idea which leads to the formation of a state in Masaryk's works . . . . It was only during the First World War that the idea of a nation state dawned upon him; even though it was not a coherent idea."[69]

In this writer's view this is a fundamental misunderstanding of Masaryk's political position and additionally of his historical interpretation as given in *The Spirit of Russia,* which condemned both the Romanov and Habsburg monarchies in its critique of "theocracy." Granted, Masaryk said at times that he thought Austria would continue to exist in the foreseeable future: but this was not a declaration of *loyalty* to the "*idea* of the Empire."

CHAPTER VI

THE NATIONALIST REVOLUTION

In the summer of 1914 Masaryk faced the most serious dilemma of his political life: should he remain in Austria, hoping for reforms in the future, or go over to the anti-German and anti-Austrian side? The decision was by no means an easy one. For a variety of reasons, Masaryk had become increasingly disillusioned with the policies and institutions of the Monarchy. The annexation of Bosnia-Herzegovina in 1908, followed by the South Slav treason affair in 1909 (in which high officials of the Monarchy were implicated in the forging of documents supposed to have proved the South Slav politicians in Austria guilty of treason), reinforced his negative view of "theocracy."[1] In his public statements before 1914 he had continued to say that for good or ill Austria would survive and that therefore there was all the more reason for needed reforms, but it cannot be inferred from this that the aristocratic and Catholic Monarchy commanded his primary allegiance. Besides, Masaryk was not an "Austrian"; he was a Czech whose commitment to his nation was paramount, and his attitude toward Austria was a function of this commitment. It was within this scale of values and priorities that Masaryk considered his options in 1914. Which side was more likely in victory to advance the cause of the Czech nation?

Ever since the epoch of the French Revolution and Napoleon, oppressed nationalities have seen in armed conflict between the Powers an opportunity to fight for their freedom. "For a universal war of peoples, we pray to Thee, O Lord," exclaimed the exiled Polish poet Mickiewicz, and his sentiment was shared by countless other nationalists. While in the history of war and diplomacy World War I is seen as a terminal event in a sequence that includes among others the Franco-Prussian War of 1870-1871, the Russian-French alliance of 1894, the Anglo-French entente, and the Bosnian annexation crisis, the nationalists have viewed the period of 1914-1918 as a phase in a process triggered off in 1848, during the "Springtime of Nations." In his "1848: Seed-plot of History," Sir Lewis Namier wrote that "every idea put forward by the nationalities of the Habsburg Empire in 1848 was realized at some juncture, in one form or another," during the following century.[2] In this respect 1914-1918 was one of the most decisive turning points.

From the very outset of hostilities, indeed since before the war had begun, some nationalists in central and eastern Europe placed their hopes in the Russo-French-English coalition, their goal being the defeat of Austria-Hungary and Germany. They included Serbs, Croats, Romanians, Slovaks and Czechs, as well as those among the Poles for whom Germany was the most dangerous of the three partitioning powers. On the other side there stood those nationalists for whom Russia was the oppressor and they were ready to work for, or with, the Central Powers. Among those anti-Russian nationalists were the Poles led by Pilsudski, and some less well known Finns, Estonians and Ukrainians.

Needless to say not all nationalistically minded members of dependent nationalities were ready to take the path of revolution. Most remained at least outwardly loyal to their respective governments. As for the masses of the people at large, they disappointed both nationalists (Pilsudski was quite bitter when the populace in Russian Poland failed to heed his call for an insurrection) and socialists like Lenin and Rosa Luxemburg, who had counted on transforming the war into an international civil war. The Czechs were not much different from the other nations. Most of those called up, served in the ranks of the Austrian army, among them Professor Masaryk's son Jan. The parties were divided, but those who remained loyal to the monarchy—Social Democrats, Clericals, Agrarians—were much stronger than those who had secretly become involved with the Russians (National Socialists and the Young Czechs led by Karel Kramar).[3] Masaryk's own party, the Realists, who were represented in the parliament by him alone, looked to their leader for guidance. What was to be done?

After a period of reflection and calculation, Masaryk reached the conclusion, which his political—and highly placed—Viennese contacts confirmed, that a victory of the Central Powers would result in the strengthening of German influence in the Monarchy at the expense of the Slavs;
the position of the Czechs had been bad enough before the war, Masaryk
felt, and a German victory would make it worse. The alternative, a pro-
Russian policy (to which, for example, Kramář was commited) held out
no better promise. Masaryk had been a consistent opponent of tsarism
—The Spirit of Russia in 1913 left no doubt on this score—and had no
wish to see Bohemia become a Russian protectorate under a Grand Duke
from the House of Romanov. He began to work out what Karel Pichlík
has called "a democratic alternative" to the pro-tsarist, Russophile, anti-
Austrian program.[4] When a German paper asked him for an anti-tsarist
declaration that might give philosophical or ideological support to the
German-Austrian cause, Masaryk refused, giving as his reason that the
French Republic and an essentially democratic England were on Russia's
side. In the end Masaryk resolved his indecision by choosing the democratic alternative represented by the West. He was now prepared to act,
no matter which side was the more likely to come out ahead.[5]

While at first Masaryk's interpretation of the emerging conflict between
the Powers was quite undoctrinaire (he denied then that a clash of philosophical principles was involved), after he had made his mind to join the
Allied side he convinced himself, and sought to convince others, especially the Allied leaders, that they represented the cause of morality, democracy and liberty. Most importantly of all, they stood for the liberation of
small nations, whereas "the German camp" stood for the exact opposite
of all those ideals.

Eventually Masaryk and other nationalists succeeded in popularizing
their program, although the statesmen, diplomats and generals of France,
Britain and Italy in private remained less impressed by those high-sound-
ing words. The Allied shift from a policy that had envisaged the survival
of the Habsburg monarchy toward one that entailed its dissolution, was
more influenced by the practical considerations of war than by Masaryk's
(or his colleagues') historico-philosophical treatises about the zone of
small nations between Russia and Germany.[6] Still, in the long run, the
nationalists proved to be more successful in ascribing a nationalistic "meaning" to the war and making of it in its final stages a war of nations, than
were Lenin and Trotsky in setting Europe aflame in a proletarian revolution.

How did Masaryk justify his leadership of a national revolution in terms of his own political philosophy? We recall that one of his most serious charges against Marxism was that it was a revolutionary doctrine. He was opposed to revolution both on political grounds, alleging that it seldom offered much improvement over the regime it displaced, and on moral grounds, because it was synonomous with violence. He felt that the question of revolution was in everyone's mind: "We hear it on all sides: social and economic revolution, political and philosophical revolution, literary and artistic revolution." To Masaryk a revolutionary was a political fetishist, putting his faith in social and political miracles; and convinced of his own charisma:

> A revolutionary is an aristocrat, an absolutist, and a tyrant, even though he goes into battle with slogans of equality and brotherhood. A revolution is characterized by secrecy. The secret police is only its official complement. A revolution is . . . political superstition. Few revolutions are truly successful, and only to an infinitesimal degree are they creative.

Therefore, Masaryk considered revolution indefensible not only historically but ethically as well: "it demands killing," he said, "something about which Marx has no scruples."[7] By 1913, after the 1905 Russian revolution and the Austrian crisis of 1908-09, Masaryk made a better case for the legitimacy of revolution. He was even able to ascribe a major role in initiating a revolution to the man who led it and to justify this role by his democratic theory:

> "There arise in all domains persons who are assigned leadership or directly and deliberately seize it."[8]

The organization of the Czech Committee in Paris in 1915 under Masaryk's chairmanship and with Edvard Beneš and Milan Štefánik as his assistants bore out this observation. Neither revolution nor rebellion was excluded from the domains in which Masaryk allowed individuals to seize leadership:

> The justification of a revolution is not furnished by the participation of the masses, but depends upon the motives of those

who. . .initiate and guide the movement. Always, however, it is essential to adduce proof that the revolution is actually in conformity with the true interests of the people, that it represents a real progress in democratic evolution. . . . Ethically considered revolution is permissible only in the last resort. Not until all other means have been tried must we have recourse to the extreme measure of revolution, and then only after the most profound searchings of conscience.[9]

Many years later, Emil Ludwig asked if the ideal revolutionary was a man guided more by reason or by passion, and Masaryk at once defined him as "a careful thinker. . . . Autonomy begins with the self. How can I govern others if I do not govern myself?"[10]

Masaryk, however, made no effort to reconcile self-rule with autocratic rule by himself; nor did he believe that the people's true interests could best be served by consulting them. In the course of the war he gave considerable thought to the organization of a postwar government in Bohemia. At that time he hoped that the Czech legions "might march with the Allied armies through Germany. . . [and] dictate peace in Berlin as the Germans dictated it in Paris or Versailles."[11] From Berlin,

> We should march by way of Dresden to Prague, I as dictator which indeed I was after the soldiers had proclaimed me as such. At the head of 60,000 men I was master of the situation and could take quick measures to convoke parliament. . . .

He cannot have envisaged parliament's functions very clearly since as dictator he hoped that he would solve pressing problems independently and "peremptorily."[12]

Masaryk wanted to see a reconstruction of Europe along national principles. Much of his wartime writings were propaganda pieces, but they were more than that. Here the politician, trying to win advantageous boundaries and other concessions for his nation, must be distinguished from the theorist who expounded his broad vision of historical development and the place of nationalism within it. By separating Masaryk the politician from Masaryk the scholar or ideologue, it becomes possible to advance a critique of his political program in which specific measures can be evaluated in the light of his general principles.

Among Masaryk's many writings of this period were memoranda for the governments of Britain, France, and the United States, but his book *The New Europe* is his most representative work and the one most worthy of attention. It combines Masaryk's arguments in support of concrete political desiderata with an outline of his philosophi~al and historical convictions. Written at the end of 1917 and given a final revision in the fall of 1918, it was privately published in London that same year and reprinted soon after.[13]

Masaryk had long feared Pan-Germanism, that is the movement working for the inclusion of all Germans (including Austria, parts of Bohemia, etc) within a Greater Germany with Berlin as its center. We have seen that in 1914 he concluded that should the Central Powers win the war, or even survive undiminished, the German element would become drastically stronger in the Habsburg monarchy. While he was writing *The New Europe,* his worst fears were realized: the German nation, with its 68 million people, was now in control of 224 million, that is, of Austria-Hungary, Bulgaria, Turkey, occupied Belgium, northern France, Serbia, Montenegro; as well as the Baltic Provinces, Poland, Lithuania, and the Ukraine. Furthermore, Masaryk said, "where it cannot employ their military strength, it exploits their economic and financial strength . . . Russia, being strategically weakened by the revolution, [has] concluded a disgraceful and dishonorable peace . . . ."[14]

Having assumed, like all sensible people, that the Bolsheviks would be defeated, Masaryk's immediate and overriding concern in those days was to forestall a peace that would leave Austria-Hungary undisturbed and thus make the rise of an independent Czechoslovakia impossible. His concern for Czechoslovakia was presented as an essential element in a larger design: the reorganization of an intermediate zone of small nations living between the Germans and Italians in the west and the Russians in the east. The peoples of East Central Europe, Masaryk pointed out, were ruled by alien powers—Germans, Hungarians, and Russians— while in the West nations were for the most part independent and ethnically homogeneous. To secure peace in Europe and prevent the resurgence of German tendencies toward hegemony, the Eastern European peoples should be granted independence from the Habsburg Monarchy, or autonomy within a federalized Russian Republic. This republic would include the peoples of the former Russian Empire, except for the Poles, who would be independent; Finland might also become independent if Russia

were to agree. The idea, now firmly entrenched, that East Central Europe
is a distinct region of the continent owes much to Masaryk for its incep-
tion. He advanced his broad conception of an anti-*Mitteleuropa* to support
the Czechoslovak political program and bolstered it by his interpretation
of European development since the French Revolution. He agreed with
Herder that nations were "the natural organs of humanity" and states
only artificial ones. Masaryk offered a truly Herderian vision of European
transformation:

> The discrepancy between State and ethnographic frontiers
> causes the unrest and wars in Europe. . . . States are instru-
> ments, the development of nations is the goal. Democracy, there-
> fore, accepts the modern principle of nationality . . . the right
> of nations to self-determination proclaimed by the Russian
> revolution demands changes of political boundaries.[15]

Masaryk's wartime politics was guided not only by his general conception of European evolution and/or his fear of German domination of
Central Europe, but also contained a clear element of strong personal
anti-Austrian feeling. The following passage is illuminating: "Prussia
especially I cannot love; but I strive to be fair to her. If I really hate
anything, it is Austrianism—or rather Viennism, that decadent aristocratism,
. . . that nationally nondescript and yet chauvinistic medley of people
known as Vienna. I do not like Prussianism, but I still prefer it, with its
robust militarism and hungry harshness of the parvenu, to the thin-blood-
ed, pleasure seeking spirit of Vienna."[16]

When he was still in Prague, Masaryk saw the war entirely in pragmatic
terms as the result of economic competition and the struggle for power
between England and Germany, but even then he was thinking of its
effect on the position of small nations and of the eventual strengthening
of democracy.[17] But in exile, he emphasized the ideological significance
of the war and passed over the more obtrusive military and economic
issues. In *The New Europe,* he said that the victory of the Allies was the
victory of democracy. This meant that no man would use another man,
nor any nation another nation, as an instrument for selfish ends. Men
and nations alike had their own individualities and their own rights.[18]
Thus a principal aim of the war had been the self-determination of peoples.

Masaryk spoke of the principle of nationality as having appeared in Europe in the eighteenth century and as having since pervaded the political and social spheres, as it had those of philosophy, art, and daily life. Herder and those who followed him had tried to identify the spirit of a nation in its folk songs. After Herder, scholars studied languages and literature to grasp the philosophical substance of their own and foreign nations; for "language is the determining factor of nationality."[19]

Masaryk regarded the understanding of the principle of nationality and the relation of nation to state as of overwhelming importance. The Pan-Germanists put the German state above individual nations and went so far as to declare that the principle of nationality had become antiquated.[20] Others considered the Church the highest organization, still others the proletarian class. Masaryk agreed with none of them; he believed that "nation and nationality should be held to be aim of social effort while the state should be the means. . . ."[21] In other words, he was in basic agreement with Herder. Masaryk also saw the nation as a spiritual and cultural organization, a free organization naturally formed; while the state has often been the oppressor of its own nations. "The nation is a democratic organization—each individual is called, each one may make himself felt; while the state is an aristocratic organization, compelling, suppressing: democratic states are only now arising."[22]

Thus to states of the old type, Masaryk opposed nations and democratic states; he did not explain, however, whether the new states would be denied the right to use force. He was not very clear on what democracy meant when it was applied to nations, as distinct from the democratic institutions of states, but he declared that national movements were among the most powerful of democratic forces because subject nations were striving for political independence and were seeking the recognition of their nationality as a higher principle than that of the state.

Political independence thus was vital for an enlightened, civilized nation, for politically dependent nationalities have always, even in the most civilized states, been oppressed and exploited economically and socially. Masaryk rejected national autonomy as a way to solve the problems of different nationalities; if Europe were to become truly democratic, a more radical solution would be needed. True, some nationalities might choose to live in mixed states as they did in Belgium and Switzerland, which were made up of two and three nationalities, respectively.[23] Minorities would remain even in a reconstructed Europe, and their rights would have to be protected. However, Masaryk emphasized that such minorities should be as small in size as possible.

Were the principle of nationality to be adhered to, the Czechs would form an independent state in those sections of Bohemia, Moravia and Austrian Silesia where they constituted a majority; Slovakia and the predominantly German section of the "historical lands" would be free to remain outside the new state is they so wished.

Against this conclusion, inescapable on his own premises, Masaryk replied that each national problem had its own particular features. Although he declared the nation, defined primarily by community of language, superior to the state and claimed that states formed in the past had been products of the spirit of conquest, and although he argued that Europe ought to be reorganized into nationally homogeneous states, he did make one exception. Sometimes, he said, political considerations were more pressing than language. Thus, as he had done twenty years earlier, Masaryk drew a distinction between linguistic and political nationalism, rather as if the former were nonpolitical. In the case of the Czechs, he saw these two elements combined. "Legally," he added, "Bohemia is still an independent State": its union with Austria and Hungary in 1526 gave it only a common sovereign; and whatever changes in its status may have occurred later had no binding legal force.[24]

Moreover Masaryk found it possible to justify the inclusion of the German minorities in his state on the basis of the parliamentary and and democractic principle. For example, in restored Poland, as well as in Bohemia, there would be German minorities. What he meant was that in the proposed independent nations of Bohemia and Poland there would be fewer Germans than there had been Czechs and Poles in prewar Germany and Austria; this arithmetic apparently made the new arrangements more "democratic and just."[25]

Masaryk's argument, based on historical rights, contradicted his principle of self-determination of nations as defined by a community of language. That the right of national self-determination which he espoused contradicted "historic rights" and justified the secession of the Germans from Bohemia was understood by some loyalist Czechs at home, like the historians Jaroslav Goll and Josef Pekař, who envisioned a Bohemia in a reformed monarchy.[26] Yet it would be wrong to assume that Masaryk was engaged here in a new argument. As we have suggested above, Masaryk's rejection of historical rights in 1900 presaged the course of action he would adopt during the war. At that time, as we recall, Masaryk joined together the historical and ethnic principles, thus making himself a target for both sides, the Czech and the German. By 1918, however, his plan had become a reality: ethnic Czechs, defined lingusitically and led by modern, middle-class politicians, had won recognition for themselves as the sole legatees of the historical, feudal and nonethnic Crown of St. Wenceslas. The entire area of Bohemia, Moravia, and Austrian Silesia was assigned to the Czechoslovak Republic.

Democracy, in accord wiht his ethical principles, meant to Masaryk that no man or nation should treat another man or nation as an instrument for selfish ends. Had he been consistent, he would have agreed with A. Pamphilet, a Belgian contributor to *New Europe,* a journal that was Masaryk's chief propaganda organ during the war, that "a nation has no more right than a sovereign to annex for its own convenience even the merest handful of men who do not wish to belong to it."[27] By Masaryk did not seem to be aware that he was promoting the interest of the Czech nation, while making another nationality its "instrument," when, to secure the inclusion into Czechoslovakia of areas where his fellow-nationals were in a minority, he was prepared to deprive several times as many "aliens" of their own statehood. His arguments justifying the incorporation of non-Czech territories and population into the new Czechoslovakia are instructive. He invoked many principles, reasons and rights. But he never found a way to organize the new multinational state so that no one nationality had the ruling hand. Under pressure of circumstances and for tactical reasons, Masaryk's wartime writings used language that lent itself to various interpretations and did not always reveal his true thoughts. This was true of his references to self-determination. Only when he dealt with its application was it the real Masaryk who spoke; and it could not be otherwise so long as he believed that one ethnic nation could use the state to promote its own welfare and keep other nations in submission.[28]

Was it more just, Masaryk asked, "that ten and a half million Czechs should be under foreign rule, or that two and a half million non-Czechs should be under Czech rule?" The alternative apparently was thought to exhaust all possible solutions. It did not; it would have been possible to delimit the frontier so that minorities would be substantially cut down. A Dutch correspondent who interviewed Masaryk in 1919 told him: "You won't leave a half-million Czechs to the Germans yet you want to have three million Germans annexed to the Czechoslovak State. How do you explain this, Mr. President?" And the answer was: "A nation of seventy million like the Germans can much more easily lose three million souls than a nation of ten million can lose half a million; and this consideration is here the only right one."[29] His deeds and words between 1914 and 1920 were also prompted by his unwillingness to trust the capacity of ordinary men, "the masses." He believed them incapable of determining their interests or deciding on appropriate action; for him there was always only one right course and that would be revealed to the expert few.

A certain uneasiness seemed to affect Masaryk when he faced the problem of a people's best interests. Thus he told the Germans that it was in their own interest for many of them to be in Czechoslovakia: "our Germans," he said, "may determine to remain with us, as the Swiss Germans have determined to stay outside Germany." It was of great political benefit to the Germans to belong to many states, just as it was to the French who belonged to France, Belgium and Switzerland, he added. But it apparently did not occur to Masaryk that it was for the Germans themselves to decide where their best interest might lie; that Bohemia's Germans had already decided what they wanted; and that those whom he called "the French" in Belgium or Switzerland were not a French minority comparable to the German minority in Czechoslovakia, but were as much Belgian or Swiss as anyone else.

Against the German claim for separation from the Czechs Masaryk wrote in *The Making of a State:* "Individual rights are not the sole governing factors in the question of whether a whole, or parts of a whole, shall be independent; the rights of others enter into it, . . . and considerations of reciprocal advantage, especially in the economic sphere."[30] This is the only passage in the book where a contractual arrangement is suggested and where Czechs and Germans are spoken of as parties with equal rights. But Masaryk really meant something else. He was concerned with the economic disadvantages likely to accrue to the Czechs from the separation of the German areas; and he claimed the right of the Czechs

as well as of the Germans to profit from these areas. The logical conclusion—that both parties should decide what was of reciprocal advantage—was not drawn.

In 1919 a Hungarian journalist asked Masaryk how the annexation of
Slovakia could be reconciled with the right of self-determination, since
the Slovak representatives to the Prague national assembly had not been
elected but were appointed by the government. When he suggested a
plebiscite, Masaryk replied:

> I regard the plebiscite as a double-edged weapon. He who agitates
> wins. And in so far as Slovakia in particular is concerned, one
> should allow no voting there at all. Slovaks have been so oppres-
> sed that they never had an opportunity to think politically and
> so they would not even know how to decide on their fate. In
> such circumstances one has to accept the view of the leaders of
> the people.[31]

Masaryk must soon have realized that a plebiscite would not be a safe
course if two parties took part. At any rate, by 1919 his opinion about
the usefulness of a popular vote had grown more conservative. The occasion was the relatively minor territorial dispute with Poland, in formerly
Austrian Silesia, the so-called "Teschen Question." In this dispute the
Czechs invoked historical rights while the Poles claimed the ethnic principle in support of their case.

> . . . We have not allowed for a plebiscite in Bohemia or in Slo-
> vakia; Silesia has for centuries been part of our State, we have
> full right to Silesia and the right does not change with canvassing
> and voting. We may cede a part of our territory . . . but we may
> not let a vote be taken about [the subject of] our legal con-
> viction.[32]

The President's views about the status of the Germans—and by implication of the other minorities in Czechoslovakia—was made public in his
inaugural message to the Czechoslovak Nation, delivered on 22 December
1918: "As to the Germans in our lands, . . . the territory inhabited by
the Germans is our territory and will remain ours . . . we have built our

State; by this is determined the consititional position of our Germans who originally came to our land as emigrants and colonists. . . ."[33] Masaryk repeated on many subsequent occasions that it was his strong desire to see the Germans and all other minorities reconciled to the new state and cooperating with the Czechs and Slovaks. He admitted that the problem of the Germans was a particularly anxious one, owing to their numbers, their economic and cultural strength and the proximity of the Reich; and he emphasized the need to treat them justly. It was crucial that they be given a due share in the administration of the States to which they belonged.[34]

In an address to Czechoslovak journalists in 1919, he repeated that the Czechs would concede to the Germans all that was rightly their due.[35] But Masaryk's statements raise several questions. First, he granted to minorities only the right to share in administration; he did not recognize their right to take part in the organization of the state. Second, he looked on the nationals of another nation as a group apart and made their right to participate even in administration dependent on particular conditions: for example, it must first of all recognize the supremacy of the state and its policies. He thus made the rights of citizens dependent on their acceptance of the state, rather than making the authority of the state dependent on the consent of its citizens. Third, Masaryk spoke of concessions to the Germans: "we will concede to them. . .their due." But were not the Germans also citizens of the state and was not he their president also? These are not circumstances in which to make concessions.

Emanuel Rádl has compared Masaryk's views in this matter with the attitudes of past enlightened despots who issued a "patent of toleration" to religious minorities.[36] It would seem that the only restriction Masaryk placed on the actions of a nation was its own sense of duty, responsibility, and sympathy fo others; in case of doubt, the judge would be the nation itself. Rádl's analysis was confirmed by Masaryk's statement that appeared in his conversations with Karel Čapek in *Masaryk on Thought and Life,* a book that enjoyed the status of a semi-official publication in Czechoslovakia. Masaryk said: "We have built that state, we must know how to manage and govern it." Because of the minorities within the state, he acknowledged the individual citizen's duty to both the State and to his own nationality. It was the Czechs' task "to win over to the idea of our democratic republic the minorities with whom we are living."[37]

Although Masaryk recognized the dual responsibilities of an individual to state and to nationality, he considered nationality the more basic identity: "language is an expression, albeit not the only expression, of the national spirit.... Conscious fostering of nationality implies therefore a comprehensive policy of culture and education...our national program must embrace the whole domain of culture."[38] It was Masaryk's hope that the Czechoslovaks would contribute to a synthesis of European and world culture; to the minorities he assigned "a weightly and honorable task" in those pursuits, hoping that they would serve as intermediaries among the different national cultures.

The question of whether Czechs and Slovaks comprised one nation or two had been discussed long before 1914, but there was general agreement that, along with differences explainable by a thousand years of separate existence, Czechs and Slovaks were very close in language and culture. Masaryk had considered Slovaks a branch of the Czech nation and their language was a form of Czech. Accordingly, Slovakia was included in his political plans. In a memorandum written in 1915 he declared that the Slovaks were Bohemians, in spite of the fact that they used their dialect as their literary language.[39] No language question would arise if Slovakia became a part of Bohemia, since Czechs and Slovaks could easily understand each other.

If we are to appreciate the originality and boldness of Masaryk's conception of Czecho-Slovak unity, it is worth remembering that as late as the last quarter of the nineteenth century few Czech politicians had considered the Slovaks a part of the Czech national aims. Preoccupied as they were with the question of historic state rights, the politically active Czechs paid little attention to the nationality problems across the Hungarian border. Masaryk, on the other hand, became active in Slovak affairs when he went to Prague; during long periods in Slovakia and through personal acquaintance with Slovak students, he tried to infuse the young Slovak intelligentsia with his social and cultural ideas. Gradually a group of young intellectuals and professionals formed around him; in 1898 *Hlas*, a Slovak periodical that promoted Masaryk's ideas appeared. They young Hlasists opposed the traditional Slovak leadership centered in Turčiansky Svätý Martin, with its romantic nationalism and Pan-Slavism. The reformers looked to the westernized Czechs as their model for bringing Slovakia into the modern age. Indeed their desire to emulate, and cooperate with, the Czechs led some of the young impatient reformers to deny a separate Slovak nationality.

Masaryk wanted a unity of the Czechs and Slovaks as much as they did. He believed that traditional Slovak aims and standards reflected the inertia of Slovak civilization; he hoped to raise the Slovak consciousness to the higher level of the Czechs. Although he really cared little whether Slovaks spoke Czech or Slovak, he could see no other device for implementing Czecho-Slovak cooperation and political alliance than by presupposing their national unity.[40] Of the two groups, he assumed that the Czechs had a claim to leadership on the basis of their cultural superiority. There were of course Slovaks who protested against Masaryk's denial of their nationality. Although Masaryk failed in his efforts to create a Czecho-Slovak nationality, his work, which started in the 1880s and ended during the war, resulted in the rise of a common state of Czechs and Slovaks.

It is doubtful whether the Slovaks, given the opportunity in 1918 or 1919, would have voted overwhelmingly for union with the Czechs, although one may suppose that a majority of those who were nationally conscious would have favored the creation of a common state as an alternative to continuing Slovakia's inclusion in Hungary. There was, however, an important difference between the view that regarded the Slovaks as a branch of the Czech nation and the view that considered them a distinct nation. The former point of view, for which Masaryk was the foremost advocate, did not require any explicit expression of the will of the Slovaks themselves. If the Czechs, who constituted three-quarters of the Czechoslovak nation, desired independence, they ipso facto committed the Slovaks to independence also, and the same majority principle would be invoked in the making of a constitution and in other matters. On the other hand, if the Slovaks were recognized as a distinct nationality, they would be entitled to autonomy in accord with the principle of national self-determination. Thus the move toward a Czechoslovak nation ignored Slovak demands by invoking rule by the majority, and it was clear that a majority, consisting of the Czechs, would reject the idea of autonomy for the Slovaks. During the war, Masaryk also fell back on historic right to justify the inclusion of the Slovaks, saying that Slovakia had been the center of the Great Moravian Empire until it was torn away by the Magyars in the tenth century.[41] How historic right invalidated the stronger historical right of the Hungarians, who could claim a ten centuries' possession, Masaryk did not trouble to explain.

Considering the situation of Slovakia in 1918-1919 in practical and not philosophical terms, it would seem that in the long run the Masaryk formula was far more advantageous to the Slovaks than either of the two alternatives.[42] Had the Communists won in Hungary and succeeded in keeping Slovakia as part of the "Socialist Federal Soviet Republic of Hungary" (for this was the official designation of Soviet Hungary), Slovakia would have been granted, following the Russian example, an autonomous-republic status. If the Scviet Russian experience is any guide, such a federated Soviet Hungary would have retained the Magyar nation in the position of the federation's leading nation, "elder brother." It depends on one's politics whether this kind of arrangement would have been preferable to the Masaryk solution. The other, more realistic alternative would have left Slovakia in Admiral Horthy's aristocratic Hungary. It seems highly questionable whether this would have provided a more favorable setting for the national self-fulfillment of the Slovak people, either.

As a matter of practical politics, the compacts Masaryk reached with the Slovak leaders in America were perhaps the most important, in particular the Agreement (*Dohoda*) signed by representatives of Czech and Slovak organizations at Pittsburgh on 30 May 1918. The agreement endorsed the creation of a common state of the Czechs and Slovaks and provided that Slovakia would have its own administration, Diet, and courts of justice. Detailed provisions were to be determined later by "the liberated Czechs and Slovaks and their legitimate representatives." The agreement was unhesitatingly signed by Masaryk, who later saw it as a local understanding between American Czechs and Slovaks endorsing his policies. He mentioned that the signatories were mostly American citizens, suggesting that technically this was a private contract made by foreign citizens and so not binding on Czechoslovakia. He did not concede, however, that his own activities during the war, which had included agreements with foreign powers, were no less private and illegal: after all, he was an Austrian citizen at the time, and his activities, legally speaking, qualified as high treason. At any rate, Masaryk regarded the problem of Slovakia definitively solved by the Constitution of 1920, which was adopted by the Slovaks as well as by the Czechs and constituted a legal endorsement of complete union.[43]

The Czechoslovak Republic came into being on 28 October 1918. A Revolutionary National Assembly met in Prague, appointed a government, elected a President, and adopted a provisional constitutional charter. This assembly was composed of those Czech members who had been elected to the Reichsrat in 1911, with the addition of party representatives who were selected in the same ratio as the distribution of seats among the Czech parties in 1911.[44] Forty (later raised to fifty-four) representatives of the Slovaks, selected with the help of Slovak supporters of centralism, also entered the parliament. This mode of selection meant that there was a disproportionately large number of Slovak Centralists as opposed to the Autonomists. It also favored Protestants over Catholics (the former represented 17 percent among the Slovaks but received one-half of their seats) and completely excluded the national minorities.[45] Allegedly because of a lack of sufficiently qualified Slovaks, seven Czechs, among them Edvard Beneš and Alice Masaryk (Masaryk's daughter), received parliamentary seats within the Slovak quota.

The Assembly abolished local self-government—with the exception of communes of the lowest grade for which elections took place in 1919 in all areas except Slovakia—and the autonomy of historical lands. Requests for Slovak autonomy were presented by those Slovaks who firmly believed that they constituted a separate nationality but these were ignored by the Prague Government.

When, late in 1918, the Germans in Bohemia and Moravia followed in the steps of the Czechs by establishing their provisional governments and deciding to unite with Austria, the Czech army was sent to occupy their areas. Although no formal offer was made, the Germans were invited to cooperate with the Czechs on condition that they would accept the new state. Alois Rašín, a prominent member of the new government, dismissed suggestions that the Germans should negotiate in respect to their joining the new state as equal partners in a phrase that became famous: "With rebels we do not negotiate." (Rašín had been tried for treason by the Austrians during the war and had been reprieved by the Emperor as recently as 1917.) The Germans clung to their opposition, now placing their hopes in President Wilson and the Peace Conference. By the terms of the peace treaty, they became Czechoslovak citizens, after which they dissolved their regional governments, then in exile in Vienna, and their leaders returned home.

In the meantime the Prague Assembly was busy preparing the Constitution; the Germans and Hungarians and the representatives of Carpatho-Ruthenia did not participate. With the adoption of the final constitution on 29 February 1920, Czechoslovakia became the only country in Europe whose constitution was adopted by a body with no elected members. Almost 40 percent of its citizens had no representation at all. When the first national assembly chosen by election met in May 1920, its non-Czechoslovak members publicly repudiated the legitimacy of a state in which, they said, they had been incorporated by force; the Constitution, they said, had been imposed on them by an *Octroy*, that is, in a manner recalling legal enactments of absolute monarchs.

The new State determined the languages of Czechoslovakia by law and regulated the status of the nationalities. According to the Constitution and other legislative acts, as well as general usage, the Czechoslovak nation comprised those citizens whose native language was "Czechoslovak," i.e., either Czech or Slovak. All others were "Czechoslovak citizens of other than Czechoslovak nationality." Thus in making this distinction—a logical inference, after all, from the prevailing ideology —the leaders of the new State made it clear that the "Czechoslovak nation" did not include all the citizens of the state. Because the Czechs alone made up half the total population, the "Czechoslovaks" were the leading, or in the idiom then current, the state-creative (*státotvorní*) nationality; therefore the Czechoslovak state had a national character of its own.

The Czechoslovak Constitution, in accord with the protection of minorities specified by the peace treaty of St. Germain, declared: "All citizens of the Czechoslovak Republic shall be in all respect equal before the law and shall enjoy equal civic and political rights without regard to race, language or religion."[46] It also guaranteed the right of a citizen to use his own language in philanthropic, religious, or social matters, and in towns and districts where a considerable fraction of the people spoke a language other than Czechoslovak. Their children were to be given every opportunity to receive instruction in their own language. A law of 29 February 1920 established language rights. Among other things, it obliged the courts, offices and agencies of the Republic, in districts where at least 20 percent of the citizens spoke a language other than Czechoslovak, to accept cases in their language and deal with them both in Czechoslovak and the language in which the cases were presented.

Thus, while the State undertook to recognize and protect its citizens' equality in most circumstances, it did not recognize the equality of its constituent nations and languages, and it even abolished the regional autonomies that had existed in the late Monarchy. In making the stipulations that they did, the Czechoslovaks were ignoring the protests of their minorities, as well as a warning from the "Committee on New States" in Paris in 1919. That body, acknowledging the acceptance by Czechoslovakia of all the obligations that the Allies had specified, nevertheless pointed out that the prosperity and perhaps almost the existence of the new State would depend upon the success with which it incorporated the Germans as willing citizens. The Committee said, "The very magnitude of this task makes it quite different in character from the mere protection of the other minorities. . . . : it is one which goes so deeply into the heart of all the institutions that the solution of it is probably best left to the Czechs themselves."[47]

The rights determined by the Constitution, except for the status of Carpatho-Ruthenia,[48] and to some extent the rights of minorities in certain districts, could be exercised only by individuals. The only other group or collective rights recognized by the Constitution were those of the Church and of the right of employees to strike, which was granted on 12 August 1921. Thus by and large only individual citizens could claim nationality rights, while entire classes of citizens were not protected by the law on nationalities.[49]

The protection offered to minorities in Czechoslovakia was of great value to its individual members if they came under Masaryk's own definition of a minority. In *The New Europe* he admitted that, even after the changes had been implemented, scattered groups of other nationalities would remain in large industrial areas and the like; such groups could not reasonably expect special provisions to be made for them. But it was another matter when a minority consisted of a compact group settled in a region they regarded as their home, their native land. Not counting the Slovaks, 34 percent of the citizens of Czechoslovakia, including three-and-a-quarter million Germans, belonged to such minorities.

Statistically Germans were a minority, just as Czechs or Poles would have been if their countries had been annexed by Germany; the Germans would not reconcile themselves, however, to being a minority in the political and legal sense. Consequently, throughout the period 1920 to 1938 all their parties had in their program a demand for making German an official state language, on an equal footing with Czech and Slovak. A more moderate demand was for local autonomy and the official use of the German language in German districts. These postulates were retained by the German parties that took part in government in 1926 and later; by the cooperation with the Czechs they hoped to win them over to their side. They continued to oppose the Constitution's legalization of the myth of a Czechoslovak language as the sole official language of the Republic.[50]

But the question of language was not simply a technical matter, one of finding the most convenient tool of communication between the ethnically diverse citizens of Czechoslovakia (who spoke at least seven languages: Czech, Slovak, German, Hungarian, Ukrainian, Yiddish, and Polish). For the nationalists, language was the distinguishing mark of a nation, and a national state properly so called had to have *one* language, regardless of expediency, political prudence or national tact. The question of language was above all ideological; similarly, ideological considerations, not economic, were decisive in the Communists' drive to control the economic life of the country. The eagerness of nationalists to seize the means of communication and education (the new regime in Slovakia rushed to close down Hungarian schools) was the East European counterpart of the excesses in which the Bolsheviks indulged during "War Communism." In both cases these actions revealed their perpetrators' conception of the proper relationship between society (defined linguistically in one case, economically, in the other) and the state, which was treated as a potent instrument for remaking society into a desired shape. In Russia, the Communists proceeded to create a powerful industry and with it a proletariat in whose name they had seized power in the first place. In the new national states, the ruling nationalists were determined not to share their power with the "aliens," but, rather, to employ it in the building of those nations for whom the states had been founded. Having made Romania, Czechoslovakia, Poland, and so on, they were now determined to make Czechoslovaks, Romanians and Poles, out of the people they ruled.

But the nationalist revolution did have an economic dimension, too, its primary concern with the language, culture and national identity notwithstanding. The nationalist revolutions carried out important socioeconomic changes, including large-scale expropriations of "alien" properties through state take-overs or land reforms. They also carried out mass layoffs of civil servants, teachers, postmen, railroad workers, etc., who did not belong to the ruling nation, but had been granted—in theory equality—as citizens of their respective new states. Clearly, nationalism offered real, tangible rewards, such as land and jobs (in government, in education, and increasingly also in industry and finance) for those who had the right ethnic affiliation. Even though East European nationalists professed their opposition to Communism and their allegiance to the principles of private property, equality before the law, and other western ideas, they violated them when it came to advancing the welfare of their ethnic community. In this regard Karl Deutsch appears to have been right when he attributed to nationalism the responsibility for first undermining and in part destroying the traditions of property in Eastern Europe. (He noted, however, that Bismarck's Germany had pioneered such behavior in its anti-Polish legislation of the 1880s)[51] Since the ownership of property and the right to work in one's chosen occupation depended in the new states more on the individual's relation to the ruling nation, and less on his desires or skills, these "policies of confiscation and repression," carried out by the professed enemies of Communism, "did much to pave the way for Communist systems of government."[52]

Czechoslovakia was no exception to this generalization, although it carried out its revolutionary measures on the whole more gradually and more peacefully, especially in the historic lands of Bohemia. (Things were more rough in the ex-Hungarian Slovakia.) It did not succeed in charting out a "parliamentary road to nationalism," insofar as the non-Czechoslovaks, among them any Slovaks who did not consider themselves Czechoslovak, did not participate in the establishment and constitution of the new state. They rejected the argument, which was factually correct, that Czechoslovakia treated its minorities incomparably better than Poland or Romania did theirs.

CHAPTER VII

MASARYK'S REPUBLIC:
NATIONALISM WITH A HUMAN FACE

This chapter examines Thomas G. Masaryk's political ideas during the period when he was President of Czechoslovakia (1918-1935), and it concentrates on two themes in particular. First, we hope to elucidate Masaryk's solution to the problem of leadership in a democratic society. Masaryk's earlier political ideas laid a strong stress on the role of political experts in government: how did he reconcile these ideas with his own role as head of a democratic state? Second, we will examine Masaryk's position on the relationship between state and nation in Czechoslovakia. How did Masaryk's world view relate to the official national ideology of the Czechoslovak state?

After the war, although he manifold duties of the presidency naturally laid first claim to his attention Masaryk remained faithful to his philosophical preoccupations. In 1925 he published an account of his wartime work in *Světová revoluce (The World Revolution)*, and in 1927 he reissued in a Czech edition his old book on suicide. During the remaining years of his life and almost until the end, Masaryk worked on revised versions of *Suicide* and *Concret Logic*. He was convinced that these two books remained essentially correct in their diagnosis of the problems of modern life, subject to the findings of more recent literature. But many of his plans were never realized. For rather obscure reasons, the final part of *Russia and Europe,* which he completed before 1914 (the first two volumes had come out in 1913), was not published. Only in 1967 was an

English translation, prepared from the original German manuscript, published in the West.

We are of course aware that Masaryk's political ideas after 1918 cannot be studied fully without access to his personal papers and to other archival materials. As President of the Republic, his freedom of speech was to some extent constitutionally restricted. Masaryk first realized this on his arrival from exile in December 1918, when the government insisted that two points be deleted from his message to the nation. One asked lenient treatment for those who had sided with Austria during the war, the other condemned anti-Semitism.[1] The old fighter seemed uncomfortable under such restraints, and occasionally in interviews with press correspondents he allowed himself a certain degree of outspokeness, which was promptly disavowed by the government. For example, when Masaryk told a foreign reporter in 1930 that Czechoslovakia might be ready to made territorial adjustments in favor of Hungary, his statement was immediately denied by the Ministry of Foreign Affairs.[2] In another interview, this time with Emil Ludwig, he was asked to comment on the fact that during a political trial in Slovakia (the so-called Tuka treason trial of 1929) communist newspapers were seized by the authorities for quoting speeches Masaryk had made in the Vienna parliament before the war. He replied: "So? But the speeches I made in those days are not an index of what will now be done . . . . Communists . . . make the President responsible for what . . . censorship does."[3] Masaryk thus acknowledged that he presided over a state where political censorship obtained, but he disclaimed responsibility for it. One must remember that Masaryk was not a dictator: on the contrary he presided over a state governed by politicians who had been his political enemies before the war.[4] A discussion of Masaryk's thought after 1918, therefore, has to be limited to pointing out the continuities between his early views and his new positions, at least so far as these were publicly stated. What his innermost thoughts were about the subjects on which he did and did *not* speak publicly will be known, if ever, only after the Masaryk papers are opened to scholars.

Yet, Masaryk was by no means a figurehead, even though such a role was originally planned for him by many influential politicians in Prague.[5] The provisional constitution of 1918 limited the president's rights severely, but Masaryk gradually won an extension of his prerogatives: the right to appoint the government; to receive written reports from it and its individual members, and to attend cabinet meetings.[6] Under pressure from Masaryk, who wanted to ensure Edvard Beneš' succession to the presidency, the age limit for a president-elect was lowered to 35 (Beneš was 35 in 1919), even though one still had to be at least 45 to be elected as senator.[7] He was unable, however, to establish direct presidential elections by the electorate or to secure for the president the right to appoint certain members of the upper chamber, the Senate.[8]

In a move not foreseen by the drafters of the constitution, Masaryk did succeed in appointing a cabinet of nonparty officials (or "experts"), headed by Jan Černý, in 1920. This was reminiscent of the actions of Emperor Francis Joseph before the war, and it showed the extraordinary powers the Masaryk presidency had acquired beyond the provisions of the constitution.[9] Masaryk also took very seriously his right to appoint various state officials of lower level. He said that before making a decision he was apt to speak with the minister of the appropriate department, publicists, journalists, and experts. "But I do not discuss questions of principle with anybody."[10]

Masaryk accepted the fact that in a democracy all power had its source in a parliament elected by the people, but he worried about the inevitable consequence that in a democratic state, with universal suffrage, non-specialists, or laymen, would surely be admitted to the government and parliament.[11] Predictably his remedy against this was to stress the necessity of training and developing wise and good leaders and indeed, of educating all citizens; for, as he said in *The Making of a State,* "whatever the form of a parliament may be, education and morality on the part of its members are essential postulates."[12] The promotion of education and morality were to take place under free conditions. To those who deprecated political freedom, including freedom of the press, Masaryk had only one remedy to suggest: more freedom, but, of course, a freedom that by no means included "freedom for anarchy . . . incompetence or ignorance." The dangers of an uninformed freedom could be checked by an enlightened leadership. "I know that universal suffrage, with proportional representation, does not produce a body of statesmen. But parliament has it uses. The deputies keep current matters before the eyes of the govenment and the public. Then the government or maybe one or two statesmen will see the right lesson that is to be drawn . . . ."[13]

Masaryk's concern for the stable leadership of expert individuals surfaced again in his comments on the *Pětka,* and extra-constitutional body made up of the leaders of the various Czech parties. They met informally to decide on proposals that were later submitted to parliament and easily approved merely by reliance on party discipline. This committee constituted another instance of his reliance on experts. "A full parliament," he said, "is not the place for work and thinking. . . . Real work will always be done in committees and in those by still smaller bodies and often by individuals; democracy cannot do without able, knowledgeable and fair experts, workers, leaders."[14] It is interesting here that Masaryk failed to distinguish between committees elected by the chamber and the *Pĕtka,* a body independent of parliament and not always even composed of its members. His term "work" apparently covered decision-making, which in a parliamentary system is vested in parliament and not in committees, still less in organs independent of parliament.[15] Masaryk's view of the *Pĕtka* was perhaps connected not only with his conception of democratic government as administration by experts but also with his mistrust of the masses, who were still, to his mind, insufficiently educated politically to bear the responsibility for leading the state.

A more recent scholar, Ladislav Lipscher, writes that the *Pĕtka* decided all important questions which properly belonged to the competency of the government and that it had the power to overthrow any cabinet. "In fact it constituted the proper government without bearing its political responsibility." Although the *Pĕtka* was never authorized by the constitution, it continued to function as a component part of the governmental structure. Under the Czechoslovak system parliamentary deputies were controlled by the party leadership, but this did not depend on the parliamentary party.[16] In this lies an essential difference between the Czechoslovak system and, say, the British practice, where the powerful party leader derives his (or her) authority from the party's members of parliament. In Czechoslovakia the party leaders themselves did not have to be parliamentarians.

Masaryk closely cooperated with party leaders, but he did not regard the parties as a sufficient pool from which to draw leaders. As president he established a *de facto* independent power center to which the public gave the informal name of "the Castle" (*Hrad*). The Castle was understood to be made up of Masaryk and his closest associates, who were drawn from diverse circles and backgrounds. Most notably this circle included Edvard Beneš, Masaryk's closest associate in World War I and his designated successor to the presidency. The actual role of the Castle in Czechoslovak politics has not yet been fully examined, although there exists a two-volume collection of studies (cited earlier in this chapter) by a group of German and Czechoslovak scholars, which appeared under the title *Die "Burg." Einflussreiche politische Kräfte um Masaryk und Beneš* ("The 'Castle.' Influential Political Forces around Masaryk and Beneš").[17] An earlier writer, Christian Willars (pseudonym of Oswald Kostrba-Skalicky), argued that Masaryk's politics were in the hands of the intelligentsia, but that in practice Masaryk and the group of personal associates around him wielded enormous power.[18] In any case, it has been suggested that a study of interwar Czechoslovak politics might well focus on such structures as the Castle, the government coalition (the *Pětka*), and the industrial-financial complex, rather than on those conventional entities, the executive, legislative and judiciary branches.[19] We would agree with F. Gregory Campbell that while "in a formal constitutional sense Czechoslovakia was a parliamentary democracy with only a weak president," in fact the country had a presidential democracy so long as Masaryk occupied that office.[20] Campbell sees the source of Masaryk's power in the fact that the majority of citizens held him in reverence as the liberator of their country. "Masaryk's countrymen were accustomed to an emperor, and he exploited their monarchial tendencies in an effort to establish the new republic on firm foundations of authority."[21]

It would seem, however, that regardless of public opinions, Masaryk himself would not have like to have been compared to Francis Joseph. Rather, he saw his political role as grounded in his broader view that the intellectuals ought to be secured a measure of political influence in modern democractic society, a view that, of course, followed the Platonic tradition as well as that of Herder, and was in Masaryk's own time supported by such writers as Karl Mannheim.[22] More specificially, if would seem that Masaryk regarded himself and Beneš as the real founders of Czechoslovakia and so claimed special prerogatives in the conduct of state affairs after 1918. In Masaryk's description of the origins of the state, "external action," that is, the activities of Masaryk and his colleagues in exile, was given greater prominence than "internal" or "home" resistance. In personal terms it meant that the claims of such leaders as Kramář and Rašín were played down, while those of the "above-party" leaders like Masaryk and Beneš were exalted. This historical interpretation was popularized in the works of Masaryk himself (especially in *The Making of a State*), the memoirs of Edvard Beneš, and the conversations of Masaryk with Karel Čapek.[23]

Masaryk had little sympathy for the view that political power should be distributed mathematically in proportion to party strength, perhaps because he had been the leader of a very small political party before 1914.[24] During his tenure in office, he worked out a compromise with party leaders under which he was granted special rights in the domains of foreign policy and defense. When Beneš was attacked politically, Masaryk retorted: "They should not forget that without Dr. Edvard Beneš there would be no Czechoslovak Republic."[25] And during the political crisis of 1925, Masaryk spoke angrily about the parties: "I brought them independence on a plate! And, besides, just imagine, a hundred generals and a thousand department heads! Isn't this enough for them? What else do they want from me?"[26] One issue on which Masaryk was uncompromising was the retention of Beneš as foreign minister, in defiance of the political parties, which were generally hostile to him. It is the conclusion of Campbell that in 1925-1926 "Masaryk's uncompromising insistence . . . protected Beneš from his political opponents and kept him on the job." Again in 1928-1929, at the time of another governmental crisis when Beneš' tenure at the foreign ministry was threatened, he was saved by Masaryk.[27] In 1935, when Masaryk resigned from the presidency at the age of 85, he formally recommended Beneš as his successor; and after complicated behind-the-scenes negotiations, Beneš was elected by a comfortable majority.[28]

There had been a time in 1926 when Masaryk considered assuming dictatorial powers under the emergency provisions of the constitution. He told the Austrian minister that "dictatorship was not necessarily irreconcilable with democracy and that it might be possible to take advantage of dictatorial powers in order to 'polish up the constitution.'"[29] This remark suggests that he contemplated more than an emergency operation. In light of Masaryk's view of himself as the founder of Czechoslovakia, such an action would have been legitimate in his eyes.

Did Masaryk's personal performance in politics help to promote democracy in Czechoslovakia? It would appear from what we know that his influence was negative, in that he prevented the operation of political forces as represented in parliament from developing freely. One critical area was foreign policy, which Masaryk reserved to himself; throughout the entire period in office, from 1918 to 1935, he secured the appointment of foreign minister to his chosen candidate. Eventually, it was due to his personal intervention (often in defiance of the preference of the parties) that Edvard Beneš was elected to the presidency. Had Beneš been dismissed as foreign minister in 1926, as he would have been without Masaryk's help, he would have most likely left the political scene; or, if he had returned, he would have owed him comeback to his own political achievements under the conditions of competition existing among the many aspiring candidates to leadership.

In his history of interwar East Central Europe, Joseph Rothschild, a contemporary American historian, summed up his review of Czechoslovak politics by concluding that throughtout those years little effort was made to give the younger generation an opportunity to participate in the decisionmaking process.[30] This no doubt was largely due to the peculiar structure of Czech party politics. However, it would appear that Masaryk's failure to leave the presidency until the age of eighty-five —based on his broader view that the founders of the republic had a special right to lead it, if necessary, in opposition to elected leaders—had a negative impact on the functioning of the Czechoslovak political system.[31]

The Czechoslovak Republic never succeeded in establishing a durable cooperation among its nationalities. This failure is variously attributed to external pressures, to unwillingness on the part of the Sudeten Germans and of at least some Slovaks to accept the Republic, and to the Czechs' failure to implement the program Masaryk had envisaged. The last point is the one of most concern to us here. In the eyes of his critics, Masaryk was out of touch with political reality. Was this the case?

One of the scholars who rejected this interpretation and held that Czechoslovakia did in fact implement Masaryk's program, but who mistakenly argued that Masaryk's ideology was supranational, was A.J.P. Taylor. He saw the governing class in prewar Czechoslovakia as united in a common humanitarian philosophy that sought to maintain an authority "above nationalities," as the Habsburg aristocracy had once done. In the *Habsburg Monarchy* he wrote:

> The Presidency of Masaryk served to answer the great "if only"
> of Habsburg history: if only the Habsburgs had been more

far sighted and democratic. Masaryk was far sighted and democratic. Czechs and Germans were not reconciled; instead it became finally clear that the two could not live within the boundaries of the same state . . . . The Czechs could outplay the Slovaks; they could not satisfy them. Masaryk had hoped that the Czechs and the Slovaks would come together as the English and the Scotch had done; the Slovaks turned out to be the Irish.[32]

Others, like William E. Griffith, ascribed some of the blame for Czechoslovakia's failure to the Slovaks, who were incapable of adjusting to the new state after a thousand years of Hungarian domination. He believed the Slovaks should have had a time of separate national existence before entering the "supranational structure"of Czechoslovakia. But Griffith also recognized such factors as the influx of Czech officials into Slovakia, the control of Slovak life by Czech banking and industry and, finally, the anticlerical policy of the Prague government. He saw the young Slovak Catholic intelligentsia, who had grown up between the wars, as "the most radical and anti-Czech element of all." In their dealings with the Slovaks as well as with the Germans, Griffith blamed the Czechs more for psychological clumsiness than for overly oppressive measures: "The First Republic, a far cry from the state 'like Switzerland' advocated by Masaryk, was a national state of Czechs and Slovaks, 'the Czechoslovak nation,' with the other ethnic minorities in an even more inferior position than the Slovaks."[33] Thus Griffith assumed a discrepancy between the actual policies of Czechoslovakia and Masaryk's conception of the state.

Elizabeth Wiskemann, writing in 1938, similarly believed that Masaryk's ideas could have served as a basis for Czech-German reconciliation:

Some common political principle which different races can respect is the cement which is needed to repair the Czech-German structure. The Humanism of Thomas Masaryk might gradually have created the necessary cohesion, and the Historic Provinces, by reconciling German with Slav, might have pointed the way towards a genuine solution of the problem of Central Europe.[34]

Although he would probably not claim to be recognized as a Czecho-slovak expert, Sir Karl Popper seems to have been more accurate in his perception of Masaryk's philosophy of the state when he wrote that "Czechoslovakia was built on the principle of the national state, on the principle which in this world is inapplicable." (Popper has argued that this principle is inapplicable because all nations and languages are too densely mixed.) And yet, he also wrote, "Masaryk's Czechoslovakia was probably one of the best and most democratic states that ever existed" despite its being a national state.[35]

This present study argues that it is misleading to call Czechoslovakia a supranational state and to compare it with old Austria; the resemblence lies only in their ethnic compositions. When Austria was ruled by the Habsburgs, none of its nationalities was the "leading" one in the structure. Czechoslovakia, of course, was governed by the Czechs, while Austria was opposed at least in principle to the supremacy of any one national group. Czechoslovakia lacked a rationale that could unite here citizens in a common loyalty that would supersede mere attachment to nationality.[36]

Certainly the Czechoslovak Republic enjoyed a democracy that her neighbors lacked; but even this regime was corrupt in the eyes of the nationals involved, because the State was thought to be an instrument in the hands of a permanent majority who were seeking to promote only the ruling nation's welfare. Even though the government of Czechoslovakia was more absolute and rigid in theory than in practice, and the Slovaks enjoyed broad cultural freedom—in particular, the freedom to speak their own language, as did the Germans and the other minorities—and even though the State, as ruled by the Czechs, granted to its citizens rights that were deservedly envied throughtout Eastern Europe in the period between the two world wars, its legitimacy continued to be questioned on nationalistic grounds.[37] It may be doubted whether Czechoslovakia could have succeeded in any case in establishing itself as a supranational state, even had there been forces willing to make the attempt. With respect to Karl Renner's pre-1914 plans, Oscar Jászi has written that in a period when the idea of a nation was no longer concerned only with cultural and ethnographical matters but represented an effort to unite traditional national settlements into an independent state, Renner's solutions were "too schematic and too bloodless" in the eyes of the fighting nations.

"These nations would have perhaps been inclined to combine their independent states with the others in a confederation but they refused to accept the competency of a superstate even in matters which they felt not strictly national."[38]

Would the other nationals have been satisfied with equality or would they still have considered it merely a step on the way to a national statehood of their own? Would the Czechs have tolerated any infringement of their full national statehood? The consequences of the nationalist theory, as Lord Acton said in 1868, practically reduced other nationalities to a subject condition; yet to grant them an equal share in the state would make it no longer national—a contradiction of its underlying principle.[39] Admittedly, a Czech national state was unacceptable to its other component nationalities because it did not admit them into the ruling authority.[40] Nevertheless, Masaryk's Czechoslovakia fully deserved its reputation as a haven of personal freedom and tolerance in Central Europe; it gave asylum to many who faced persecution elsewhere because of their political, national, religious or cultural allegiances, while its own citizens enjoyed a wide range of political liberties and social rights. But none of these benefits neutralized the challenges against the state's legitimacy when the prevailing ideology was that national character could be a state's only foundation.

To understand Czech-Slovak and Czech-German friction, it must be remembered that national oppression is perceived for the most part as something very different from the simple lack of personal liberty or representative government. As Isaiah Berlin wrote in 1958, "I may feel unfree in the sense of not being recognized as a self-governing individual human being; but I may feel it also as a member of an unrecognized or insufficiently respected group. . . ."[41] Furthermore, even Masaryk shared the common belief of his time that the emancipation of one's own nation could be achieved only in a sovereign national state.

It should be noted that the concept of the state as a vehicle of national self-realization imparts certain special features to the overall political character of the state, including those institutions not related per se to nationality. Most expressly this applies to the principle of democratic majority rule. Thus while the Czech politicians, Masaryk among them, identified democracy with government by the majority, they defined such a majority as permanent; in this case, the Czechoslovaks would always constitute the majority. As A.D. Lindsay has observed, the majority in a democratic government should not be a determinate one—a genuine majority is one that surfaces as the result of an election, and so is subject to change. In other words, "Democratic government and party conflict presuppose that each party is trying to gain the support of the general public which may vote in one way or another."[42]

Also, in considering the conditions of a permanent political society, one should recognize, as J.S. Mill did, both the quality of loyalty and a cohesive principle. Mill pointed out the necessity, in any state, of "*something* which is settled, something permanent, and not to be called in question; . . .when the questioning of these fundamental principles is . . .the habitual condition of the body politic . . .the state is virtually in a position of civil war. . . ."[43] A feeling of common interest was alike essential, so that no one part of the community would consider itself foreign to the rest. Therefore: "where the sentiment of nationality exists in any force, there is a *prima facie* case for uniting all the members of the nationality under the same government. . . ." When a people is ripe for free institutions, moreover, there is every reason to support them, for "Free institutions are next to impossible in a country made up of different nationalities. Among a people without fellow-feeling, especially if they read and speak different languages, the united public opinion, necessary to be working or representative government cannot exist. . . ."[44] Mill had the Habsburg Monarchy in mind when he spoke of the State as a power above nationalities. The Czechoslovak State differed in that it was not "the common arbiter," but this circumstance neither helped to sustain democracy in Czechoslovakia nor did it contribute to understanding among its peoples. As Joseph Rothschild has argued, Masaryk and Beneš had committed Czechoslovakia's system to two mutually incompatible ideological propositions: a democracy that granted equal political rights to all individuals, and the national Czechoslovak character of the state. Hence only two solutions to the ethnic conflict were realistic: the territorial truncation of the state or the expulsion of the disloyal minorities.[45] It emerges from our view that Masaryk failed to work out a viable alternative to this choice.

In concluding our discussion of Masaryk's stand on the question of "state and nation," several comments about the historical context of his ideas are in order. First, it should be noted that the nationalist theory of his time regarded the national state as an axiom. In this regard, Masaryk was firmly in the mainstream. Where he differed was in his insistance that the national minorities, especially the Germans, should be given an opportunity to participate in government. No other East European country adopted or followed the Masaryk example, and in some, such as Poland, the parties of the ruling nation in fact made a formal agreement always to exclude the nationalities from government ("The Lanckorona Pact").[46]

Second, the experience of western Europe in dealing with ethnic, religious or regional "subcultures" was neither as well developed as it became after World War II nor sufficiently known to be used as a model for countries like Czechoslovakia. To be sure, the example of Switzerland was often cited, but it seemed clear to most that there was no way in which one could realistically introduce by a legislative fiat what it had taken centuries to produce there. It is significant that for many years after the Second World War, western political science assumed that "political development" in the Third World would signify gradual assimilation of ethnic groups to the dominant one. It was thus assumed that it was necessary first to transform society through government intervention rather than adjust government to the realities of society.[47]

In more recent decades the traditional view which assumed a basic contrast between the advanced western nations—which were supposedly ethnically homogeneous—and the rest of the world, where ethnic and linguistic diversity prevailed, has been seriously revised. It is accepted now that western nations contain many different and enduring "subcultures," and the experience attained by those western nations in coping with problems arising from this fact has opened new ways for looking at the question of ethnicity and democracy. To summarize a complex issue in the most simple terms, the phenomenon of "consociational democracy" has made an entry on the scene. "Consociational democracy," to quote salient passages from a representative work, is defined by four characteristics. One of them is "government by a grand coalition of the political leaders of all significant segments of the plural society." The others are the mutual veto rule, which serves to protect vital minority interests; "proportionality as the principal standard of political representation, civil service appointments, and allocation of public funds;" and finally, "a high degree of internal autonomy for each segment."[48]

As we can see, Masaryk's Czechoslovakia, while it basically failed to approximate this form of arrangement, did make some tentative moves in the right direction, when, for example, it included German politicians in government or recognized the special status of Ruthenia. It did not produce a Grand Coalition, however, because the *Pětka* excluded non-Czech political leaders. But the experience of the *Pětka* seems to have been followed after 1945 in Austria, where the two major parties formed a lasting cooperative relationship in a similar body.[49]

To go back to Masaryk: contrary to what has been suggested by some, there is no reason to suppose that he abandoned his conception of the national state after he had become disillusioned, allegedly, with how the system worked in practice.[50] Despite the state's shortcomings, it must have seemed to him basically sound. On the contrary, it would seem that Masaryk had good reason to consider Czechoslovakia a success in terms of his criteria for a good state. First, it was led by wise and good leaders. Second, the state had a national character.[51] Third, political conditions were sympathetic to the reception of his intellectual and religious ideas, although the memory of his failure to win support for his doctrines before the War, the inevitable limitations to his freedom of action imposed by his official post, and, not least, his advancing age, probably all combined to prevent Masaryk from reviving his earlier campaign for a Czech philosophy that would serve as a force of national integration. His past writings, however, were being reissued during the 1920s and 1930s, and occasionally he used his influence to support actions that seemed to implement some of his old postulates. Not all of them were altogether noncontroversial. When the Government officially proclaimed a celebration on the occasion of the anniversary of Jan Hus's death at Constance, it provoked not only a diplomatic conflict with the Vatican but also did much to offend the Catholics. Some critics complained that coercion was being applied to make men honor freedom of conscience. The Catholics, who were particularly devout and were in fact in a majority in Slovakia, were displeased, and the Germans were offended because Hus was presented as a fighter against the Germans. On the other hand, the celebration gratified the "Czechoslovak National Church," a new confession launched in 1918 with Masaryk's support, which, because it combined religion with nationality, was very close to his heart.[52]

Masaryk's religious philosophy, which he linked to his conception of a nation, and its association with the official political ideology of the republic after 1918, conflicted with the principles of a modern liberal state, which Czechoslovakia proudly proclaimed itself to be. However, the realities of the state did not quite correspond to what Masaryk had preached in the 1890s. Thus it was possible for the members of the liberal-democratic and secular intelligentsia, including those of German-Jewish background, to work in the state and at times for the state, despite their lack of identification with the message of Hus, Žižka, Dobrovský and Havlíček. Theoretically (as we noted in Chapter IV), Masaryk's national "brotherhood" excluded non-Czechs. In the reality of the political scene of Czechoslovakia after 1918, there was no other place for such intellectuals to be but in association with the Castle—and they did associate themselves with it for reasons unconnected with Masaryk's religious philosophy.[53] A realistic alternative to Masaryk's humanitarian nationalism and intellectual leadership was the more extreme nationalism of politicians who had no sympathy with Masaryk's elevated ideals.

While these elements of the state's stability were less impressive in respect to the non-Czechs, Masaryk's own personality and the legend that had arisen around him exerted a more extensive influence. Masaryk was a man who had won and retained the personal confidence of Czechoslovak citizens of all languages and races, and these citizens believed with reason in his good will toward them. He always felt a direct sympathy for, and fought for, any individual who was oppressed, discriminated against or abused. He spoke out on many occasions, before and after 1918, against all discrimination or persecution on grounds of race, language, nationality or belief, and against prejudice or hatred of any sort. If Czechoslovakia did not treat her nationalities exactly as did her neighbors, with whom she shared her nationalists theories, this was due in part to the political sense and experience of the Czech people and their leaders, but, in particular, to the moral authority of Masaryk. Yet, it is easy to exaggerate this moral authority. There was one major segment of the Czechoslovak electorate that was skeptical, to say the least, of Masaryk's moral or philosophical ascendancy—this was the Communist contingent. Throughout the interwar period they consistently remained a major force, drawing 13.2 percent of the vote countrywide in 1925 (the first time they presented a separate slate), 10.2 in 1929, and 10.3 in 1935.[54]

The Czech Communist party had emerged in 1920, after a group of right-wing leaders of the Social Democratic party organized an internal party coup to prevent the election of a pro-Communist leadership at their party congress. They surreptitiously transferred legal ownership of the party's presses, headquarters, and so on, to themselves, then they engineered a postponement of the congress itself and the expulsion of the Left Wing from the party. However sympathetic one may be to their motives, it is difficult to avoid the impression that those anti-Communists were pursuing the tactics often thought to be typical of the mode of operation of the Communists whom they opposed. In any event, the Leftists refused to recognize this maneuver, and "claiming to represent a majority of the membership, proceeded to occupy the party head-quarters and printing plant." An appeal to the authorities resulted in the eviction of the Leftists by the government of "experts" headed by Černý and appointed Masaryk. A general strike followed. In the Kladno area it reached near-revolutionary proportions and was smashed by force.[55]

The point here is that Masaryk fully supported the maneuvers of the right-wing minority, the subsequent intervention of the authorities which bestowed the party properties on the anti-Communists, and finally the suppression of the potential insurrection at the time of the strike.[56] Masaryk frequently addressed himself to working-class audiences at this time, castigating Bolshevism as unsuited to the conditions of Czechoslovakia—in the Czechoslovak context, he said, it would be "inorganic."[57] The fact remained that Masaryk had difficulties in reconciling a major segment of the industrial working class to his policies, and there was little understanding or communication between the president and the Communist party. At times workers' discontent surfaced in clashes with the police; the Communists were accused of encouraging unrest, while they blamed police brutality. "From time to time they addressed Masaryk to inquire how the methods of the police fitted into his philosophy of humanism. The Communists never made their peace with Masaryk's republic."[58] All this leads to the inevitable conclusion that however strong Masaryk's moral authority or personal charisma may have been, there were clear limits to what he could do in the complex, socially and ideologically differentiated, and conflict-ridden society of Czechoslovakia after 1918. It was not the country and not the time for Masaryk to play the role of a Louis Napoleon or a Peron—nor indeed did he seem to aspire to this sort of leadership.

Masaryk's nationalism, however deficient in certain of its aspects, was always moderated and restrained by other values that may be encompassed by the name of humanism. We may see how different this was from the classical pure nationalism of his time by comparing it with the views of some of his closest collaborators.

His chosen successor, Edvard Beneš, was convinced that Europe and the world were living in the era of nationalist doctrines, movements, states, and wars, which gave to the twentieth century its distinctive mark as the religious wars had to earlier epochs. He spoke of the evolution of Germany, particularly in the era of Hitlerism, as a problem of nationalist German unification, and of Italy after 1922 as being in the grip of a struggle for unification by nationalist Fascism. His conclusion was that ". . . the March on Rome in 1922, and the whole Fascist regime, constitute the latest stage in the Italian Risorgimento. The same in true about Hitlerism in the centralizing evolution of Germany today."[59] Beneš remained faithful to this point of view even after World War II. In 1945 he said, ". . .let us never forget that we are carrying through first of all a national, an ethnic revolution . . . ."[60]

Speaking in the 1930s, Beneš said that the times demanded that the Czechs and Slovaks should aim for a "strong, united, sure, uniform nation, for ever homogeneous like cement and steel . . . . It is our duty to develop as soon as possible a full and definite Czechoslovak national unity." Referring to the separatist movement in Slovakia, he continued:

> It would be tragic, not only absurd, if in this great moment
> of history, when Fascism and nationalism organize powerful
> uniform movements of great nations on our borders, the same
> nationalist ideology operated in our country in the spirit of sepa-
> ration and particularism, instead of the spirit of unification.[61]

Time would work in favor of the Czechs if only the existing political balance in Europe could be preserved: "In thirty, forty years from now Czechoslovakia may have twenty million citizens, of whom fifteen million will be Czechoslovaks (this means that minorities will drop from a third to the total today to a quarter)." Indeed some evidence encouraged his optimism: as another of the contributors to the *Idea of the Czechoslovak State* hopefully pointed out, the ratio of Czechoslovaks increased during the decade after 1921 by 13.8 per thousand while the Germans dropped by 10.4 per thousand.[62]

The appeals that Beneš addressed to the Slovaks made little impression. When they asked for recognition of their national identity, they were still ready and willing to preserve the political union of Slovaks with Czechs— a union based on mutually recognized rights and obligations. They rejected a centralized state which justified itself by alleging that the Czech and Slovak languages were identical or by pointing to Slovakia's past in the Moravian Empire while ignoring the will of its people. Thus the leaders of Czechoslovakia, having first denied a Czechoslovak nationality to the Germans and Hungarians on the grounds of their origins and language, found their doctrine turned against them where they had most hoped for support: in the end it was on ethnic principles that the Slovaks claimed to be a separate nation.

The Czech, or more accurately Eastern European, concept of nationality differed from that of Western Europe where "all the citizens of the State compose the nation, irrespective of their origin or their mother tongue, and to be a subject of the State means to possess its nationality." This conception was quite alien to the Czechs, who defined a nation as a group of people who spoke their own traditional language; a nation was not composed simply of a country's inhabitants.[63]

According to Kamil Krofta, a professor of history who served as foreign minister under President Beneš, the ethnic concept of the Czechs had prevailed through their entire history, even in the Middle Ages. After the loss of their independence in 1620, the Czechs were only strengthened in their commitment to a "strong and living national consciousness, independent of State consciousness but based on...language." In the case of both Czechs and Slovaks, it was:

> a conception which regards the nation as a community of all who are bound together in the first place by the same tongue but also by common traditions and culture, by common morals and ideals...a community that does not depend upon external conditions so that it is not extinguished even by the lack of State independence or political freedom. This conception of nation which came to us...particularly from Germany and fully coincided with our old native tradition...became the ...guiding principle of our Czech and Slovak national pioneers.

In conformity with this view, both the old Bohemian State and the modern Czechoslovak Republic "were in essence the state of the Czechoslovak nation."

> It is perfectly natural that the members of these other peoples, not excluding the Germans, have not the same vital interest in this State, this profound consciousness of responsibility for its fortunes, this elemental love of parent and child, as it were, for this State as we have.

It is worth noting that Krofta singled out Switzerland as a country "where relatively small fractions of three great nations live in common, nationalities that have elsewhere...their own independent States and thus possess complete opportunities of living their life in full and of fulfilling their historical mission elsewhere."[64] If one were to take Krofta's argument literally, the Swiss who spoke German, French or Italian (and this comprised practically all of them) could not regard Switzerland as their country in the full sense of the word. An element of inequality was thus built into Krofta's, as it had been into Masaryk's, definition of the relationship between nationality and state. The Czechs did not seem to realize that, despite the genuine and substantial differences between their own values and practices and those of the German nationalists, they in fact shared with the latter a common philosophical ground in the matter of state and nation.[65] Most of them (with some notable exceptions, such as Rádl), also failed to perceive that precisely because they couched their state's legitimacy in ethnic terms, they were thereby subverting its right to demand loyalty from those citizens, such as the Germans, who were ethnically neither Czech nor Slovak.[66]

A year after Masaryk's death, in October 1938, his Czechoslovak Republic ceased to exist: its predominantly German areas were occupied by the Third Reich; smaller parts of the country were annexed by Hungary and Poland; and Slovakia, as well as the Sub-Carpathian Ukraine, received autonomy. Unitary Czechoslovakia was succeeded by Czecho-Slovakia. In consequence of these changes—the most important of which, the ceding of the Sudetenland to Germany, was imposed by threat of force—the German minority problem ceased to exist. After twenty years of dealing with the German question in an independent state which they controlled, the Czechs saw a solution imposed upon them, and the Germans and Czechs became separated by an international boundary. Masaryk's proud assertion, made in the early days of the Republic, that the Czechs would give their Germans "their due" and would not be forced to make concessions to them under external pressure, was belied by the events of 1938.

The Slovak problem remained unresolved at the time of the Munich crisis. Slovak nationalism was on the rise in the 1930s, and the nationalists took advantage of the state's difficulties to press their own demands. This is not to deny, however, that Slovak dissatisfaction with Czechoslovakism as a theory and as a pragmatic experience under the republic had preceded the rise of Hitler and was genuine and widespread. If anything, Masaryk's dream of ethnic unity between the Czechs and Slovaks had tended to aggravate Czech-Slovak tensions rather than to promote a resolution of them within the republic.

If the events of 1938 laid bare the failure of Masaryk's republic to resolve its most important nationality problems on the basis of his precepts, the handling of the Nazi challenge by Edvard Beneš demonstrated that his leadership was of quite a different sort from that of Masaryk. President Beneš accepted the terms of the Munich *Diktat* rather than refuse to yield and call upon his people to resist the invasion that would have followed. His later self-justification was that the Czechoslovaks had to surrender because their allies had betrayed them. However, Rothschild, who has seen in Beneš' action "a profound failure of psychological and political nerve," has wisely commented: "There are, in the final analysis, certain ultimate historical decisions that determine the moral even more than the material fate of future generations; such decisions the political leaders of even a small nation cannot 'rationally' or 'logically' abdicate to their Great Power patrons without simultaneously surrendering their own integrity."[67] Who can know whether Masaryk would have reacted in another way? But a study of his life, thought and deeds leads one to feel sure that he would have done so.

One of the main lessons Masaryk sought to teach his nation was that force should be resisted with force; he never said that it should resist only a weaker opponent. We have seen that he was wont to invoke the name of Jan Žižka to remind the Czechs that in the past they had had leaders who fought against powerful enemies, and Masaryk was himself an embodiment of his teachings. What were his struggles against the Manuscript forgeries, his campaign in defense of Hilsner, his exposure of Austrian plots in the Balkans or finally his decision to fight Austria in 1914, if not lessons by example in political behavior?

In Masaryk's organization of an independent Czechoslovak armed force, the Legions, it is possible to detect an educational or symbolic rather than simply a military significance. The Legionaries were to demonstrate to future generations that Czechoslovakia's national tradition included one of forthright struggle. Indeed the Legionaries, because they were citizens of Austria, were subjected to greater risk than ordinary soldiers: they could not claim even the protection provided by international law to combatants taken as prisoners of war.

Rothschild has spoken of the limited military role the Czechoslovaks played in the war and of its corollary, that fact that it was the Allied victory that brought independence to Czechoslovakia, as a cause of that "heavy psychological mortgage" which left the Czechoslovak leaders, Beneš in particular, "with an exaggerated sense of dependence on the West and inadequate confidence in the nation's own resources."[68] Had Masaryk's lesson been well taken, precisely because their actual role in World War I was so modest the state's leaders twenty years later would have been determined to act more forcefully. Instead, Beneš' capitulation in 1938 was an act directly opposed to Masaryk's own exhortations on leadership. If Beneš' actions had any effect on the attitudes of his compatriots, it was to underline the tradition of passivity, of surrender under the threat of force, thus repudiating the doctrines of the president he had succeeded.

The territorial settlement imposed on Czechoslovakia by the Nazis did not outlast their defeat; but it proved impossible in 1945 to restore Masaryk's Czechoslovakia. The victorious Czechs agreed with the Germans that they could no longer live in a common State. The Czechs chose to put this conclusion into practice in their own way: rather than allowing the Germans to secede form Czechoslovakia, they put out the Germans but kept their land as settlements for Czechs and Slovaks. The postwar republic in 1945 had at last to recognize the Slovaks as a nation coequal with the Czechs (ironically enough, President Beneš never accepted this arrangement in his heart). Thus after the war Masaryk's pronouncements as to Czecho-Slovak relations had to be renounced also.

In 1948, after a Communist coup, Czechoslovakia formally abandoned the principles of "bourgeois" democracy and was proclaimed a proletarian dictatorship. Masaryk's name and his legacy were condemned to oblivion —except when they were publicly vilified.[69] At that time it would have been difficult to imagine that a movement of reform could grow in Czechoslovakia less than twenty years later that would invoke Masaryk's political ideas as its spiritual ancestry. This was a process quite without parallel in Eastern Europe, for while all the countries of the region reacted against the theory and practice of Soviet communism, none went so far in their reform movements as the Czechoslovaks. They were the only ones to declare their affinity with the prewar ideological and political structure of their country.[70]

After their liberation from long years of Stalinism, the Czechs and Slovaks looked back to Masaryk's republic. They might have said, as Winston Churchill did about democracy, that the democracy of Masaryk's time was the worst imaginable form of government—except for all the other regimes they had lived through since its collapse. They might have added, "and except for all the regimes that other Eastern European nations have known in the twentieth century." Virtually everything Masaryk and the First Republic stood for—freedom of conscience, of association, of assembly; a multiparty system that allowed the Communists free operation; cultural pluralism, openness toward foreign cultures, contacts with East and West without restrictions by the state; protection of religious, political, ethnic and other minorities; the rights of labor; independence of the courts, and much more—contrasted sharply with Stalinism. In this case, an alternative model did not have to evolve from intellectual speculation: it lay in the Czechs' recent past, and it could be recovered.

The attraction of the Masaryk legacy was reinforced by the circumstance that the question of the Germans and the Slovaks, those two problems that Masaryk's republic failed to solve, was no longer an issue. The German problem had ceased to exist altogether once the Germans were expelled, and the Slovak problem, once the national identity of the Slovaks had been recognized, was fully open to a solution within the framework of a democratic and pluralistic system that the "Prague Spring" seemed to be establishing for the Czechs and Slovaks alike. The founding of a Slovak Socialist Republic in 1968 could be seen as a long delayed implementation, under changed circumstances, of what Masaryk had promised (but failed) to do in the Pittsburgh Declaration of 1918.

The search for historical antecedents to his own political and cultural program had been one of Masaryk's preoccupations. His contemporaries had remained unpersuaded when he told them that Hus, Žižka, and the national Awakeners of the eighteenth and nineteenth centuries had been direct precursors of his social and political ideas. Yet Masaryk succeeded overwhelmingly in convincing later generations that his program for the state he had led was not only an integral part of Czechoslovak national tradition but was also a living force in their own time. Masaryk's real victory came in 1968, when the Czechs and Slovaks acknowledged that they were his spiritual and political heirs; rather than in 1918, when they trusted and admired him—but in fact knew and understood him little.

NOTES

Notes for Introduction

1. R.H.S. Crossman, *The Charm of Politics* (London, 1958), pp. 36-7.

2. This approach differs from the interpretation of Antonie van den Beld, *Humanity: The Political and Social Philosophy of Thomas G. Masaryk* (The Hague and Paris, 1975), who examines Masaryk's thought in light of his concept of humanity, which van den Beld considers its central and fundamental element, "the key concept." He treats, in succession, Masaryk's views on nationalism, socialism, democracy, and revolution, in relation to that central concept, as its applications and concretizations. This work, on the other hand, identifies the crisis of authority in modern society as Masaryk's central concern and sees Masaryk's politics, including his position on socialism, democracy and nationalism, as changing over time in response to changing conditions.

3. *Modern Man and Religion,* tr. by Ann Bibza and Dr. Vaclav Beneš (London, 1938); pp. 37-8. (Punctuation and translation have been modified.) Masaryk considered Roman Catholicism and Greek Orthodoxy to be "the two medieval forms of Catholicism." (*Ibid.,* p. 38).

4. George Lichtheim, *Marxism: An Historical and Critical Study* (London, 1961), pp. 24-5.

5. Frank E. Manuel, *The Prophets of Paris* (Cambridge, Massachusetts, 1962), p. 307.

6. Fritz Stern, *The Politics of Cultural Despair: A Study of the Rise of the Germanic Ideology* (Garden City, New York, 1965), p. 79.

Notes to Chapter I

1. This chapter has no ambitions to serve as young Masaryk's biography in a proper sense of the word. Accordingly, no effort is made to interpret his outlook by reference to his personality, or to his relationship with others. A biography would require access to materials that are not accessible and skills this writer does not possess. Thus, while his mother, Theresie Masaryk, and his wife, Charlotte Garrigue, obviously were very important in the formation of Masaryk's personality and outlook, we have no way of finding out exactly what their role in fact was. The most recent work that ventures tentatively into an exploration of Masaryk's personality and attempts to place him not only in a historical perspective but also in the setting of his family and other personal relationships, is Zbyněk Zeman, *The Masaryks: The Making of Czechoslovakia* (London, 1976). However, Zeman relies exclusively on published sources. These include Paul Selver, *Masaryk: A Biography* (London, 1940) and A. Werner, *T.G. Masaryk: Bild seines Lebens* (Prague, 1934), which remain to this day the best English and German biographies respectively. Edward Polson Newman, *Masaryk* (London and Dublin, 1960) is based on secondary non-Czech works exclusively. The uncompleted biography by Zdeněk Nejedly, *T.G. Masaryk,* 4 vols. (Prague, 1930-1937), covers its subject to 1887. It is of enormous value. Jan Herben, *T.G. Masaryk,* 3 vols. (Prague, 1926-27), is also useful.

2. Zeman, *The Masaryks,* p. 17: "Josef Masaryk married an older woman and he married above his station. His bride was pregnant on their wedding day. There has been speculation as to the true paternity of the Masaryks' first-born son, Thomas. His mother had worked in the Redlich household, and a certain family resemblance between Masaryk and Josef Redlich—presumably Masaryk's half-brother, who became a distinguished Austrian politician—has struck a number of writers with a taste for the more scandalous turns of history." See also Thomas D. Marzik, "Masaryk's National Background," in *The Czech Renascence of the Nineteenth Century,* ed. by Peter Brock and H. Gordon Skilling (Toronto, 1970), p. 242.

3. Masaryk's autobiography ("Curriculum vitae"), written in 1875 and reprinted in Werner, *T.G. Masaryk,* p. 127. This document is quoted here and later not only as a source of information about Masaryk's past but

also as a help in understanding him at the age of twenty-five, when it was written for the University. Zeman, *The Masaryks,* pp. 7-14, gives another translation of this document.

4. "Curriculum vitae," Werner, *T.G. Masaryk,* p. 129, and Selver, *Masaryk,* p. 18.

5. Werner, *T.G. Masaryk,* p. 130.

6. K. Čapek, *President Masaryk Tells His Story* (London, 1934), p. 60. "From that time I retained a certain attachment to the faith of my childhood and youth and an aversion for Protestant militants and Catholic pseudoapostates," he wrote in 1875 (Werner, *T.G. Masaryk,* p. 133).

7. Milan Machovec, *Tomáš G. Masaryk* (Prague, 1968), p. 35. See also pp. 30-37. (Italics in the original.)

8. Čapek, *President Masaryk,* p. 63.

9. *Ibid.*

10. Nejedlý, *Masaryk* (Prague, 1949), I, pp. 271-72.

11. M. Procházka, *Otázka delnická* (Prague, 1898), p. 13, as quoted in Nejedlý, *Masaryk,* I, p. 279.

12. Nejedlý, *Masaryk,* I, 289-90. Cf. Čapek, *President Masaryk,* pp. 76-7.

13. *Ibid.* Masaryk's class was much later described as a *Wunderklasse:* among its members were two future cabinet ministers, a prime minister (Max von Beck), and a President of the Republic. Werner, *T.G. Masaryk,* p. 19. We might add that among Masaryk's fellow students, although not in his own grade, there was a young Czech (moreover at that time a Czech nationalist) who would later become the world-renowned German socialist leader, Karl Kautsky. Kautsky, born in 1854, attended the Academic Gymnasium from 1866 to 1874. See Gary P. Steenson, *Karl Kautsky, 1854-1938: Marxism in the Classical Years* (Pittsburgh, 1978), pp. 14-20.

14. After his first term he ranked eleventh; after the second he was twenty-first, later on twenty-eighth, and twenty-ninth, to rise finally to eighteenth.

15. J. Doležal, "Masaryk *na* studiích ve Vídni," *Masarykuv Almanach* (Vienna, 1925), p. 22, gives details of Masaryk's progress in school.

16. "Curriculum vitae" in Werner, *T.G. Masaryk,* p. 136.

17. T.G. Masaryk, *Inteligence a náboženství* (Prague, 1906), pp. 64-5.

18. Nejedlý, *Masaryk,* I, pp. 310-11. Berlinger, who did not care what beliefs his pupils held, wrote in the school register that Masaryk was

"Greek-Uniate." After some time he was registered as a Catholic again.

19. Werner, *T.G. Masaryk*, p. 136. Masaryk felt at that time that he would like to do something "um frei für mich, obzwar nicht auf eigene Faust, philosophieren zu können," i.e., "so that I might be free to pursue philosophy, though not on my own." (In Preston-Warren, *Masaryk's Democracy* [Chapel Hill, N.C., 1941], p. 12, this was rendered as: "To be able freely, yet not really as a Faust [sic], to philosophize.")

20. Herben, *Masaryk* (Prague, 1910), p. 21. (Note: This is the 1910 edition, not to be confused with the same writer's later book, referred to in Note 1.)

21. *Naše doba*, 20th October 1900, pp. 1-2. Reprinted in Doležal, *Masarykova cesta životem* (Brno, 1920-1921), II, p. 45.

22. Herben, *Masaryk*, p. 21.

23. Werner, *T.G. Masaryk*, p. 137.

24. *Ibid.*

25. "If Comte had not written his 'Sociology' I would have written it myself. . . ." *Festschrift. T.G. Masaryk* (Bonn, 1930), vol. II, p. 14.

26. Nejedlý, *Masaryk*, I, p. 356.

27. Because of this deep faith of his childhood and youth, Masaryk wrote, he liked the writings of Comte at a later time. Werner, *T.G. Masaryk*, p. 133.

28. "His way was not that of psychological analysis and sharp logical enquiry," wrote Brentano's pupil, Professor Oskar Kraus, in *Masarykuv Sborník*, II (1925), p. 53. Nejedlý, *Masaryk*, I, p. 463, says that while philosophy was Brentano's goal, it was only a means for Masaryk, who thought primarily about the "praxis," politics. See Viera Hudečková, "Príspevok k vymedzeniu vztahov T.G. Masaryka a F. Brentana," *Sborník Prací Filosofické Fakulty Brnenské University*, B16 (1969), 86-93, and a selection from the Brentano-Masaryk correspondence (*ibid.*, pp. 94-103), by Josef Jirásek.

29. The letter was reproduced many years later in V. Vlček, "Jan Herben et cie," *Osvěta* (1899), 629.

30. Werner, *T.G. Masaryk*, p. 137.

31. "Consequently," continued Brentano, "the thesis as a whole is very imperfect, though in detail the treatment of some difficult question often is thoughtful and instructive, and even where the author's love for Plato leads him to choose the more favorable to the more probable

explanation. . .it [is] not without interest." Brentano's opinion was reprinted in the original, *Masarykuv Almanach*, pp. 28-30.

32.   It is rather strange, however, that Masaryk's command of German should have been so insufficient after he had completed his studies at a German university preceded by eight years in German high schools and several more in elementary. Perhaps his thesis displayed that lack of precision which can be found also in Masaryk's other Czech writings which display, incidentally, a rather inadequate knowledge of Czech. J.L. Fischer, "T.G. Masaryk. Počátky a vlivy," *Česká Mysl*, XXVI (1930), 130-60, gives a critical examination of Masaryk's earliest published works and speaks of the "mental chaos" to be found in them. See also Nejedlý, *Masaryk*, II, p. 308.

33.   *Zora*, Brno 1896, pp. 80-110; reprinted in Doležal, *Masarykova cesta životem*, II, pp. 157-75.

34.   The relevant passages are quoted by Nejedlý, *Masaryk*, II, 314 n. and Fajfr in *Masarykuv Sborník*, I, p. 184.

35.   See Nejedly, *Masaryk*, II, p. 321. "He did not care at all for what Plato said. . .Masaryk never was a mere interpreter of the letter and he wasn't one here." (Also Fischer, "T.G. Masaryk," quoted by Nejedlý, *ibid.*, said that the views Masaryk presented "were not those of Plato.")

36.   Nejedlý, *Masaryk*, II, pp. 303-04.

37.   See Thomas D. Marzik, "Masaryk's National Background," *The Czech Renascence*, pp. 239-53, for Masaryk's ethnic background.

38.   "Slovenské vzpomienky" (1917), in J. Doležal, *Masarykova cesta životem*, II, p. 19.

39.   Nejedlý, *T.G. Masaryk*, I, pt. 1, pp. 106ff, gives examples which he quotes from F.A. Slavík, *Moravské Slovensko*, p. 83.

40.   Masaryk liked to talk about "great enmity" between boys from Čejkovice and Potvorov and called this "nationalism in miniature." Čapek, *President Masaryk*, p. 66.

41.   Nejedlý, *Masaryk*, I, p. 107.

42.   Herben, *T.G. Masaryk*, p. 40.

43.   *Světová revoluce* (Prague, 1925), p. 395. This passage was bowdlerized in the English translation, *The Making of a State* (London, 1927), pp. 294-95.

44.   Doležal, *Masarykova cesta*, II, p. 21. English translation in Selver, *Masaryk*, p. 32.

45. Doležal, *Masarykova,* II, p. 142. English translation in Selver, *Masaryk,* p. 40.

46. In 1911 Masaryk wrote down his Jewish reminiscences in "Our Mr. Fixl" (*Náš pan Fixl*), *Besedy Času,* 24 February 1911, reprinted in Doležal, *Masarykova cesta životem,* II, p. 37.

47. Čapek, *President Masaryk,* p. 70.

48. *Ibid.,* pp. 66-67. J.K.R. Herlos (Herloszsohn) was a Bohemian-German writer (1804-1849), sometimes called a "German Walter Scott." He was very popular among the Czechs for his love of the Bohemian *vlast* exhibited in a number of historical novels, e.g., *Der letzte Taborit oder Böhmen im XV Jahrhundert* (2 vols.), *Böhmen von 1414 bis 1424* (in two parts: "Johannes Hus" and "Der blinde Held," altogether 4 vols.), etc. (See *Ottuv Slovník Naučný,* XI [Prague, 1897], pp. 173-75.)

49. *Ibid.,* pp. 69-70. In one of his speeches during the Great War he said: "Langiewicz and Pustowojtówna were my heroes. . .I read everything Polish I could get. . . ." P. Maxa, ed., *Masarykovy projevy a řeči za války* (Smíchov, 1919), p. 55.

50. Wilhelm Engel's letter to Doležal in Masarykuv Almanach, p. 20.

51. Nejedlý, *Masaryk,* II, 302-03.

52. He adopted a most patriotic name, "Vlastimil," and during vacations spent in Hungary in the summer of 1871, he was looking for "relics of the Great Moravian Empire." "I did not find much." Doležal, *Masarykova cesta,* II, pp. 22-23.

53. *Ibid.,* p. 22.

54. This antagonism between the nationalist Bohemia and practical, "realistic" Moravia, also found expession in politics during the 1870s, and it lasted until the end of the Habsburg Monarchy. A significant example is the so-called "Moravian Compromise" of 1905 in which the Czechs of Moravia independently reached an agreement with the Germans.

55. W. Engel's letter to Doležal, in *Masarykuv Almanach,* p. 20.

56. Doležal, *Masarykova,* pp. 10-11.

57. Referring to Masaryk's intellectual interests at that time, Nejedlý remarked: "It is particularly strange that in the 'Conversations' nothing in fact is said on these years." *Masaryk,* II (1949 ed.), p. 298n.

58. As noted earlier, the full text of this important statement is in Werner, *Masaryk.* See p. 132. See also Doležal, *Masarykova,* II.

59. J.S. Mill, *A System of Logic* (London, 1865), II, pp. 518-19.

60. Nejedlý, discusses the passage from *Curriculum* quoted above in *Masaryk,* I, part 2, pp. 9-26, where, in our view, he produces an illuminating anlaysis of the difference between the "cosmopolitan" and "nationalist" concepts, and in this context speaks about Masaryk as a *cosmopolitan.* Nejedlý, admits that "until then Masaryk knew *little,* almost nothing of the Czech life" (p. 25), and treated, at least until the middle of 1875, the question of nationality only *theoretically,* without reference to the Czech question, but he also alleges that Masaryk did not recognize *Great Austrianism,* the acceptance by the Austrian people of the interests and ideas of Empire.

61. In an article published in 1911 Masaryk wrote: "I grew up a a a high school pupil and a student in Moravia and Vienna, spent a year in Leipzig [1876-1877], then went back to Vienna, and because of that I wasn't under the influence of Prague and the parties in Bohemia; I did not regard myself either a Young Czech or Old Czech." "Muj poměr k Jul. Grégrovi," in Doležal, *Masarykova,* II, p. 26.

62. In his first published work, *"Theorie a praxis,"* published serially in *Moravská Orlice* (first part on 23 April 1876, the last on 13 June 1876). Reprinted in Doležal, *Masarykova,* II, pp. 181-96.

63. About this the Editor of *Moravská Orlice* remarked in a note: "There can be legitimate reasons which may, regardless of the prospects of success or not, lead a party to withdraw from participation in a certain parliamentary assembly." The note appeared necessary as Masaryk missed the point of the dispute on the constitutional character of the Reichsrat and the compatibility of the Czech presence there with their claim for the rights of the "Crown of Bohemia."

64. Doležal, *Masarykova,* p. 181.

65. "I do not care much for buildings nor am I greatly attracted by statues," he wrote. "What I demand is life, and that if afforded only by pictures." Nejedlý, *Masaryk,* II, p. 351.

66. It was to be based on Funck-Brentano's *La Civilisation et ses lois. Morale sociale* (Paris, 1876).

67. *Almanach na oslavu 70 narozenin Al. Vojt. Šembery* (Vienna, 1877), pp. 137-83 (signed: Dr. Th. Vlastimil Masaryk); reprinted in Doležal, *Masarykova cesta,* II, pp. 198-217.

68. Reprinted in *Masarykuv Sborník,* I (1925), pp. 38-52.

69. "It is a workers' [society] . . . . The students who come there are

as vulgar as workers, nay, even more. That's sad." And a few months later: "I don't come to the club here and therefore don't see our papers." From letters to Zdeňka Šembera. Nejedlý, *Masaryk*, II, p. 438.

70.   Letter to Z. Šembera in Nejedlý, *Masaryk*, II, p. 464.

71.   Čapek, *President Masaryk*, p. 115.

72.   Doležal, *Masaryk osmdesátiletý* (Prague, 1931), p. 137.

73.   Masaryk lost interest in his friend when Husserl later became too much what Masaryk and always little respect for: a *Kathederphilosoph*, a "school philosopher." Josef Jirásek published a selection of Masaryk's letters to Husserl (the first dated 1877, the last 1930), in "Masarykovy dopisy Husserlovi (Dokumenty filosofického přátelství)," *Sborník Prací Filosofické Fakulty Brněnské University*, B17 (1970), 157-64. See especially letter of January 1, 1902.

74.   Names given in a biographical sketch written by Masaryk in 1877. Werner, *T.G. Masaryk*, p. 140, and Čapek, *President Masaryk*, p. 105.

75.   *Ibid.*, pp. 115-116, Masaryk continued: "But I need hardly say that I was not impressed by spiritualism and occult apparitions . . . . there are some apparitions that we do not understand—but what, after all, do we understand?"

76.   He also read some of Fichner's works and later quoted them in his own writings and recollections: *Das Büchlein vom Leben nach dem Tode, Die drei Motive und Gründe des Glaubens,* and *Über die Seelenfrage.*

77.   Nejedlý, *T.G. Masaryk*, II, pp. 483 and 398.

78.   He developed those ideas in *Der Selbstmord* (Vienna, 1881), p. 189.

79.   A letter of 17 July 1877, quoted in Nejedly, *T.G. Masaryk*, II, p. 488.

80.   *Ibid.*, p. 513.

81.   *Ibid.*, II, pp. 530-31.

82.   Čapek, *President Masaryk*, p. 119. An important consideration also was money: Masaryk had no regular income as yet in Vienna, and he had to ask his father-in-law for support. The young couple received help also in Vienna, until Masaryk got a chair in Prague.

83.   Čapek, *ibid.*, p. 121.

84.   *Ibid.*, pp. 120, 122, and Zeman, *The Masaryks*, p. 54.

85.   Of the surviving children, Herbert lived to be thirty-five, dying of typhus in 1915 while working for war refugees in Prague. He was a

painter by profession. He left a widow and two daughters, Anna and Herberta. Jan died in 1948, in Prague, while foreign minister of Czechoslovakia. In his youth he was the family's black sheep, a rebel against his father's, and it appears his parents', style of life. After graduating without distinction from high school, he did not go to university. Instead he spent some ten years in America doing various odd jobs and returned to Prague just before the summer of 1914. During the war he served in the Austrian army but remained close to his mother. (This was the time when Thomas Masaryk, accompanied by Olga, was abroad, working for the destruction of Austria, and when Alice was for a time in an Austrian prison.) Jan married an American in the 1920s, but the marriage, which was childless, ended in divorce after five years. In his later years, Jan developed a great admiration for his father and was a loyal collaborator of his father's political heir, Edvard Beneš. Alice never married, and her active life was spent in social and public service. In the interwar years she headed the Czechoslovak Red Cross. She died in a Chicago Czech nursing home in 1967. The youngest child, Olga, as we mentioned, after the war's outbreak left Prague to accompany her father into exile. She married a Swiss, Dr. Revilliod, after the war, and did not return to Prague. She visited her own country regularly, however, and there are well-known pictures of the old Masaryk playing with her two sons, Leonard and Herbert, in one of his summer vacation places. During World War II, Olga and her family lived in England. Leonard was killed in action while flying with the RAF, and Herbert died after a long illness. In the 1970s, by then a widow, Olga Masaryk-Revilliod moved to England for the third time. (Her first stay had been during World War I, when she and her father lived in Hampstead.) She had traveled rarely, coming to the United States only twice: first to visit her sister in Chicago in the 1950s and then to attend her funeral. She died in Beaconsfield, Buckinghamshire, on 12 September 1978, while a resident of a small private nursing home. In her last years she lived in obscurity and her death was reported in *The Times* only on September 18. With her death the direct line of the Masaryk family became extinct. (These biographic data are based for the most part on Zeman, *The Masaryks, passim.* For Olga Masaryk-Revilliod, see *The Times,* 18 September 1978, and J. Josten, "Olga Masaryková-Revilliodová," *Vestnik Československé Národní Rady Americké,* 279 (Sept. 1978), pp. 4-5).

86. "Curriculum vitae," 1877, reprinted in Werner, *Masaryk*. Masaryk concluded: "This is all I have to relate. Were I to speak still further I would indeed make my wishes for the future. They form the conclusion to the premises of an early life, full in experience, struggle and work." A translation of W. Preston Warren, *Masaryk's Democracy* (Chapel Hill, 1941), p. 13. The thesis was submitted in November 1877.

87. Herben, *T.G. Masaryk*, attributed the failure to negligence on the part of the registry which had allegedly put the thesis aside, not expecting Masaryk ever to return to America. Nejedlý, *Masaryk*, II, pp. 32-33, thinks there were other more important reasons. First, sociology was not well regarded in Viennese university circles; second, it was only an introduction to further study on suicide, "and this the gentlemen in the university apparently did not like." This interpretation proves inadequate when for "the circles" and the "gentlemen in university" one substitutes the names of Masaryk's examiners.

88. Again, to explain the difficulties it has been said that the thesis that contained Masaryk's estimate of the condition of modern civilization was thought to have been "a socialistic work" (Čapek, *President Masaryk*, p. 124) which obviously it was not; or not to such a degree that the examiners could fail to notice it. Herben, *T.G. Masaryk*, p. 48, said that "the social tendency of Masaryk's seemed to be a bit too red." See Nejedlý, *Masaryk*, II, pp. 47-48. Herben seems to assume that the examiners did not read the work.

89. *Ibid.*, p. 48.

90. During the next terms (until 1882) he taught: the System of Plato's Philosophy, the first five chapters of the *History of Civilization* by Buckle, Philosophy of Comte, An Introduction to the Philosophy of History, Mill's *Logic* (Book Six).

91. Whom he mentioned in the autobiographical sketch of 1877 (not to be confused with that of 1875) but came to know at first hand only later.

92. Nejedlý, *T.G. Masaryk*, p. 72. The calmness ("perfidious calmness") of a man's mind combined with his atheism appeared to be something unusual. The "Inquiry concerning the Principles of Morals" appeared in 1882 in a *German* translation by Masaryk and his wife.

93. Čapek, *President Masaryk*, p. 98.

94. A Czech student in Vienna, J. Penižek, corrected Masaryk's style, which still left much to be desired.

95. Many years later he said: "I say there that life without faith loses strength and certainty, and with that I have really said everything. To-day I could say it better, but in essence I could not add anything." Čapek, *President Masaryk*, pp. 132-33.

96. Nejedlý, *Masaryk*, II, p. 247.

97. Masaryk was not interested in theological questions as such and therefore he looked at Protestantism as a whole without caring for important differences within its ranks.

98. *Ibid.*, pp. 258-61. Reminiscences of Masaryk's friend, Dr. Oelzelt-Newin, quoted, p. 263.

99. See reminiscences of his friend, Sigmund Münz, "Erinnungen an Thomas G. Masaryk," *Masarykuv Almanach* (Vienna, 1925), p. 50; ". . . he felt that in Vienna he lived much more freely than the case would be in Prague where the primadonnas of the university were clerical or nationalist while he was a freethinker with religious sympathies and, at most, a cosmopolitan with a sympathy for nationality." "Was I glad to go? I was almost sorry . . . I shrank from the conditions prevailing there in literature and philosophy." Čapek, *President Masaryk*, p. 130.

100. See Nejedlý, *Masaryk*, II, pp. 295-97.

101. Doležal, *Masaryk osmdesátiletý*, p. 70.

102. See Čapek, *President Masaryk*, p. 130, on what would have happened to him as a Czech had he gone to Germany or to Czernowitz: "I thought it all out very clearly: if I went to Germany I should become a German writer; I should have to publish German books: but I myself should remain a Czech, even if only a 'lost Czech' like one of our tailors in Berlin or a farmer in Texas. A man remains what he was born." But he was wrong here: there would have been no Masaryk the world has known had he not gone to Prague to become a *Czech professor*. Green, *Masaryk*, p. 213, recognizes the critical importance of the years 1880-1883 in Masaryk's professional and national orientation.

Notes to Chapter II

1. Milan Machovec, *T.G. Masaryk* (Prague, 1968), p. 62. Machovec rightly presents Masaryk as a philosopher of "human existence" and concentrates on the existential and ethical aspects of his work but he does not treat his major philosophical, sociological, or historical works as ex-

pressions of his broad political and social concerns, nor does he trace in their succession the development of his political orientation, which is the interpretation argued in this study. Antonie van den Beld, *Humanity*, p. 4, agrees that Masaryk's "importance to the philosopher does not lie in the first instance in his contributions in the fields of logic, epistomology or metaphysics," nor indeed in his philosophy of religion; to van den Beld the more important fact is that Masaryk was an early student of Marx. But he, likewise, does not see either *Suicide* or *Concrete Logic* as statements of Masaryk's position on the state of modern society or as attempts to suggest ways to overcome its crisis. Political problems in relation to Masaryk's philosophy are discussed by Lubomír Nový, "T.G. Masaryk v českém myšlení," *Filosofický časopis*, XIV, 1 (1966), 22-44, and L. Richta, "O podstatě sociologické a filosofické soustavy masarykismu'," in *Filosofie v dějinách českého národa* (Prague, 1958). For Masaryk's philosophy and sociology see also Olga Loužilová, "Masarykova filosofie člověka" (*Acta Universitatis Carolinae*, Philosophica et Historica, Monographia XVII (Prague, 1967); Olga Loužilová, "Problém osobnosti v Masarykově filosofii člověka," *Filosofický časopis*, XVI, 6 (1968), 852-69; René Wellek, "Masaryk's Philosophy," in *Essays on Czech Literature* (The Hague, 1963), pp. 62-70; Ferdinand Kolegar, "T.G. Masaryk's Contribution to Sociology," in Miloslav Rechcigl, Jr., ed., *Czechoslovakia Past and Present* (The Hague and Paris, 1968), II, pp. 1526-39; Josef Král, "Masaryk als Philosophe und Soziologe," and Oskar Kraus, "Die Grundzüge der Welt—und Lebensanschauung T.G. Masaryks," *La pensée de T.G. Masaryk (Internationale Bibliothek für Philosophie*, III, No. 3/5, Prague, 1937), pp. 77-104 and 105-13.

2. T.G. Masaryk, *V boji o náboženství* (Prague, 1947), p. 12. Lubomír Nový, *Filosofie T. G. Masaryka* (Prague, 1962), pp. 62ff. discusses Masaryk's treatment of faith and knowledge, including the question of non-rational or extrarational sources of knowledge.

3. John Day, "Authority," *Political Studies* (Oxford), XI, 3 (1963), p. 258. "To acknowledge the authority of a scholar involves accepting his opinion on matters which fall within his special field. To acknowledge the authority of a church over oneself implies accepting its judgment on morals and theology . . . . To acknowledge the authority of a government . . .means principally obeying its commands . . . .When one person acknowledges another's authority, it cannot be because he is forced to" (258-59).

4. Roberto Michels, "Authority," *Encyclopaedia of the Social Science* (New York, 1936), II, 321.

5. Day, "Authority," p. 268.

6. Thomas Garrigue Masaryk, *Der Selbstmord als sociale Massenerscheinung der modernen Civilisation* (Vienna, 1881).

7. Anthony Giddens, "Introduction," in Thomas G. Masaryk, *Suicide and the Meaning of Civilization,* William B. Weist and Robert G. Batson, tr. (Chicago and London, 1970), pp. xxxiv, xl-xli. Masaryk's work appeared in a series entitled "The Heritage of Sociology," edited by Morris Janowitz. Giddens' introduction to this English edition of *Der Selbstmord* places Masaryk's work in the context of the history of suicide studies. Olga Loužilová, "Masarykuv problem sebevraždy," *Acta Universitatis Carolinae,* Philosophica et Historica I (1968), pp. 83-97 deals with the place of suicide in Masaryk's philosophy of man.

8. *Modern Man and Religion,* pp. 15-17.

9. *Der Selbstmord,* p. 63.

10. *Ibid.,* pp. 65-66. On the contrary, the educational level of men who attained an intellectual standard higher than that of a simple peasant and lower than that of a university professor was nothing but semi-education (*Halbbildung*) and this posed the greatest danger.

11. Simon Rosengard Green, *Thomas Garrigue Masaryk: Educator of a Nation* (Unpublished Ph. D. dissertation, University of California-Berkeley, 1976), p. 167.

12. *Der Selbstmord,* p. 71n. The particular immorality of suicides consisted, in Masaryk's description (p. 76), "in their particular hopelessness, desperation, in their lack of trust and faith that the conditions of humanity can be improved, in their lack of energy to work with others toward improvement of those conditions."

13. *Ibid.,* pp. 84, 85.

14. *Ibid.,* p. 84.

15. *Ibid.,* pp. 84, 85. Masaryk remarked that "Mill wants no Christianity, but he wants religion." "Obviously he lacks himself most of all a warm and true religious feeling. Comte, who founded the Religion of Humanity did possess this feeling. A man like Mill . . . will naturally achieve to a certain degree what some of the better religions could give him . . . but how many souls are equal to Mill's?"

16. *Ibid.,* p. 85, 141.

17. *Ibid.,* p. 142.

18. This comparison was possible because of the distinction Masaryk made between *Selbstmord* and Selbsttödtung." ". . . the primitive peoples know no *Nervosität*, no psychosis, no pessimism and therefore no tendency to suicide." The cases that take place are "self-killings" and not"self-murders," and the definite cases of suicide do not give any evidence of a morbid love for death. *Ibid.*, pp. 143, 146.

19. *Ibid.*, pp. 168, 174.

20. *Ibid.*, p. 233.

21. *Ibid.*, p. 175.

22. *Ibid.*, pp. 157-58.

23. *Ibid.*, p. 160, 162.

24. *Ibid.*, pp. 162-63.

25. J.L. Hromádka, *Masaryk as European* (Prague, 1937), p. 21, emphasized that "Masaryk has not analysed and compared the forms of Christianity according to their fundamental theoretical and religious ideas, their conception of God, faith, Revelation and Christological dogma. He . . . has not gone as far as the point where the real struggle between the Churches is carried on."

26. *Der Selbstmord*, pp. 164-66.

27. *Ibid.*, p. 175. See "Masarykovy dopisy," *Listy filologické*, 56 (1929), 144.

28. *Der Selbstmord*, p. 241. But (he added) things could turn out differently: the history of mankind is as yet too brief to warrant forecasts of the future. It might well happen that a new growth of religious fervor could take place without any ecclesiastical unity at all; perhaps religious individualism could take hold permanently under an organization like congregationalism. *Ibid.*, pp. 234-35.

29. *Ibid.*, p. 241.

30. János Kristóf Nyíri, "Philosophy and Suicide Statistics in Austria-Hungary," *East Central Europe*, V, 1 (1978), p. 74, comments on Masaryk's book's aim: "In search of a religion that would constitute a defense against suicide, and in search of ethical perfection at the same time, Masaryk hoped for a unification of the Catholic *belief in authority* and Protestant *individualism*—a religious third way." This comment may be applied more broadly to Masaryk's intellectual search—rather than just to this particular book.

31. *Der Selbstmord*, pp. 236-40.

32. *Ibid.*, pp. 232, 235.

33. E.g., Nejedlý, *Masaryk*, II (1949), pp. 367, 394-95.

34. In his conversations with Čapek when speaking of Italy and Italians Masaryk said: ". . . Of their philosophers I especially like Vico." Čapek, *President Masaryk*, p. 101.

35. *The New Science of Giambattista Vico*, T.G. Bergin and M.H. Fisch, trs. (Ithaca, N.Y., 1948).

36. See, e.g., the comments by V. Cathrein, *Moralphilosophie*, I (6th ed. Leipzig, 1924), p. 59n.

37. J.B. Kozák, "Masaryks Stellung zur Metaphysik," *Masaryk Festschrift*, II (Bonn, 1930), p. 200, examined some of the contradictions in Masaryk's thought, and particularly that between the "scientific basis" and Masaryk's "deepest ethical and moral convictions." He observed that it was a lifetime's task for Masaryk to resolve this contradiction. This is also the conclusion of van den Beld, *Humanity*, pp. 23-24, who sees a *non sequitur* in Masaryk's simultaneous belief in determinism and in a free individual will, "between what shall be and what ought to be."

38. *Der Selbstmord*, pp. 141-42.

39. *Versuch einer concreten Logik* (Vienna, 1887), p. 235.

40. *The Making of a State* (London, 1927), pp. 397-98.

41. Emil Ludwig, *Defender of Democracy: Masaryk Speaks* (London, 1936), pp. 241-42.

42. "Plato jako vlastenec," *Zora*, 1876, pp. 80-110, reprinted in *Česká mysl*, XVII, (1919), 1-18, and in Doležal, *Masarykova cesta životem*, II, pp. 157-75.

43. *Ibid.*, p. 169.

44. *Ibid.*, p. 185.

45. Graeme Duncan, *Marx and Mill: Two views of social conflict and social harmony*, (Cambridge, 1973), pp. 261-62, 259.

46. "Plato jako vlastenec," pp. 164, 171. "Plato was often reproached for not caring about freedom of will, freedom of individuals; but we must remember that Plato wanted to bring everyone up to a position he had been best fitted for by nature, and then we shall see that he paid great attention to the selection and examination of individuals."

47. *Ibid.*, p. 170.

48. Masaryk dismissed the accusation against Plato for preaching "theocracy." "They [the critics] forget that he wanted philosophers, not priests, to be rulers."

49. *Ibid.*

50. *Ibid.*, pp. 170, 174.

51. *Der Selbstmord,* p. 231. "Almost all theorists and practical men have tried to remove the evils of modern society by means of economic and political reforms. . . but I am not able to share these hopes. . . . The attempts and struggles of our [i.e., Austrian, not only Czech] parliamentarians, politicians and economists often appear to me exceedingly petty and futile; in any case political and economic concessions, reforms or piecemeal reforms will not save society. A greater or smaller dose of law will not remove a pessimistic weariness with life."

52. *Ibid.* Even in much later work, *Russland und Europa* (1913), tr. as *The Spirit of Russia* (London, 1919), II, p. 525, Masaryk wrote: "Such differences as exist between the Prussian monarchy and the Russian monarchy can be accounted for by the differences between [them] . . . in respect to ecclesiastical and religious institutions."

53. *Die philosophischen und sociologischen Grundlagen des Marxismus* (Vienna, 1899), p. 558, 559. "Thus Schopenhauer rejected God and accepted blind Chance as the essence of the world. Engels discovers quite consistently that blind Evil constitutes the motive power of the world. . . . there is no place left, no time for joy and love. . . . When Christ had breathed his last, the Evangelist recounts, darkness set in on Earth and the sun was eclipsed—also the inmost soul of man grows dark when God has died in him or if he has killed Him in his soul. And the Hegelian Left killed God as Schopenhauer did, too. Hegel's work was completed by Feuerbach, Strauss, Stirner, Marx." See also the later *The Spirit of Russia* for similar sentiments.

54. Zdeněk Nejedlý, "T.G. Masaryk a Revoluce," *Masarykuv Sbornik,* II (1925-26), 149-150. It may be fitting to add that Mill, to whom we have referred earlier in clarification of Masaryk's position, was similarly "critical of the economic and social—as well as the ideological—conflict that he saw about him, and sharply attacked market notions of human society. He was repelled by much of the liberal culture and by the idea of 'a society only held together by the relations and feelings arising out of pecuniary interests.'" (Graeme Duncan, *Marx and Mill,* p. 274.) (The quotation within quotation is from Mill's *Principles of Political Economy,* IV, vii, xi, p. 760.) It hardly needs saying that Mill did *not* share Masaryk's view of the crisis of modern civilization—or of the crisis per se as Masaryk perceived it.

55. *Der Selbstmord*, pp. 219-21.

56. *Ibid.*, pp. 49, 115n.

57. *Ibid.*, p. 49. Democracy in church organization "could be seen as an ideal" but in the country in which it was applied, Switzerland, it had a harmful effect (p. 203).

58. *Ibid.*, p. 62.

59. It is clear that Masaryk's idea of the good life did not include the principle that Mill declared to be "of as universal truth and applicablity as any general proposition which can be laid down respecting human affairs"; that is, that "human beings are only secure from evil at the hand of others in proportion as they have the power of being, and are, self-protecting." J.S. Mill, *On Liberty and Considerations on Representative Government* (Oxford, 1946), p. 142.

60. *Der Selbstmord*, pp. 110-11.

61. T.G. Masaryk, *Modern Man and Religion* (1896) (London, 1938), p. 49.

62. *Der Selbstmord*, pp. 231-33. "We too shall find rest for our souls if we become good." "It is obvious, of course," he added in a footnote, "that the oppressive want and degrading poverty now in existence must be removed." However, the economic issue was not central: "Poverty can be borne well if man is reasonable" (*Ibid.*, p. 58).

63. *Základové konkretné logiky* (Prague, 1885), pp. 170-71.

64. *Versuch*, pp. 275-76. As noted earlier, the present study does not deal with Masaryk's philosophy as such, as his philosophical ideas are reviewed here as an aspect of his political concerns. Nejedlý, *Masaryk*, IV (Prague, 1937), pp. 172-245, gives a detailed summary of this book and compares the Czech and German versions. He argues that the German version should be considered the more authoritative. Also Green, *Masaryk*, devotes a whole chapter to this work. For detailed critiques of Masaryk's methodology of science see, e.g., Lubomír Nový, *Filosofie T.G. Masaryka* (Prague, 1962); Lubomír Nový, "Masaryk jako sociolog," *Sociologicky časopis*, 4, 3 (1968), 297-306; J.B. Kozák, "Masaryks Stellung zur Metaphysik," *Masaryk Festschrift* (Bonn, 1930) II, and J.B. Kosák, "Masaryk as Philosopher," *The Slavonic Review*, VIII (1930); W. Preston Warren, *Masaryk's Democracy* (Chapel Hill, N.C., 1941); Robert Flint, *Philosophy as Scientia scientiarum and a History of Classifications of the Sciences* (Edinburgh and London, 1904), pp. 282-83, and the reviews of Masaryk's book by J. Witte (*Zeitschrift für Philosophie und philosophische Kritik*,

95 (1889), 123-24), R. Schubert von Soldern (*Literarisches Zentralblatt,*
1887, no. 41, p. 1400), and G. Žába in *Krok,* 1887, reprinted in *Masarykuv Sborník,* III (1927), pp. 267-72.

65. *Modern Man and Religion* (London, 1938), p. 212.

66. J.B. Kozák, "Masaryk as Philosopher," p. 494: ". . .his [Mas-
aryk's] powers seem to be unequal to describing what the religious life
really is. We continually hear what religion is *not*—not dogma, not philosophy and science, not morality, not liturgy or attachment to a church . . . ."

67. *Modern Man and Religion,* pp. 9-10.

68. *The Making of a State,* p. 397.

69. *Versuch,* pp. 215-17, 265.

70. *Versuch,* pp. 14, 17-20, 58-59, 187-218.

71. *Ibid.,* p. 219. Masaryk argued more fully that artistic knowledge
was superior to scientific knowledge in *O studiu děl básnických* (1884)
(2nd ed., Prague, 1926), pp. 13-19. This argument was considered unclear
and incompatible with his other views by G. Žába, *Krok,* 1887, reprinted
in *Masarykuv Sborník,* III (1927), pp. 267-72.

72. *Versuch,* pp. 232-33.

73. *Ibid.,* p. 205. "Concrete logic determines the subject matter of
particular sciences, the method which they follow, what parts they consist of, and shows what place they occupy in the system of knowledge."
For a full description see pp. 205-06.

74. *Ibid.,* pp. 272-73. However, "philosophy is not something erected
above special disciplines. . . . there is philosophy in all sciences, and all
sciences are philosophical. The scientific philosopher is a specialist in one
or more sciences . . . the greater the philosopher, the more significant he
was as a specialist."

75. *Ibid.,* pp. 269, 273-74.

76. *Ibid.,* p. 269. According to this "law," the first to develop were
the abstract sciences, which were followed by the concrete and practical
ones (VCL, 284), while the scientific world outlook as a whole was developing out of the mythical outlook (VCL, 277-87).

77. *Ibid.,* p. 274.

78. *Ibid.,* pp. 270-73.

79. *Ibid.,* pp. 274-75. In his detailed analysis of Masaryk's concrete
logic, Green (*Masaryk,* p. 329) comments: ". . . two . . . notions deserve
stress: the potentially authoritarian nature of pedagogy as Masaryk sees it,

and the educational, and therefore fundamentally ethical nature of sociology. The first serves as a good counter to those who just see Masaryk as the great democrat, and the latter is very pertinent to the issue of the role of the academic expert in the modern world."

Notes to Chapter III

1. For Czech politics in the nineteenth century and Masaryk's role in it, see H. Gordon Skilling, "The Politics of the Czech Eighties," and Stanley B. Winters, "Kramář, Kaizl, and the Hegemony of the Young Czech Party, 1891-1901," in Peter Brock and H. Gordon Skilling, eds., *The Czech Renascence of the Nineteenth Century* (Toronto, 1970), pp. 254-81, and 282-314, respectively. The earlier study by Jurij Křížek, *T.G. Masaryk a česká politika: Politické vystoupení českych "realistu" v letech 1887-1893* (Prague, 1959) deals with political activities of "Realists" (Masaryk, Kramář, Kaizl) in 1887-93. Otakar Odložilík, "Enter Masaryk: A Prelude to His Political Career," *Journal of Central European Affairs*, X (1950) is an earlier work. For the general background and setting, the most comprehensive is Garver's book, which provides detailed information on social and economic conditions, constitutional and legal structure, cultural institutions, etc., of the Bohemian lands after 1860. Gary B. Cohen, "Recent Research on Czech Nation-Building." *Journal of Modern History,* 51 (December 1979), pp. 760-772, gives an informative survey of current scholarship.

2. The most recent account is in Zeman, *The Masaryks,* and Green, *Masaryk.* Both authors are heavily indebted to Nejedlý although Green has gone through Masaryk's publications on his own.

3. Green, *Masaryk,* pp. 213, 222, 233-34. Green also notes, as have earlier biographers, that Masaryk made a conscious effort to establish contact with his students outside the formal classroom framework by holding soirees at home. "His charisma in the classroom took some time to take effect, but more importantly his informal discussions quickly brought him a coterie of energetic and bright students. The very act of having Friday soirees was important, but more significant was the fact that Masaryk would have much greater influence and was much freer to deal with practical problems in this setting." (*Ibid.,* p. 213.) . . . .

4. Zeman, *The Masaryks*, pp. 45-48, 57, and Jurij Křížek, *T.G. Masaryk a česká politika*, p. 35.

5. Masaryk's letter to Edward Albert, 29 September 1888, as quoted in Křížek, *Masaryk a česká politika*, pp. 36-37. Masaryk indicated that his opponents had viewed the university as a national concession to the Czechs, an institution that would be dominated by, and serve as a source of support for, "various patriots." Neither those patriots nor the Vienna government, Masaryk said, understood "what a modern university is and can be." (*Ibid.*, p. 36.)

6. Full details about those initiatives are to be found in Nejedlý, *Masaryk*, IV, and, in English, in Green, *Masaryk*, p. 249ff.

7. H.G. [H.G. Schauer], "Naše dvě otázky," *Čas*, 1:1 (20 December 1886), 1-4. The memoirs of Jan Herben, *Kniha vzpomínek* (Prague, 1936), pp. 278-90, deal with the "nihilist" affair. There is an interesting discussion of the problem raised by Schauer in Józef Chlebowczyk, "Marks i Engels a problem małych narodów w Europie środkowo-wschodniej," *Z pola walki*, No. 2 (50), 1970, pp. 41-43.

8. Zeman, *The Masaryks*, p. 58. It my be worth adding that since the Braf memoirs contained passages critical of Masaryk, the editor wrote to the then President, asking whether they should be omitted. On 6 June 1919, Masaryk replied: "As far as I am concerned, I should like to see it published, because it is a part of the whole: Bráf did not understand me, that is true, but others did not understand me either, and I did not understand myself. At that time, I should say, I was chasing an ideal, which was not as clear to me then as it became during the war, and I then made—I know this best—many mistakes. Especially, I antagonized people." Zeman, *The Masaryks*, quoting from Albín Bráf, *Paměti*, Josef Gruber, ed. (Prague, 1922), editor's preface.

9. Graver, *The Young Czech Party*, p. 209.

10. For this reason, Masaryk's ideological position in the 1880s, in the period of *Concrete Logic*, may be compared to that of J.S. Mill. See Maurice Cowling, *Mill and Liberalism* (Cambridge, 1963), p. 136, as quoted by Duncan, *Marx and Mill*, p. 284: "Mill's situation, as a highly articulate, intellectually ambitious member of a middle-class, literary intelligentsia with little opportunity to exercise open, conventional political power, made it likely that his claims to political authority would be based, if based on authority as they were, on intellectual rather than social

superiority. Looked at from one point of view, that is what his moral and political writings are—claims to supersede leadership based on social, by leadership based on intellectual, superiority." Another similarity which suggests itself is with the Fabians, who sought to secure to the intelligentsia a leading position in the modern industrial and scientific social order. See on this George Lichtheim, *Marxism in Modern France* (New York, 1966), p. 121n. and E.J. Hobsbawm, *Laboring Men: Studies in the History of Labour* (London, 1964), pp. 250-74.

11. T.G. Masaryk, *The Spirit of Russia,* two vols., Eden and Cedar Paul, tr. (London, 1955), II, pp. 557-59. This work was first published in English in 1919 from the German original, *Russland und Europa, Studien über die geistigen Strömungen in Russland.* 2 vols. (Jena 1913).

12. *The Spirit of Russia,* I, pp. 481, 486.

13. *Ibid.,* I, pp. 22, 209.

14. *Ibid.,* II, p. 493.

15. Trotsky reviewed Masaryk's book in "Professor Masaryk über Russland," *Der Kampf,* VII, 11-12 (1914), 519-27. The review was reprinted in translation in *Masarykuv Sbornik,* (1924-25), 78-93. While this journal was dedicated to the study of the life and works of the then President of the Czechoslovak Republic, it published material, such as the Trotsky piece, that at times was highly critical of its subject.

16. Cited in the "Translator's Foreword," *The Spirit of Russia,* I, pp. vii-viii.

17. The final part, dealing with Dostoyevsky per se, was first published, in English only, as *The Spirit of Russia,* vol. III (London, 1967), George Gibian, ed., Robert Bass, tr. It was not only the Russian Marxists, such as Trotsky, who criticized Masaryk's book; S.L. Frank, *Biografiia P.B. Struve* (New York, 1956), p. 229, commented: "Having written a book in the history of Russian thought, Masaryk . . . in the essence did not understand anything in our spiritual and social problems." A contemporary Polish historian, Ludwik Bazylow (*Ostatnie lata Rosji carskiej. Rządy Stołypina* [Warsaw, 1972] , p. 21), agrees with Semen Frank: "Masaryk, the author of a book on the development of Russian thought, understood nothing as far as the essence of the most important processes in that area is concerned." For Masaryk and Dostoyevsky see an essay by George Gibian, "Masaryk and Dostoyevsky," in Miloslav Rechcigl, Jr., ed., *Czechoslovakia Past and Present* (The Hague and Paris, 1968), II,

pp. 951-61, and Donald W. Treadgold, *The West in Russia and China, I: Russia, 1472-1917* (Cambridge, 1973), pp. 202-03.

18. *The Spirit of Russia*, I, pp. 210, 521.

19. See for instance *ibid.*, II, pp. 494-97, 503-04, 518-19, etc.

20. *Ibid.*, II, pp. 496, 523.

21. *The Ideals of Humanity*, pp. 187-88.

22. J.P. Mayer, *Max Weber and German Politics* (London, 1956), p. 78: "While Luther directed the German individual soul to its mystical depth, he accepted 'order' and 'authority' with regard to the worldly state. Personal religiosity and State were thus fundamentally separated. Once the religious soul was assured of its intimate mystical union with its God, the individual could submit to State obedience . . . . So the 'free Christian' easily became the slave of the State."

23. *The Ideals of Humanity*, pp. 187-88: The Germans "show a great consensus of opinion in aims and tendencies, manifesting itself in various ways."

24. *The Spirit of Russia*, II, pp. 522-23.

25. *Ibid.*, II, p. 553. The differences between the Prussian and Russian monarchies corresponded to their respective ecclesiastical and religious institutions (p. 525).

26. *Ibid.*, II, pp. 562-63.

27. *Ibid.*, p. 516.

28. *Nesnáze demokracie* (Prague, 1913), pp. 8-9.

29. In political, economic, social, religious, linguistic and national spheres. *The Spirit of Russia*, II, pp. 506-07, 510.

30. *Ibid.*, II, pp. 506-10.

31. *Ibid.*, pp. 507-08. Masaryk proposed to prevent democracy from turning into an *aristocratic* oligarchy by means of a "mutualist federation of organizations."

32. *Nesnáze demokracie*, p. 6. František Fajfr, in "Masarykova filosofie demokracie," *Masarykuv Sborník*, I, 3 (1924-25), 217, observed: "[Masaryk] does not carry this idea further; but were the mechanics and technique of social coexistence necessarily, *ipso facto*, artistocratic and oligarchic, it would mean that democracy could not be realized and that for purely technical reasons society could not be organized democratically."

33. *Nesnáze demokracie,* p. 10.

34. *The Spirit of Russia,* II, p. 516.

35. *Ibid.* "Kant posited in his categorical imperative an infallible, ethical authority; but this authority is subjective and individual, even though it proclaims itself universal as well as necessary."

36. *Ibid.,* p. 517.

37. *The Making of a State* (London, 1927), pp. 397-98.

38. *Nesnáze demokracie,* pp. 10-11, 15.

39. *The Spirit of Russia,* II, pp. 467, 511.

40. *Nesnáze demokracie,* pp. 11-12, 41-42.

41. *Die philosophischen und sociologischen Grundlagen des Marxismus* (Vienna, 1899), pp. 495, 585.

42. *Ibid.,* pp. 229-30, 496.

43. *Ibid.,* p. 218.

44. *Sociální otázka* (Prague, 1898), p. 579.

45. *Die Grundlagen,* p. 234. Masaryk explained synergism in a later work: God created man after his own image; conscious synergism for man is collaboration with the divine will. In acquiring knowledge of Nature, man, and natural laws, both spiritual and historical, we participate in the divine creation and direction of the world. "Synergism with the divine will gives man his measure of freedom and of determinism." *Masaryk on Thought and Life,* pp. 74-75.

46. R.R. Betts, "Masaryk's Philosophy of History," *The Slavonic Review,* 26 (1947), 38, referring to Masaryk's words about the laws of history and freedom, rightly pointed out that his intellectualism was here in conflict with his ethical voluntarism.

47. *Die Grundlagen,* p. 558; *Masaryk on Marx,* pp. 356-57. This quotation refers back to his *Suicide* (1881).

48. *Die Grundlagen,* pp. 229, 485-87.

49. *Ibid.,* p. 492.

50. *Ibid.*

51. "Ke klasifikaci věd," *Česká mysl,* III (1902), pp. 1-2.

52. *Die Grundlagen,* pp. 227-28.

53. *Ibid.,* p. 578.

54. *Ibid.,* pp. 191, 578.

55. *Ibid.,* pp. 191, 194. I am not here concerned as to whether or not Masaryk had correctly understood Marx and Engels.

56. In so doing he ignored Rousseau's warning in the "Origin of Inequality": "It is useless to ask what is the source of natural inequality, because that question is answered by the simple definition of the word. Again, it is still more useless to inquire whether there is any essential connection between the two inequalities; for this would be only asking, in other words, whether those who command are necessarily better than those who obey . . . ; a question fit perhaps to be discussed by slaves in the hearing of their masters, but highly unbecoming to reasonable and free men in search of the truth." See J.J. Rousseau, *The Social Contract, Discourses*, G.D.H. Cole, tr. (London, 1958), p. 160.

57. *Die Grundlagen*, p. 405.

58. *Nesnáze demokracie*, p. 6.

59. *Die Grundlagen*, pp. 191, 406.

60. *Ibid.*, p. 578.

61. *Ibid.*, pp. 192, 578-79.

62. *Ibid.*, pp. 192, 194-95.

63. *Ibid.*, p. 495.

64. T.G. Masaryk, "Potřeba pokrokové politiky" (1908), *Masarykuv Sborník*, I, 2 (1924-25), 170.

65. *Ibid.*, pp. 170-71.

66. K. Krofta, *Masaryk's Political Democracy* (Prague, 1935), p. 2.

67. T.G. Masaryk, "Potřeba pokrokové politiky," p. 172.

68. *Naše nynější krise*, p. XLI.

69. See, e.g., T.G. Masaryk, *The Speech on the Tenth Anniversary* (Prague, 1928), p. 15.

70. This is not a caricature. See *The Spirit of Russia*, II, 512: "Knowledge, critical knowledge, is democracy; aristocracy is the offspring of the mythological outlook."

71. Masaryk, *Světová revoluce* (Prague, 1925), p. 608. Also earlier (*The New Europe*, p. 74): "Caesar or Jesus—that is the watchword of democratic Europe."

72. E. Rádl, *Der Kampf zwischen Tschechen und Deutschen* (Reichenberg, 1928), p. 85; K. Vorovka, *Dvě studie o Masarykově filosofie* (Prague, 1926), p. 24.

73. *The Making of a State*, pp. 308-09. By "democratic art" Masaryk meant that art which gave "the possibility of influencing. . . large numbers of persons simultaneously" (*The Spirit of Russia*, II, p. 513).

74.   In 1933 Masaryk told a Reuter correspondent: "In fascism, indeed, there is an element of democracy. To be successful fascism must refer to public opinion and interest. Mussolini has put monarchy aside. He has formed a sort of republic." *Dokumenty o protilidové a protinárodní činnosti T.G. Masaryka* (Prague, 1953), p. 247.

75.   Masaryk told E. Ludwig that he would use state authority to raise the minimum age for marriage to twenty-eight for men and twenty-four for women, to encourage chastity and prevent divorce, and to forbid birth control (Ludwig, *Defender of Democracy*, pp. 242-45).

76.   E. Rádl, *Der Kampf*, p. 196. To that philosophy Rádl opposed one that limited the rights of the state by the rights of individuals and not by the sentiment and goodwill of the sovereign.

77.   F.Fajfr, "Masarykova filosofie demokracie," *Masarykuv Sborník,* I, 3 (1924-25), 212, 214.

78.   In his *Système de politique positive* Comte spoke of a society of the future where only duty would be operative, with a total elimination of "rights."

79.   K. Krofta, *Masaryk's Political Democracy*, p. 2.

80.   *Masaryk on Thought and Life*, p. 192. Likewise, equality was based on a religious foundation, a belief in the immortal soul: this was "true, metaphysical equality" (*ibid.*, pp. 190-91).

Notes to Chapter IV

1.   Čapek, *President Masaryk*, p. 175: "I wanted to made a new policy, a policy of the future, and impress myself on the thought of our people." For Masaryk's political involvement before and after 1893, see Bruce M. Garver, *The Young Czech Party 1874-1901 and the Emergence of a Multi-Party System* (New Haven and London, 1978). For the circumstances of Masaryk's break with the Young Czechs in 1893, see pp. 186-87 and 458. An earlier but still useful Czech work is Jurij Křížek, *T.G. Masaryk a česká politika: Politické vystoupení českých 'realistu' v letech 1887-1893* (Prague, 1959).

2.   See Anthony D. Smith, *Theories of Nationalism* (New York, 1971), pp. 247-54, for a discussion of nationalism in terms of "dual legitimation" and for the concept of a "secular 'chosen people.'" Smith does not specifically refer to Masaryk but his generalization is applicable.

Masaryk's discovery of the nation as that social unit predestined to promote his program reminds one of Marx's discovery of the proletariat as
the social force that would identify itself with, and implement, *his* philosophy. In Marx's declaration that "as philosophy finds its *material*
weapons in the proletariat, so the proletariat discovers its *intellectual*
weapons in philosophy . . . .," Masaryk might have substituted the "Czech
nation" for the proletariat, and his own program for Marx's "philosophy."
See George Lichtheim, *Marxism: An Historical and Critical Study* (New
York, 1962), p. 53; Alfred G. Meyer, *Marxism: The Unity of Theory
and Practice* (Ann Arbor, 1963), pp. 96-100.

    3.   Garver, *The Young Czech Party*, pp. 206-16; especially pp. 214-5.

    4.   Antonie van den Beld, *Humanity*, pp. 55-6.

    5.   *Versuch*, p. 283.

    6.   T.G. Masaryk, *Česká otázka (The Czech Question), O naší ny-
nější krisi (On Our Present Crisis), Jan Hus* (Prague, 1924). (*Česká otázka*
and *Naše nynější krise* were first published in 1895; *Jan Hus* in 1896).
A selection of Masaryk's writings on Czech history is available in English.
See Tomáš G. Masaryk, *The Meaning of Czech History*, René Wellek, ed.;
Peter Kussi, tr. (Chapel Hill: University of North Carolina Press, 1974).

    7.   T.G. Masaryk, *Karel Havlíček* (Prague, 1896), pp. 477-78.

    8.   *Česká otázka*, p. 11.

    9.   Čapek, *President Masaryk*, pp. 186-87.

  10.   Masaryk, *Karel Havlíček*, pp. 443 ff; 477-78.

  11.   *Česko otázka* (Prague, 1895), p. 9.

  12.   *Ibid.*, p. 4.

  13.   *Ibid.*, p. 116.

  14.   *Ibid.*, pp. 152-54. An interesting illustration of Masaryk's point
of view is seen in the way he handled the criticism by Sobestiansky of
Moscow of the idealization of the ancient Slavs by Johann Gottfried
Herder and Jan Kollár. Masaryk dismissed the evidence cited by Sobestiansky. He argued that Dostoevsky and Leroy Beaulieu had described the
nineteenth-century Russians (i.e., Slavs), and their description of modern
Slavs conformed to the picture of ancient Slavs drawn by Herder and
Kollár. Therefore the observations of Dostoevsky or Ivan Kireevsky on
nineteenth-century Russians were just as relevant as statements collected
from old sources (*ibid.*, p. 73). A prominent Czech historian, Josef Pekař,
pointed to this and other methodological principles of Masaryk in his

celebrated essay, "Masarykova česká filosofie," *Český Časopis Historický*, vol. 18 (1912), 170-208.

15. *Česká otázka*, p. 155.

16. According to Masaryk, the significance of Czech history was contained in the succession of names: Hus, Chelčický, Kˆmenský, Dobrovský, Kollár, Palacký, Havlíček. It might be useful here to consider Masaryk's definition of "sociological law." In general, he was in agreement with Häckel's "biogenetic law," according to which individual evolution is a rapid repetition of the slow evolution of tribes or races. See *Selbstmord*, p. 187n.

17. *Česká otázka*, pp. 9-10. For the influence of the German philosophers on the Czechs, especially Kollár, see pp. 23-4 and 58-9.

18. *Ibid.*, pp. 13, 15, 115.

19. *Ibid.*, p. 10.

20. *Ibid.*, pp. 15-20-21. Masaryk had been interested in Slavophilism as early as the 1880s. His estimate then was very favorable, although he did not share its "mysticism and clericalism." He thought that Orthodoxy, Catholicism, and Protestantism were the three religions from which a new synthesis might develop one day: "The society and the age when this happens will save mankind" (T.G. Masaryk, *Slovanské studie 1. Slavjanofilství I. V. Kirejevského* [Prague, 1889], pp. 39-40). Theodor Syllaba, "Na okraj Masarykova 'Ruska a Evropy,'" *Filosofický časopis* (Prague, 1958), No. 6, p. 14, suggested that Masaryk had been inspired by the Slavophiles when he produced "the counterrevolutionary interpretation of the Czech problem as a religious problem."

21. Pekař, "Masarykova česká filosofie," pp. 180-84.

22. *Jan Hus*, 3rd ed. (Prague, 1925), p. 136. ". . . from the fourteenth century until the eighteenth, for over four hundred years (from the time of Charles IV until Joseph II and Maria Theresa) the problem of religion has always been outstanding in our national development . . . is it possible that this problem which moved the nation for four hundred years, in which the nation reached its maturity and its most glorious period, . . . should be suddenly broken down because we have other troubles today—no, this is not even thinkable. Religion has its own development . . . , it is our task to seek the direction in which it is proceeding. . . ."

23. *Palackys Idee des böhmischen Volkes* (Prague, 1898), pp. 10-11. See also *Naše nynější krise* p. xvi.

24. *Česká otázka*, p. 221. "In 1487 greed for power and wealth won in Bohemia a victory over Czech heart and reason." Masaryk implied that 1620 was a punishment deserved.

25. *Ibid.*, pp. 215-15. Masaryk added that this dual Czech nature had not escaped the attention of Czech patriots of the past: one of them, Rokyčana, used to pray to God for the golden mean. Masaryk did not agree; something else was needed: a harmonious merging of the two qualities into a higher spiritual unity. Then men will appear who ". . . will burn with that true active love: not a romantic and sentimental love, will it be, but brave, sure, golden and soft, like gold . . . ."

26. *The Ideals of Humanity and How to Work* (London, 1938), pp. 123-25.

27. *Grundlagen des Marxismus*, pp. 435-36.

28. *Naše nynější krise*, XVI. ". . .the conviction that a nation as a whole has, along with church and state, a cultural mission appears among wider circles only at the end of the last century" (*Česká otázka*, p. 23).

29. *Naše nynější krise*, XV.

30. *Česká otázka*, p. 150.

31. *Ibid.*, pp. 195-96. But the Cyrillo-Methodian controversy furnished Masaryk with a supplementary proof that the religious question was indeed the most important one, since even indifferent liberals could not help sensing it in their odd idiosyncratic way (pp. 194-95).

32. *Naše nynější krise*, p. 60.

33. "Jan Hus" in: *Česká otázka*, pp. 364-365. This was so, Masaryk said, in spite of the fact that the Brethren consituted no more than one-tenth of the whole Czech people (p. 378). Earlier, in his prenationalist phase, Masaryk's estimate of the religious condition of his country was very different: "The Czechs are an especial example of religious superficiality . . . . Hussitism remains a liberal pastime . . . but is no longer a religious tendency, only rationalistic superficiality and unsteadiness (aufklärerische Halbheit und Haltlosigkeit) . . ." (*Selbstmord*).

34. *Česká otázka*, p. 366. It may be added that one could also be an unwitting follower of the Brethren; in his last book, published in 1925, Masaryk wrote, "though King George opposed the Brotherhood, he proclaimed the ideal of universal peace, and was thus in agreement with the Brethren's fundamental doctrine" (*The Making of a State*, p. 424).

35. *The Ideals of Humanity,* pp. 13, 15-16, 89.

36. *Národnostní filosofie doby novější* (Jičín, 1905), p. 15. Schopenhauer, as well as Herder, represented German national character: his pessimism was "the foundation of German national philosophy" (p. 21). For Masaryk's relation to Herder, see A. Gillies, "Herder and Masaryk: Some Points of Contact," *Modern Language Review,* XL (1945), 120-28.

37. *The Ideals of Humanity . . . ,* pp. 17-18.

38. *Ibid.,* pp. 89-91.

39. *Česká otázka,* p. 23, and *The Ideals of Humanity,* p. 17.

40. *Česká otázka,* pp. 8-9.

41. *The Ideals of Humanity,* pp. 172-73. "The Young Czech party wishes to publish . . . German writings. This signifies a great lack of sincerity. What is at the core of our ethics? We have our national pride on our lips yet do not perceive what is worst for our country" (p. 173).

42. "*Liberalism in its essence* is a philosophical rationalism which . . . rejects the religious and ethical meaning of life and culture; socially it is an aristo-plutocratic philosophy. Liberalism developed in the eighteenth century, notably in France, and carried through the Great Revolution and subsequent smaller ones, particularly those of 1848; the forces of reaction were not equal to it; they themselves were in essence liberal, wishing to return to old political regimes for reasons of expediency. Therefore in reality they strengthened liberalism. Liberal and revolutionary political constitutionalism became accepted and its philosophical foundation was also accepted or tolerated . . . . Liberalism tends to keep the society of our times on shallow revolutionary principles, . . . no thorough revision or reform—that's the motto of all liberalism." *Česká otázka,* pp. 325-26.

43. *Ibid.,* pp. 326-27. "The humanitarian *Czech* ideal has its historical and essential foundation in our reformation, not in the French revolution; liberal humanism is not the same as the humanity of our reformation. He who wants to think and feel truly *Czech* must be aware of this distinction" (p. 327).

44. *Ibid.,* pp. 47, 347. Masaryk condemned also the "Voltaireian-Wielandian liberalism." In *The Czech Question* he admitted that Voltaire's philosophy was humanitarian but "not suitable for us."

45. *Ibid.,* pp. 193-94.

46. *The Ideals of Humanity,* p. 50. But on p. 49, Masaryk wrote: "In

Czech literature anarchism also plays a part, but in view of our cultural conditions this part is different from that played by anarchism in Germany or Russia . . ."

47. *Česká otázka,* pp. 230-31.

48. *Ibid.,* pp. 222-26.

49. *Naše nynější krise,* p. XXI.

50. *Česká otázka,* pp. 227-28. He especially addressed the Czech nobility: for it was they who now had a chance and duty "to undo the wrongs of 1487."

51. See *The Ideals of Humanity,* pp. 170, 187-88 (a lecture delivered in 1898): "One thing especially should be clear to our political educated classes, namely that everywhere in all parts of our Czech country, people should understand each other, even if they are not formally united by party or caste, that there should be among them a *tacitus consensus.* The nation lacking such accord is in a bad way. Every nation, sect, State, society, or organization is lost if it has no members who understand each other without explanations. Why cannot a person in Prague, one in Pilsen, and one in Opava come to logically similar conclusions? Because this unspoken agreement is not there . . . . We lack the political discussions of other nations, especially the large ones; for instance, the Germans show a great consensus of opinion in aims and tendencies, manifesting itself in various ways, giving them national strength, and endangering such nations as lack it."

52. Čapek, *Masaryk Tells His Story,* pp. 175-76.

53. J. Pekař, "Masarykova česká filosofie," *Český časopis historický,* XVIII (1912), 202-03.

54. See Ivan Franko, "Moje styky s Masarykem" (written in 1910), *Masarykuv Sborník,* IV (1930), pp. 15-18, for Masaryk's influence among the Galician Ukrainians. Masaryk had exerted a similar impact on the South Slavs. For a recent recognition of this fact see Václav Žáček et al., *Češi a Jihoslované v minulosti: Od nejstarších dob do roku 1918* (Prague 1975), especially the essays by Karel Herman and Miroslav Tejchman. For a comprehensive study of Masaryk's view of the nationality question, with special reference to the Ukrainian problem, see O.I. Bochkovs'kyi, *T.G. Masaryk. Natsional'na problema ta ukrains'ke pytannia* (Poděbrady, 1930).

55. Ernest Denis, in *Masarykuv Sborník,* IV (1930), p. 11.

56. Josef Kaizl, *České myšlenky* (Prague, 1896).

57. E. Denis, *La Bôheme depuis la Montagne-Blanche*, 2 vols. (Paris, 1903), II, pp. 14n, 576n.

58. S. Harrison Thomson, "T.G. Masaryk and Czech Historiography," *Journal of Central European Affairs*, X (1950), 49-50, 52. Jaroslav Werstadt, *Odkazy.dějin a dějepiscu* (Prague, 1948), p. 30, notes that along with Josef Kaizl, all leading historians of Bohemia (among them Jaroslav Goll, E. Denis, J. Pekař, J. Vlček) disagreed with Masaryk. R.G. Plaschka, *Von Palacký bis Pekař* (Graz-Cologne, 1955), p. 81, rightly observes: "While Pekař conducted his counterattack for history as it was . . . Masaryk was concerned with the totality of his national political progam, his philosophical-political catechism, its historical proof." The Masaryk-Pekar controversy was discussed by František Červinka, "Spor o smysl českých dějin 1912," *Plamen*, 1 (1969), 14-23. See also František Kutnar, *Prehledné dejiny českého a slovenského dejepisectví*, II (Prague, 1977), pp. 35-37; Milan Hauner, "Recasting Czech History," *Survey*, 24, No. 3 (Summer 1979), pp. 214-225, and Tomáš Vojtěch, "Česká historiografie a pozitivismus do roku 1918," *Československý časopis historický*, 28 (1980), pp. 78-105.

59. Thomas G. Masaryk, *The Meaning of Czech History*, edited with an introduction by René Wellek, Peter Kussi, tr. (Chapel Hill: The University of North Carolina Press, 1974), p. xi.

60. *The Meaning of Czech History*, p. xxii.

61. *Ibid.*, pp. xiv, xvii.

62. *Ibid.*, pp. vii-viii.

63. K. Marx and F. Engels, *The Holy Family or Critique of Critical Critique* (Moscow, 1956), p. 53.

Notes to Chapter V

1. From the opening paragraph of the Realists' political program. See *Rámcový program české strany lidové (realistické)* (Prague, 1900), p. 1.

2. This has been noted by K. Krofta, "Masaryk und unser politisches Programm," in *Masaryk–Staatsmann und Denker* (Prague, 1930), pp. 36-37.

3. Austria. Reichsrat. Haus der Abgeordneten. XI Session. Steno-

graphische Protokolle über die Sitzungen des Hauses der Abgeordneten in dem Jahre 1892 (Vienna, 1892), pp. 7857, 10779. (Hereafter cited SPHA.)

4. SPHA, XVI Session, p. 1258.

5. Quoted by J. Křížek, *Masaryk a Česká politika* (Prague, 1959), p. 304, from an unpublished manuscript.

6. SPHA, pp. 7850, 10783.

7. SPHA, p. 6846, cf. p. 7850.

8. Robert A. Kann, *Multinational Empire*, vol. I, p. 206.

9. There is a good summary of the Czech-German conflict and a review of the literature in D. Perman, *The Shaping of the Czechoslovak State: Diplomatic History of the Boundaries of Czechoslovakia 1914-1920* (Leiden, 1962), pp. 8-14.

10. A.J.P. Taylor, *The Habsburg Monarchy*, p. 221.

11. *Rámcový program*, pp. 112-18; T.G. Masaryk, *Právo přirozené a historické* (Prague, 1900), pp. 35-37, 42.

12. *Právo přirozené*, p. 31.

13. *Rámcový program*, p. 5.

14. *Ibid.*, p. 24.

15. *Ibid.*, pp. 1-2, 19.

16. *Ibid.*, p. 1. Presumably the territorial division of States for political, administrative, economic, etc., purposes would be undertaken without regard for nationality.

17. *Ibid.*, p. 19.

18. *Ibid.*, pp. 7, 47.

19. Perman, *The Shaping of the Czechoslovak State*, p. 12: "Czech politicians genuinely feared that an ethnographic divvision of administration would close the German areas to the swelling Czech population and confine the Czech nationals to the role of an insignificant Slav minority within German Austria." See also R.J. Kerner, ed., *Czechoslovakia, Twenty Years of Independence* (Berkeley, 1940), p. 45.

20. *Rámcový program*, p. 5.

21. *Ibid.*, pp. 7-8, 118.

22. *Ibid.*, pp. 2, 4.

23. *Národnostní filosofie doby novější* (Jičín, 1905), p. 14. Masaryk did not then believe in the practical feasibility of an independent Czech state for at least two reasons. One was a product of his reflections about

the evolution of Europe; the other corresponded to his view of the function of the State in social life. When one of the smaller political groups, the Progressivits, declared that an independent Bohemia in union with other Habsburg lands was their ultimate goal, Masaryk declined to accept their program: "I am not able to put into a real political program something that I am convinced I will not see in my life-time" (*Naše nynější krise*, p. 97). One is reminded of Lenin's letter to Swiss workers, written early in 1917, in which he said he did not expect to live long enough to see the revolution.

24. *Rámcový program*, pp. 122, 124.

25. This letter apparently has not been published to this day. It is cited here as quoted in the indictment presented by the prosecution at a trial of several Czech nationalists, Masaryk's followers, in 1916 in Vienna. See "K.K. Militäranwalt des Militärkommandanten in Wien. Anklageschrift gegen Johann Hájek, Cyril Dušek, . . . ," Vienna, Kriegsarchiv, Militärkanzlei Seiner Majestät, A 3641/15, 57-3/15-3, ex-1916, pp. 31-32. Masaryk's letter was dated 9 January 1899. The prosecution also pointed out that it was significant, in light of what transpired later, that when he testified before a Vienna court in 1909 (The Friedjung Affair), Masaryk declared that in relation to modern legal and political concepts the concept of high treason had lost "all practical significance" (p. 24). Herben, *T.G. Masaryk*, p. 230, argued that Masaryk moved to the anti-Austrian position in the 1890s.

26. Alois Czedik, *Zur Geschichte der k.k. österreichischen Ministerien, 1861-1916* (Teschen, Vienna and Leipzig, 1917-20), IV, pp. 233-34.

27. For an analysis of the demographic transformation of Czech lands, and of Prague, which since the beginnings of the Czech national revival had served as the center of Czech culture and politics, see Jan Havránek, "The Development of Czech Nationalism," *Austrian History Yearbook*, vol. III, pt. 2 (1967), pp. 223-28, and *idem*, "Social Classes, Nationality Ratios and Demographic Trends in Prague 1880-1900," *Historica* (Prague), vol. XIII (1966), pp. 171-208.

28. For a brief historical account and a review of the literature see Friedrich Prinz, "Die Böhmischen Länder im Zeitalter der modernen Industriegesellschaft," in Karl Bosl, ed., *Handbuch der Geschichte der Böhmischen Länder* (Stuttgart, 1968), vol. III, pp. 154-235. See also Havránek, "The Development," *passim*, and Joseph F. Zacek, "Nationalism

in Czechoslovakia," in Peter F. Sugar and Ivo J. Lederer, eds., *Nationalism in Eastern Europe* (Seattle and London, 1969), pp. 183-86. The recent article by Trevor Vaughan Thomas, "Bohumil [i.e., Bohumír] Šmeral and the Czech Question 1900-14," *Journal of Contemporary History*, XI (1976), 79-98, deals with the problem of socialism and nationalism in depth. Šmeral (1880-1941) was a socialist leader and a founder of the Communist Party of Czechoslovakia.

29. For a survey of the Czech party system in the early twentieth century, see Bruce M. Garver, *The Young Czech Party 1874-1901*, pp. 277-308.

30. "Zur deutschböhmischen Ausgsleichsfrage," *Die Zeit*, VII, 82 (1896).

31. *The Ideals of Humanity*, p. 19.

32. *Die philosophischen und sociologischen Grundlagen des Marxismus*, pp. 406, 577. Masaryk did not always clearly separate progressive autonomization as an historical event and progressive autonomization as a desired course of events. Perhaps one would often be right to interpret his statements as containing both meanings.

33. *Rámcový program*, p. 122.

34. *Grundlagen des Marxismus*, p. 151.

35. Cf. *The Spirit of Russia*, vol. II, p. 557; E. Ludwig, *Defender of Democracy*, pp. 177ff.

36. *Naše nynější krise*, p. XXXIX-XL.

37. *Ibid.*, p. XXXIX. (This translation attempts to preserve Masaryk's style, including punctuation.)

38. *Ibid.*, pp. XXXVIII, XXXIX.

39. J. Kaizl, *Politické myšlenky* (Prague, 1896), pp. 113-15.

40. *Česká otázka*, p. 169.

41. Written from the perspective of time, the following passage perhaps does more justice to Austrian liberals: ". . .it should not be forgotten that the Liberals had a fine conception of that German civilization which they praised so highly, and further that it was thanks to them that police rule gave way to the reign of law and the recognition of individual rights including those of the Jews." E. Wiskemann, *Czechs and Germans* (London, 1938), p. 35.

42. *Naše nynější krise*, p. XLIII.

43. *Grundlagen des Marxismus*, pp. 405-06.

44. *Speech on the Tenth Anniversary* (Prague, 1928), p. 31.

45. *The Making of a State*, p. 409.

46. Zeman, *The Masaryks*, p. 60.

47. See J.B. Kozák, "Masaryks Stellung zur Metaphysik," *Masaryk Festschrift*, vol. II, pp. 210ff., and Lubomír Nový, "Masaryk jako sociolog," *Sociologický časopis*, vol. 4, no. 3 (1968), esp. pp. 297-303, for a discussion of the revisions introduced by Masaryk in his work "Rukovět' sociologie," *Naše doba*, VII (1900-01). Nový cites several other relevant works. Masaryk remained convinced of its great importance, and as late as 1930 wrote to Husserl that he was working on a second edition. See *Sborník prací filosofické fakulty Brněnské university*, B17 (1970), p. 164. (Letter of 10 March 1930.)

48. Karel Čapek, *President Masaryk*, pp. 179-80.

49. Draga B. Shillinglaw, *The Lectures of Professor T.G. Masaryk at the University of Chicago, Summer 1902* (Lewisburg and London, 1978), p. 97.

50. Shillinglaw, *The Lectures*, p. 98.

51. For full accounts of the Hilsner affair, see František Červinka, "The Hilsner Affair," *The Leo Baeck Institute Year Book*, XIII (1968), pp. 142-57, and Ernst Rychnowsky, "The Struggle Against the Ritual Murder Superstition," in *Thomas G. Masaryk and the Jews*, Benjamin R. Epstein, tr. (New York, 1941), pp. 148-234. (This latter book was a translation from *Masaryk und das Judentum*, Ernst Rychnowsky, ed., Prague, 1931.) The Hilsner affair is discussed in all Masaryk biographies. Zeman, *The Masaryks*, p. 53, notes: "Masaryk became...the most isolated figure in Czech public life. Even some of his friends from the small 'realist' circle turned away from him. Anti-Semitism was used to stimulate the animosity which had accumulated against Masaryk during his seventeen years' stay in Prague. In the comparison with the Hilsner affair, the earlier manuscript controversy had been gentle discourse between civilized men." However, in the Masaryk literature there exists a tradition which suppresses the fact that the Czech public opinion was anti-Semitic and speaks of "the Germans" and the German press as having been anti-Hilsner. This tradition is not dead even in our days. Thus, Draga B. Shillinglaw writes in the introduction to her edition of Masaryk's Chicago lectures: "His [Hilsner's] trial had aroused outbursts of anti-Semitism, including a German press campaign against the Jews." Shillinglaw

also attributes to Masaryk discovering and publishing "proof that Hilsner was innocent," resulting in a retrial and acquittal of Hilsner. (Nothing of the sort happened: Hilsner was again found guilty of murder, but not ritual murder, and was amnestied only in 1918.) See Shillinglaw, *The Lectures*, p. 27. (In 1969, Anežka's dying brother confessed he had murdered her.)

52.   Peter G.J. Pulzer, *The Rise of Political Anti-Semitism in Germany and Austria* (New York, 1964), p. 215.

53.   Robert Weltsch, "Introduction," *The Leo Baeck Institute Year Book*, XIII (1968), pp. xi-xii. "It is significant that Masaryk's involvement in the Hilsner affair is referred to [in Masaryk's Conservations with Čapek] only casually on one single page of the book." (*Ibid.*, xii *n*).

54.   See on this particular question F. Gregory-Campbell, *Confrontation in Central Europe*, pp. 85-86, who notes that the Prague Jews were often targets of "anti-German" demonstrations, for example, in 1918, when Czechoslovakia became independent.

55.   T.G. Masaryk, "Ernest Renan o židovství jako plemenu a náboženství," *Sborník Historický*, I (1883), pp. 120-27, reprinted in *Masarykuv Sborník*, ((1925), pp. 61-68. Masaryk disagreed with Renan's argument that the Jews in modern times were no longer an ethnic (or racial) but merely a religious group consisting of persons of very different ethnic backgrounds. While he admitted that in the more distant past the Jews in fact did "mix" with the other nationalities (via conversion to Judaism or intermarriage), he thought they were less "mixed" than other modern nations, and "we must consider them as a nation quite different from ourselves" (*Ibid.*, pp. 67-68).

56.   Felix Weltsch, "Masaryk and Zionism," *Masaryk and the Jews*, p. 76.

57.   Weltsch, "Masaryk," pp. 76-77, and Masaryk, *Die Grundlagen des Marxismus* (Vienna, 1899), pp. 452-55. This was the German translation of *Otázka sociální. Základy marxismu filosofické a sociologické* (Prague, 1898). See *ibid.*, 5th ed. (Prague, 1948), II, 180-82.

58.   Christoph Stölzl, "Die 'Burg' und die Juden," *Die Burg*, II, pp. 102-03. For Havlíček's rejection of assimilation, see Ruth Kestenberg-Gladstein, "The Jews between Czechs and Germans in the Historic Lands, 1848-1918," in *The Jews of Czechoslovakia, Historical Studies and Surveys* (Philadelphia and New York, 1968 and 1971), vol. I, pp. 22-23 and 61-62. For the pro-Czech assimilationist current see Egon Hostovsky,

"The Czech-Jewish Movement," in *The Jews of Czechoslovakia*, II, 148-54. See also Jaroslav Rokyčana, "Friends in Need," *Masaryk and the Jews*, pp. 235-47.

59. Stuart A. Borman, *The Prague Student Zionist Movement 1896-1914* (unpublished Ph.D. disseration, University of Chicago, 1972), pp. 33-40.

60. Toennies himself, however, placed both state and nation (but not *volk*) under the *Gesellschaft* heading in distinction from those more closely-knit groups which represented *Gemeinschaft*. See on this Joanna Kurczewska, *Naród w socjologii i ideologii polskiej* (Warszawa, 1979), p. 304. Cf. Toennies, *Community and Society*, tr. Charles P. Loomis (New York, 1963), pp. 231 and 258-59.

61. Herben, *T.G. Masaryk* (Prague, 1926), I, pp. 231-32.

62. For Masaryk's attitude toward Clericalism, see *Rámcový program*, pp. 77-78. See also "Svobodomyslní Čechové v Americe," *Naše doba*, X (1902-1903), 1-7, and "Lev XIII," *ibid.*, 801-807.

63. Paul Selver, *Masaryk: A Biography* (London, 1940), p. 198.

64. *Věda a církev. Církevně politický význam Wahrmundovy affairy* (Prague, 1908); *Freie wissenschaftliche und kirchlich gebundene Weltanschauung und Lebensauffassung. Die kirchenpolitische Bedeutung der Wahrmundaffaire* (Vienna, 1908).

65. Masaryk's candidature was endorsed by the *Oesterreichisch-Israelitische Union*, which, Pulzer explains, was founded in 1886 "because the Liberals could no longer be relied upon to fight anti-Semitism." Candidates supported by the Union "were not necessarily Jewish or even Liberal. Kronawetter was supported, as was Masaryk." (Pulzer, *The Rise*, p. 212.)

66. See Masaryk's May 25, 1908 speech in the "Galician debate." *Stenographische Protokolle uber die Sitzungen des Hauses der Abgeordneten*, XVIII Session, 75 Sitzung, pp. 4887-95. Reference to "Monarchomachs" is on pp. 4888-89.

67. See the brochure *Der Agramer Hochverratsprozess und die Annexion von Bosnien und Herzegovina* (Vienna, 1909): Masaryk's Reichsrat speeches of May 14 and 18, 1909.

68. See Vienna, *Kriegsarchiv*, Militär-Kanzlei Franz-Ferdinand, files Nos. 5344 and 6300 for 1913, and Nos. 741 and 1604 for 1914, for the correspondence between Vienna and Stockholm and Copenhagen *re* Masaryk's prize.

69. van den Beld, *Humanity,* pp. 65-66; see also pp. 68-69, 141-44. A similar statement is made by Karl W. Newman, *European Democracy between the Wars,* tr. from the German by Keith Morgan (London, 1970), pp. 74-75. In this, Newman follows R.A. Kann. Kann, says Newman, "has proved definitely that no trace of reservations about the continued existence of the Habsburg monarchy is to be found in either Masaryk's or Beneš' pre-war writings." Newman cites R.A. Kann, *The Multinational Empire: Nationalism and National Reform in the Habsburg Monarch, 1848-1918,* 2 vols. (New York, 1950), I, p. 215. To rely solely on Masaryk's speeches but to disregard such books as *The Spirit of Russia,* would be as correct as to deduce Hitler's long-term plans from his interviews for American and British newspapers in the 1930s, but to forget about *Mein Kampf.*

Notes to Chapter VI

1. Karel Pichlík, *Zahraniční odboj 1914-1918 bez legend* (Prague, 1968), pp. 21, 35, 38. Pichlík convincingly argues that Masaryk's faith in Austria's capacity for self-reform rapidly declined after the Bosnian crisis, but that at the same time Masaryk remained an opponent of tsarism and could not associate himself with the pro-Russian stand of radical nationalists or with the neo-Slavism of the Young Czechs. Even before the war's outbreak, for example in 1913, he had been seeking to develop a program that would place the nationality problems of Austria in a European and democratic framework. Pichlík's book, based on archival and printed sources, is indispensable to a study of Masaryk's work in 1914-1918. (An earlier valuable work by Pichlík is "První projekt samostatného Československa z podzimu 1914," *Historie a vojenství,* 3 (1966), 356-407, which surveys the post-1948 Masaryk literature in Czechoslovakia as well as his work in 1914.

2. Lewis Namier, *Vanished Supremacies: Essays on European History 1812-1918* (New York, 1963), p. 28.

3. Bruce M. Garver, *The Young Czech Party 1874-1901,* p. 358, gives electoral results for 1911, in which the Socialists gathered 357,263 votes, and the Agrarians 257,714 votes, out of a total of 1,099,171 votes cast for Czech parties. Other parties winning more votes than Masaryk's own party, for which about one percent of Czechs voted, included National Socialists, National Catholics, Christian Socialists, and Young

Czechs. For a review of the political scene in Czech lands before 1914, see *idem*, pp. 277-308. For Masaryk's political isolation in 1914 see Victor S. Mamatey, "The Union of Czech Political Parties in the Reichsrat, 1916-1918," in *The Habsburg Empire in World War I*, Robert A. Kann, ed. (Boulder, Colorado, 1977), p. 6. For the parties' stand in 1914, see Zbyněk Zeman, *The Masaryks*, pp. 64-69, 72, and *idem, The Break-Up of the Habsburg Empire* (Oxford, 1963), esp. pp. 76-94. Paul Vyšný, *Neo-Slavism and the Czechs 1898-1914* (Cambridge, 1977), in a full-scale study of the pro-Russian current in Czech politics. For the socialists' dilemma, see Zdeněk Kárník, *Socialisté na rozcestí: Habsburk, Masaryk či Šmeral?* (Prague, 1968).

4. Pichlík, *Zahraniční odboj*, pp. 21, 35, and 38. Among other works, Victor S. Mamatey, "The Establishment of the Republic," in Victor S. Mamatey and Radomir Luza, eds., *A History of the Czechoslovak Republic 1918-1948* (Princeton, 1973), pp. 3-38, outlines the history of the struggle for Czechoslovak independence during World War I and Masaryk's role in it; its bibliography is most useful. An excellent bibliography on World War I and the establishment of Czechoslovakia is in *Handbuch der Geschichte der böhmischen Länder*, Karl Bosl, ed. (Stuttgart, 1968), III, pp. 239-273. The post-1919 period is covered in *Handbuch*, IV (Stuttgard, 1970), pp. 3-98. For a detailed account of Masaryk's plans and activities see R.W. Seton-Watson, *Masaryk in England* (Cambridge, 1943) and Ernest Birke, "Das neue Europa in den Kriegsdenkschriften T. G. Masaryks 1914 bis 1918," Wilhelm Berges, ed., *Zur Geschichte und Problematik der Demokratie: Festgabe für Hans Herzfeld* (Berlin, 1958), pp. 551-75. An earlier, but still valuable, work in Czech is Karel Stlouka, *Československý stát v představách T.G. Masaryka za války* (Prague, 1930).

5. Pichlík, *Zahraniční odboj*, pp. 87, 115.

6. It is outside the consideration of this work to examine Masaryk's political activities and their effect at winning the Allies over for the Czechoslovak cause. This subject belongs to the diplomatic history of the war, as does that of the evolving attitude of the Western powers toward the problem of Austria-Hungary and its component nationalities. For relevant examples of recent works, see Kenneth J. Calder, *Britain and the Origins of the New Europe* (Cambridge, 1976), Wilfried Fest, *Peace or Partition: The Habsburg Monarchy and British Policy, 1914-1918* (London

1978), and Josef Kalvoda, "Masaryk in America in 1918," *Jahrbücher für Geschichte Osteuropas,* 27, No. 1 (1979), 85-99.

7. *Masaryk on Marx, An Abridged Edition of T.G. Masaryk, The Social Question: Philosophical and Sociological Foundations of Marxism,* Erazim V. Kohák, ed. and tr. (Lewisburg, 1972), pp. 345-47.

8. *The Spirit of Russia,* II, p. 539.

9. *Ibid.,* pp. 538-539, 541.

10. Ludwig, *Defender of Democracy,* p. 108.

11. *The Making of a State,* p. 418. Apparently the opposition between the forces of theocracy and those of democracy did not go so far as to prevent democracy from dictating peace treaties.

12. Ludwig, *Defender of Democracy,* p. 149.

13. *The New Europe: The Slav Standpoint* (London, 1918). This work was recently reissued under the editorship of W. Preston Warren and William B. Weist, with an introduction by Otakar Odložilík (Lewisburg, 1972). Rudolf Nadolny, *Germanisierung oder Slavisierung? Eine Entgegnung auf Masaryks Buch Das neue Europa* (Berlin, n.d. [1927]), is a book-length critique of Masaryk's wartime arguments against Pan-Germanism.

14. *The New Europe* (1972 ed.), p. 35.

15. *Ibid.,* pp. 127, 177, 186. For Herder's view see p. 62.

16. *Ibid.,* p. 127. A passage like this helps us to understand what Masaryk meant after 1918 by the necessity to de-Austrianize (*odrakouštět*) the Czechs. See K. Čapek, *Hovory s T.G. Masarykem* (Prague, 1946), pp. 312-13.

17. Pichlík, *Zahraniční odboj,* pp. 86-87, 98-99.

18. *The New Europe: The Slav Standpoint* (London, 1918), p. 69.

19. *Ibid.,* pp. 16-17. "And language has a tremendous social significance—makes possible the contact of man. Nationality, national spirit, manifests itself therefore in literature; . . . great poets are looked upon as the most expessive representatives of their nations. But even science and philosophy have their national character—even mathematics, an abstract science, differs in the different countries."

20. *Ibid.,* p. 18. In 1905, however, Masaryk wrote: "For the Germans nationality is a higher principle than the state." *Národnostní filosofie,* p. 14.

21. *The New Europe,* p. 18. See A. Gillies, "Herder and Masaryk:

Some Points of Contact," *Modern Language Review,* XL (1945), 120-28. The Czech philosopher E. Rádl in his *Der Kampf zwischen Tschechen und Deutschen,* p. 132, noted significant parallels in the thought of Herder and Masaryk.

22. *The New Europe,* p. 19.

23. *Ibid.,* pp. 19, 28. How uncertain, however, Masaryk must have been about one at least of those "exceptions" may be seen from what R.W. Seton-Watson (*Masaryk in England,* p. 49) wrote about a conversation with Masaryk in 1914. Masaryk feared it might prove impossible to secure the restoration of Belgium. "If the final settlement followed purely ethnographic lines, was there not a danger of Belgium being divided between France and Holland?" Even if his fears were premature, from the perspective of the 1980s it is undeniable that Masaryk perceptively diagnosed Belgium's ethnic divisions as potentially threatening its survival.

24. *The New Europe,* pp. 47, 29.

25. *Ibid.,* p. 29.

26. Victor-Lucien Tapie, *The Rise and Fall of the Habsburg Monarchy* (New York, 1971), p. 392.

27. A. Pamphilet, "A Corrective to the Principle of Nationality," *The New Europe* (London), XII (1917), 197.

28. *The New Europe* (London, 1918), p. 53.

29. T.G. Masaryk, *Cesta demokracie,* three vols. (Prague, 1933-36), I (1933), p. 84. Moreover, the whole question might have been approached in other terms.

30. *The Making of a State,* pp. 385-86.

31. *Cesta demokracie,* I, p. 71.

32. Ferdinand Peroutka, *Budování státu,* 4 vols. (Prague, 1932-36), II, p. 1269.

33. T.G. Masaryk, *Poselství* (Prague, 1930), pp. 17-18.

34. *The Making of a State,* pp. 387, 389.

35. Address to Czechoslovak journalists, 7 June 1919, quoted by E. Rádl, *Der Kampf zwischen Tschechen und Deutschen* (Reichenberg, 1928), p. 197.

36. *Ibid.* We have followed here Rádl's critique of Masaryk's postwar standpoint. See especially pp. 195-97.

37. Čapek, *Masaryk on Thought and Life,* pp. 210-11.

38. *The Making of a State,* p. 390.

39. "Independent Bohemia," in R.W. Seton-Watson, *Masaryk in England*, p. 125.

40. Samo Falt'an, *Slovenská otázka v Československu* (Bratislava, 1968), pp. 72-78, observes that while Masaryk recognized Slovakia's linguistic and literary peculiarity, he failed to grasp the Slovaks' national development as a nation of its own. In this respect his perception of Slovakia ignored the developments since the middle of the 19th century. In consequence of this position, Masaryk spoke of incorporating the Slovaks into the body of the Czech, later "Czechoslovak", nation. Masaryk did not even think of Slovaks as a "younger brother" of the Czechs but as members of the Czech nation itself. An earlier work specifically devoted to this problem is A. Pražák, *Češi a Slováci* (Bratislava, 1929). See also, among others, the unsigned editorial, "Česká politika a Uhry," in Masaryk's journal *Naše doba*, XI (1903-04), 1-2, which states his belief that Slovaks were a part of the Czech nation and emphasizes the importance of Slovakia in strengthening the Austrian Czechs in their struggle against the Germans. Ludwig von Gogolák, "T.G. Masaryks Slowakische und Ungarländische Politik," *Bohemia: Jahrbuch des Collegium Carolinum*, IV (1963), 174-227, saw the central importance of Slovakia in Masaryk's political program and emphasized that Masaryk was unique among his Czech contemporaries in his grasp of the Slovak problem and its implications. Noting the absence, before 1918, of any "Czecho-Slovak institutions or associations on which Czechoslovak unity could be built," Jan Hajda concluded: "The establishment of Czechoslovak society was the embodiment of an idea rather than the outgrowth of gradual political or economic processes." See Jan Hajda, "The Role of the Intelligentsia in the Development of the Czechoslovak Society," in Miloslav Rechcigl, Jr., ed., *The Czechoslovak Contribution to World Culture* (The Hague, 1964), p. 311. Cf. *O vzájomných vztáhoch Čechov a Slovákov* (Bratislava, 1956), and Vladimír Kulíšek, "O činnosti a významu Českoslovanské jednoty přěd vznikem ČSR," *Historický časopis*, X (1962), 351-68. Masaryk's relations with the Slovaks have also been covered by Zdeněk Urban, *Problémy slovenského národního hnutí na konci 19. století* (Acta Universitatis Carolinae, Philosophica et historica, monographia XXXVII, Prague, 1971). Selected items of correspondence between Masaryk and various Slovak personalities were published by Josef Jirásek, "Z korešpondencie predstaviteľov českého a slovenského narodného hnutia na

prelome 19 a 20 storočia," *Historický časopis,* XVII, 2 (1969), 270-84, and 3, 427-37. See also Thomas D. Marzik, "T.G. Masaryk and the Slovaks, 1882-1914," *Columbia Essays in International Affairs: The Dean's Papers,* Andrew W. Cordier, ed. (New York and London, 1966), pp. 155-74.

41. *The New Europe,* p. 51.

42. For a systematic examination of what actually happened after 1918, see Owen V. Johnson, *Sociocultural and National Development in Slovakia, 1918-1938. Education and Its Impact.* Unpublished Ph.D. dissertation, University of Michigan, 1978.

43. *The Making of a State,* pp. 208-09.

44. The distribution of parliamentary seats, not the share of popular vote in 1911, was the principle followed in assigning seats in the Assembly of 1918: this favored the Agrarians and the Young Czechs but discriminated against the Socialists and Catholics, who held fewer seats than their votes would have secured for them in 1911. See on this Garver, *The Young Czechs,* p. 358. Thus the Social Democrats with 357,263 votes won 25 seats in 1911 while the Agrarians had 38 seats but only 257,714 votes.

45. For the Slovaks and Slovakia during Czechoslovakia's formative period, see Václav L. Beneš, "Czechoslovak Democracy and Its Problems, 1918-1920," in Mamatey and Luza, *The Czechoslovak Republic,* especially pp. 56-58, 73-86, 92-98. See also Ladislav Lipscher, "Klub slovenskych poslancov v rokoch 1918-1920," *Historicky časopis,* XVI (1968), 133-68.

46. Art. 128. It further stated that differences in religion, language, etc., would constitute no obstacle to any citizen's entering public office and service, attaining promotion or recognition, and that all citizens would be free to choose the language they would use in private and business interactions, in the press and all publications, and in public assemblies. This did not affect the rights conferred on the State bodies in these matters by laws already in force or those that might be enacted in the future in regard to public order, security of the State or effective control.

47. E. Wiskemann, *Czechs and Germans* (London, 1938), pp. 91-92.

48. Paul Robert Magocsi, *The Shaping of a National Identity: Subcarpathian Rus 1848-1948* (Cambridge, Mass., 1978), pp. 76-102.

49. To make this point clearer, E. Rádl (*Der Kampf*, pp. 111-12) showed what the rights granted to citizens "whose language was not Czechoslovak" meant in practice by an analogy, substituting "workers" for "citizens." Thus the Constitution could be paraphrased: "Workers are equal to other citizens; workers may be employed in state service if they meet the required conditions of employment; workers may publish newspapers," and so on. In reality the rights of workers were rights to form labor unions, right to strike, guaranteed minimum wages and insurance, rights of working women and minors, and so on. Whether a worker claimed them or not, or even knew of them, these rights had to be respected by employers and by the State. But comparable regulations to protect nationalities had been omitted from the Czechoslovak Constitution. If we exclude Subcarpathian Ruthenia—promised autonomy in 1919, secured in 1938—the two most important minorities were Germans and Hungarians.

50. As no Czechoslovak language existed, the law stated that in the historical lands Czech, and in the former Hungarian provinces Slovak, would be used.

51. Karl W. Deutsch, *Tides Among Nations* (New York and London, 1979), p. 226.

52. *Ibid.*, p. 227.

Notes to Chapter VII

1. Emanuel Peroutka, *Budování státu* (Prague, 1932-36), I, p. 473, and Helmut Slapnicka, "Die Rechtsstellung des Präsidenten der Republik nach der Verfassungsurkunde und in der politischen Wirklichkeit," *Die "Burg." Einflussreiche politische Kräfte um Masaryk und Beneš*, Karl Bosl, ed., 2 vols. (Munich and Vienna, 1973-74), II, p. 9. (Hereafter cited *Die Burg.*)

2. Edward Polson Newman, *Masaryk* (London and Dublin, 1960), pp. 213-14, refers to one such interview, published in *Saturday Review*, November 1, 1930. According to Newman, "Masaryk's wings were clipped by the extreme nationalism of those by whom he was surrounded."

3. Ludwig, *Defender of Democracy* (London, 1936), p. 188. It goes without saying, of course, that Masaryk cannot be held responsible for how the administration of the state, of such branches as the military,

the foreign service, or the police, operated. Not enough research has been carried out on the actual working of the Czechoslovak bureaucratic machinery in terms of its conformity with the constitutional principles or law in general. There is also not enough research on the operation of the highest levels of the political structure of Czechoslovakia. For a suggestive approach to the latter theme see Antonín Palecek, "The Good Genius of Czechoslovak Democracy: Masaryk and Beneš, or Švehla?," *East European Quarterly*, XIII, 2 (June 1979), 213-234. For interesting insights on how Czechoslovak-British relations functioned on the day-to-day basis, see Jonathan Zorach, "The British View of the Czechs in the Era Before the Munich Crisis," *Slavonic and East European Review*, 57, 1 (January 1979), 56-70. Zorach suggests that Czech military and diplomatic agencies resorted at times to what may be described as "dirty tricks" both toward British diplomats and toward Czechoslovak citizens of German nationality.

4. Machovec, *Masaryk,* p. 170, commented that the Presidency was a device for restricting the freedom of "the old fighter," while actual power belonged to the clericals and nationalists. In this form Machovec's assertion is exaggerated, as we shall show below, but the entire subject of Masaryk's role calls for a special study.

5. Peroutka, *Budování státu,* I, 254-55.

6. Slapnicka, "Die Rechtsstellung," *Die Burg,* II, pp. 10-11; Friedrich Prinz, "Die Burg, ihre Entstehung und Struktur als Forschungsaufgabe," *Die Burg,* I, p. 21.

7. Slapnicka, "Die Rechtsstellung" pp. 13-14. This change in the constitution was opposed especially strongly by the National Democrats, whose leader was Karel Kramář.

8. Ladislav Lipscher, "Zur allgemeinen Analyse des politischen Mechanismus in der ersten Tschechoslowakischen Republik," *Die Burg,* I, pp. 149-50.

9. Prinz, "Die Burg," p. 17. Taylor (*The Habsburg Monarchy*, p. 255) wrote: "The parallel [with the Habsburg Monarchy] was complete when Masaryk resorted to Francis Joseph's device of a cabinet of officials independent of parliament." (In actuality, the Masaryk-appointed cabinet did have a tacit support of the parliament.) This might have been not exactly in conformity with the constitution, but it was necessary, or so Masaryk felt, to save the state from a possible Communist uprising. The

cabinet of officials appointed by Masaryk took those measures which a party-based cabinet before it did not dare to take. (See on this below, text to note 55.)

10. E. Ludwig, *Defender of Democracy*, pp. 160-61.

11. *The Message on the Tenth Anniversary* (Prague, 1928), p. 15.

12. *The Making of a State*, p. 392.

13. Ludwig, pp. 236-37.

14. *Cesta demokracie*, II (1934), pp. 209-10.

15. These criticisms are made by R.N. Foustka, "Otázka fašisace zákonodárství buržoasní Československé republiky." *Rozpravy Československé Akademie Věd*, Řada SV, 68, 8 (1958), 50-51.

16. Lipscher, "Zur allgemeinen Analyse," *Die Burg*, I, pp. 150 and 152. Lipscher notes (p. 154) that party controls over the deputies contrdicted a constitutional provision forbidding members to receive orders from the outside. The courts established that a parliamentary seat belonged to the party, not to the individual who held it. See also F. Gregory Campbell, *Confrontation in Central Europe: Weimar Germany and Czechoslovakia* (Chicago and London, 1975), p. 207, and Edward Taborsky, *Czechoslovak Democracy at Work* (London, 1945).

17. In addition to those already cited, the essays by Martin K. Bachstein and Hans Lemberg in *Die Burg*, I, pp. 47-68 and 69-84, raise a number of interesting questions and cite the literature extensively. See also Dagmar Horna-Perman, "The Castle," *East Central Europe*, 4 (1977), 93-105.

18. Christian Willars, *Die Böhmische Zitadelle. ČSR–Schicksal einer Staatsidee* (Vienna and Munich, 1965), pp. 261-62, and *Die Burg*, II, p. 153.

19. Vojtěch Mencl and Marmila Menclová, "Náčrt podstaty a vývoje vrcholné sféry předmnichovské československé mocensko-politické struktury," *Československý časopis historický*, 16 (1968), 341-68, and Piotr Wandycz, "Pierwsza Republika a Druga Rzeczpospolita," *Zeszyty historyczne*, 28 (1974), 3-20. Wandycz offers stimulating suggestions for a comparative study of Polish and Czechoslovak institutions and policies before World War II.

20. Campbell, *Confrontation*, p. 207. See also F. Gregory Campbell, "Central Europe's Bastion of Democracy," *East European Quarterly*, XI (1977), 2, 167-69. The methods to which the Castle resorted in its

practical activities did not exclude blackmail of hostile politicians on the basis of "detailed dossiers" assembled by an intelligence service. ("Enemies of the Castle"?), Compbell, *Confrontation,* pp. 169, 208, 316-17. See also Jonathan Zorach, "The Enigma of the Gajda Affair in Czechoslovak Politics in 1926," *Slavic Review,* XXXV, 4 (December 1976), 683-698. For Masaryk's role in an attempt to compromise Kramář see Julius Firt, "Die 'Burg' und die Zeitschrift Přitomnost," *Die Burg,* II, 124.

21. Campbell, *Confrontation,* p. 208. The same point had been made earlier by Taborsky, "The Roots of Czechoslovak Democracy," in Miloslav Rechcigl, ed., *Czechoslovakia Past and Present,* I, p. 118, who revealed the prevalence of undemocratic popular attitudes: he observed that the bulk of the population continued to view Masaryk as a "father-like protector and the sure guarantor of their country's independence and well-being." Needless to say, in a democracy the elected officials are not "protectors" but public servants responsible to the people. The people themselves are the "guarantors" of their "independence and well-being."

22. F.M Barnard, *Herder's Social and Political Thought* (Oxford, 1967), p. 82, notes that after Herder the nationalist movements of East European nations allowed a major political role to the intellectuals. Karl Mannheim, *Ideology and Utopia,* Louis Wirth and Edward Shils, trs. (New York, 1963), pp. 154-55ff. argued that the intelligentsia is a "relatively classless stratum" which might be capable, because of its educational and social background and the nature of its work, of rising above particularistic points of view and interests. Interestingly enough, Herder thought in a similar vein. (Barnard, p. 145.)

23. Prinz, "Die Burg," pp. 13 and 19-21.

24. *Ibid.,* p. 21. Prinz comments (p. 22) that allocating power according to the relative strength of the parties is a fundamental principle of a democratic state.

25. Julius Firt, "Die 'Burg' aus der Sicht eines Zeitgenossen," *Die Burg,* I, pp. 90-91.

26. František Kubka, *Mezi válkami. Masaryk a Beneš v mych vzpomínkách* (Prague, 1969), p. 54.

27. Campbell, *Confrontation,* pp. 170-71; 207. Masaryk's role in keeping Beneš in office was publicly recognized by Beneš when he spoke of the "moral dictatorship" exercised by Masaryk and his insistence that Beneš should remain as Minister. E. Beneš, *Gedanke und Tat,* three vols. (Prague, 1937), III, pp. 15-16.

28.   Victor S. Mamatey and Radomír Luža, eds., *A History of the Czechoslovak Republic, 1918-1948* (Princeton, 1973), pp. 155-56. Slapnicka, "Die Rechtsstellung," p. 27, argues that Masaryk exceeded his prerogatives when in his letter of resignation he recommended Beneš' election to the presidency.

29.   Campbell, *Confrontation*, pp. 169 and 316, summarizing an unpublished report by the Austrian minister to the Ministry of Foreign Affairs, Vienna, 18 March, 1926.

30.   Joseph Rothschild, *East Central Europe Between the Two World Wars* (Seattle and London, 1974), p. 135.

31.   Dagmar Horna-Perman, "The Castle," p. 94, writes: "He was a champion of democracy: yet it was rumored that he undermined the democratic development of Czechoslovakia by exercise of political power and stifled the political initiative of his contemporaries." Although Perman does not answer this question herself, our own answer, regretfully, is in the affirmative. This is not to deny, though, that Masaryk had exerted an enormous positive influence on the promotion of individual liberty, cultural and religious toleration, advancement of academic and artistic freedom, interest in and appreciation of foreign cultures, etc.

32.   Taylor, *The Habsburg Monarchy*, pp. 254-55.

33.   William E. Griffith, "Myth and Reality in Czechoslovakia History," *East Europe*, XI, 3 (1962), 34.

34.   Elizabeth Wiskemann, *Czechs and Germans* (London, 1938), p. 283.

35.   K.R. Popper, *The Open Society and Its Enemies*, 3rd ed. (London, 1957), II, 312. According to Popper (*ibid.*, 50-51), Masaryk and Woodrow Wilson both fell a victim to the philosophy of Hegel and Fichte but what he offers as an explanation of why this happened really begs a question: "How anybody with the slightest knowledge of European history . . . could ever have put forward such an inapplicable principle [the principle of the national state] , is hard to understand. The explanation is that Wilson, who was a sincere democrat (and Masaryk also, one of the greatest of all fighters for the open society), fell a victim to a movement that sprang from the most reactionary and servile political philosophy that had ever been imposed upon meek and long-suffering mankind. He fell a victim to his upbringing in the metaphysical political theories of Plato and Hegel, and to the nationalist movement based upon them." (See also *ibid.*, II, 318.)

36. Taylor (*The Habsburg Monarchy*, pp. 260-61) wrote: "Democratic federal Yugoslavia translated into practice the great might-have-been of Habsburg history. Marshal Tito was the last of the Habsburgs: ruling over eight different nations, he offered them "cultural autonomy" and reined in their nationalist hostility. Old Yugoslavia attempted to be a Serb national state; in new Yugoslavia the Serbs received only national equality and tended to think themselves oppressed."

37. This conclusion was reached by Campbell, "Central Europe's Bastion of Democracy," pp. 158-59, who noted that the shift of the German population toward fascism—so strikingly different from what was happening among the Czechs—was to be explained by "the social psychology of the two groups." The Czechs enjoyed the consciousness of belonging to the governing nationality; "the Sudeten Germans acutely felt their minority status." ". . .the Czechoslovak republic failed to make its mission understandable in terms that the Sudeten Germans could accept and support." Czech dominance in the country was all too obviously reflected in the "symbols of the state" while the "proclivity of Czech political leaders for talking about 'our Germans' hardly helped matters. Public rhetoric thus tended to obscure the real advantages such as personal freedoms, political democracy, and social welfare support that the Sudeten Germans enjoyed in the republic." But of course "public rhetoric" was what Masaryk regarded as an essential element in educating the Czechoslovaks in the spirit of their past. (Campbell speaks of the glorification of such figures as Přemysl, St. Wenceslas, Jan Hus, and Jan Žižka, in illustration of this "rhetoric.")

38. Oscar Jászi, *The Dissolution of the Habsburg Monarchy* (Chicago, 1961), p. 180. After 1918, Renner paid close attention to Czechoslovakia, arguing that since it so closely resembled Austria-Hungary (but was ruled by such a democrat as Masaryk) it ought to introduce equality of all nations, not only equality of individuals, as its constitutional principle. All its nations ought to become joint owners of the state; after all, the Germans had lived in the country since before 1492, the date of the discovery of America. Was it not long enough to have them accepted as full citizens? See Karl Renner, *Das nationale und das oekonomische Problem der Tschechoslowakei* (Prague 1926), esp. pp. 11-15. Renner simultaneously advocated close economic cooperation of Czechoslovakia with Germany and Austria—a step which could not but make the Czechs

feel that they would become economically dependent on the Germans just as in the recent past they had been under their political and cultural influence. (*Ibid.*, pp 18-19.)

39.   Lord Acton, "Nationality," in *Essays on Freedom on Power* (London, 1956), p. 168.

40.   As C.A. Macartney, *Hungary and Her Successors* (London, 1937), p. 150, wrote: "It may well be that the experiment (which, had it succeeded, would have ranked among the happiest in the modern times) was too hazardous; that equality would not have satisfied the Magyars and Germans accustomed so long to domination. But rightly or wrongly it was not tried."

41.   Isaiah Berlin, *Two Concepts of Liberty* (Oxford, 1958), pp. 41-2.

42.   A.D. Lindsay, *The Modern Democratic State* (London, New York, Toronto, 1943), I, pp. 200-01. Carl Cohen, *Democracy* (New York and London, 1971), pp.71-72, writes: "What really rules, in a moderately healthy democracy, is not the majority, but majori*ties*... constantly changing in membership. I call this 'rule of fluctuating majorities.' [It] is operative when membership in a decisive majority is experienced by all (or almost all) of the community's members at one time or another, and when...any member is likely to find himself a constituent of the ruling majority on some issues and of a ruled minority on others."

43.   J.S. Mill, *A System of Logic* (London, 1865), II, p. 517.

44.   J.S. Mill, *On Liberty, Considerations on Representative Government* (Oxford, 1946), p. 292.

45.   Rothschild, *East Central Europe*, p. 134.

46.   Antony Polonsky, *Politics in Independent Poland 1921-1939* (Oxford 1972), pp. 114-15.

47.   Arend Lijphart, *Democracy in Plural Societies: A Comparative Exploration* (New Haven and London, 1980), p. 24.

48.   *Ibid.*, p. 25.

49.   *Ibid.*, pp. 32-33.

50.   Wenzel Jaksch, *Europe's Road to Potsdam,* Kurt Glaser, tr. (New York and London, 1963), pp. 230-31.

51.   It is not our intent to deal with the political problems, domestic or international, which resulted from the national character of the state. Let use merely note in passing that the leaders of the Czechoslovak state

seemed to be throughout the years strangely oblivious to the threat of German nationalism, while they were fully aware of the threat it posed to Poland. It is hard to understand why they hoped that the Germans would not seek to "redeem" Austria or the Sudetenland while at the same time they were certain that Poland was doomed because of its German minorities. See on this especially Campbell, *Confrontation*, pp. 183-89.

52. This is not to imply that the Czechoslovak church was not a genuine religious organization. See, e.g., Rudolf Urban, *Die tschecho-slowakische Hussitische Kirche* (Marburg/Lahn, 1973), and Ludvik Nemec, *The Czechoslovak Heresy and Schism: The Emergence of a National Czechoslovak Church* (Philadelphia, 1975). See also Augustinus Kurt Huber, "Die 'Burg' und die Kirchen," *Die Burg*, II, pp. 181-96.

53. Christoph Stölzl, "Die 'Burg' und die Juden," *Die Burg*, II, pp. 104-08. Before 1914 Masaryk believed that the Jewish nationality was the logical national identification for a person of Jewish religion in Bohemia (pp. 102-03).

54. Rothschild, *East Central Europe*, pp. 110, 116, and 126, and Josef Korbel, *Twentieth-Century Czechoslovakia* (New York, 1977), pp. 71-74.

55. Rothschild, *East Central Europe*, pp. 104-05, and Vera Olivová, *The Doomed Democracy: Czechoslovakia in a Disrupted Europe 1914-1938*, George Theiner, tr. (London, 1972), pp. 130-34.

56. van den Beld, *Humanity*, pp. 148, 152.

57. *Ibid.*, pp. 147-54, summarized Masaryk's arguments against Bolshevism and its applicability to Czechoslovak conditions. See also Zeman, *The Masaryks*, pp. 136ff.

58. *Ibid.*, p. 148. Zeman remarks that nobody in the government and few in the parliament knew much about the leaders of the Czechoslovak communist party. Klement Gottwald, secretary-general of the party after 1929 and member of parliament, "knew Masaryk slightly better than many years ago, Masaryk had known, say, Emperor Franz Joseph" (p. 147.) Gottwald would of course become president of Czechoslovakia in 1948, presiding over the liquidation of what was left of the "bourgeois democracy" of Masaryk's vintage.

59. E. Beneš, "Náš největší úkol národní," in *Idea Československého Státu* (Prague, 1936), II, p. 224.

60. *Svobodné slovo,* 16 October 1945, as quoted in Z. Jičínský, *K politické ideologii buržoazní ČSR* (Prague, 1965), p. 235.

61. Beneš, in *Idea,* II, p. 225.

62. *Ibid.,* pp. 72, 223.

63. Kamil Krofta, *The Germans in the Czechoslovak Republic* (Prague, 1937), pp. 17, 19 (address delivered at Karlovy Vary, 13 December 1936.)

64. *Ibid.,* pp. 11, 19-20, 27.

65. Josef Chmelař has written of the Germans: "One of the fundamental ideological and programmatic points of German National-Socialism is . . . *the idea of the unity of the whole German nation;*" National Socialism stresses national unity "in the form of emphasis upon community of race—*Volksgemeinschaft*—which represents both racial and cultural aspects, . . ." Chmelař quoted a Nazi statement that "it was not citizenship but community of blood, of type [race?] and language which determined and ensured Germanity" and commented that this doctrine, if applied, would be destructive of the order and stability of other states. He did not seem to realize that he advocated an identical view. See Josef Chmelař, *The German Problem in Czechoslovakia* (Prague, 1936), pp. 52-53 (Emphasis in the original.)

66. If one required the Germans to be loyal to Czechoslovakia, what right did the Czechs have to "betray" Austria? On this see Karl W. Newman, *European Democracy between the Wars,* pp. 151-52, who refers also to S. Rabl, *Staatsbürgerliche Loyalität in Nationalitätenstaaten* (Munich, 1959). Emanuel Rádl's remedy was as simple as it was logical: he proposed to make all citizens of Czechoslovakia, especially the Germans, "Czechoslovaks," and the German language one of the Czechoslovak languages, like Czech or Slovak.

67. Rothschild, *East Central Europe,* p. 132. This is the conclusion of Josef Korbel too: "As one sifts out all the arguments either defending or criticizing the capitulation, one cannot but conclude that the valiant ethos of the nation demanded from its leaders the ethical, not the practical position. The Munich dictate should have been rejected, no matter what the consequences." (Korbel, *Twentieth Century Czechoslovakia,* p. 148.)

68. Rothschild, *East Central Europe,* p. 77.

69. But one has to be careful in making judgments here. For some time after 1948, the treatment of Masaryk was not entirely hostile. The

University of Brno bore the name of Masaryk throughout that time and was not renamed until *after* Stalin's death in the 1950s. It is possible to argue that even the Communists had to some extent succumbed to the Masaryk mystique, their negative estimate of the prewar republic notwithstanding. And there is some significance in the fact that Gottwald and his successors chose to have themselves elected to the Presidency, an institution so closely associated with the President-Liberator. (In the Stalinist 1940s-1950s, all countries of Communist East Europe abolished the institution of the Presidency in favor of a collective Presidium or Council of State, following the Soviet model—all except Czechoslovakia.) A final point concerns the freedom of the Czechoslovak Communists to determine their position, including their view of Masaryk and his legacy: to what extent was the anti-Masaryk campaign dictated by Moscow? See H. Gordon Skilling, "Communism and Czechoslovak Traditions," *Journal of International Affairs*, XX, 1 (1966), 118-36, for a discussion of some aspects of this problem.

70.   There are many studies of the Czechoslovak reform movement in the 1960s. Besides the standard work of H. Gordon Skilling, *Czechoslovakia's Interrupted Revolution* (Princeton, 1976), they include Galia Golan, *Reform Rule in Czechoslovakia* (Cambridge, 1973); Vladimír V. Kusín, *The Intellectual Origins of the Prague Spring* (Cambridge, 1971), and his *Political Grouping in the Czechoslovak Reform Movement* (Cambridge, 1972); and Ivan Sviták, *The Czechoslovak Experiment, 1968-1969* (New York and London, 1972), and others. For works that examined the role of Masaryk's thought in the Czechoslovak revival of the 1960s, see Wolf Oschliess, "Masarykismus: Konservative und Progressisten in der Auseinandersetzung um das demokratische Vermächtnis des tschechoslowakischen Staatsgründers," *Politische Studien*, 21, 194 (November/December 1970), 668-85. David W. Paul has placed the period of the sixties in a broader context of Czech history in "Nationalism, Pluralism, and Schweikism in Czechoslovakia's Political Culture" (Ph.D. dissertation, Princeton University, 1973).

71.   This does not mean that Masaryk has ceased to be controversial. Anonymous, "Getting Along in Czechoslovakia," *The New York Review of Books*, November 9, 1978, pp. 37-38, reports that an unpublished manuscript by the late professor Jan Patočka, highly critical of Masaryk's philosophy of history, circulates in Czechoslovakia. Patočka was one of

the leaders of the human rights movement ("Charter 77") until his death in 1977. Patočka's work, banned in Czechoslovakia, has appeared in the West. See Jan Patočka, *Dvě eseje o Masarykovi* (Toronto, 1979) and Jan Patočka, "Pokus o českou národní filosofii a jeho nezdar," in *Hodina naděje: almanach české literatury 1968-1978.* Jiří Gruša, Milan Uhde and Ludvík Vaculík, eds. (Toronto, 1980), pp. 15-44. A discussion of Masaryk's thought and action and its role in modern Czechoslovak history has recently begun among the Czechs and Slovaks in the West. By way of example, see Erazim Kohák's review article of Patočka's book in *Proměny,* 16, 3 (August, 1979), pp. 88-95, Václav Černý, "Nekolik portrétu," ibid., pp. 21-39, and Milič Čapek, "Současnost Masarykova myšlení," *ibid.*, 17, 2 (April, 1980), 9-30.

BIBLIOGRAPHY

Acton, Lord. *Essays on Freedom and Power.* London: Thames & Hudson, 1956.

Anon. "Getting Along in Czechoslovakia." *The New York Review of Books,* November 9, 1978.

Austria. Reichsrat. Haus der Abgeordneten. *Stenographische Protokolle über die Sitzungen des Hauses der Abgeordneten.* Vienna: Hof- und Staatsdruckerei, 1861/2-1917/18.

Barnard, F.M. *Herder's Social and Political Thought.* Oxford: Oxford University Press, 1967.

. "The Prague Spring and Masaryk's Humanism." *East Central Europe,* 5 (1978).

Bazylow, Ludwik. *Ostatnie lata Rosji carskiej: Rządy Stołypina.* Warsaw: Panstwowe Wydawnictwo Naukowe, 1972.

Beneš, Edvard. *Gedanke und Tat.* 3 vols. Prague: Orbis, 1937.

. "Naš největší úkol národní." In *Idea Československého Státu.* Edited by Jan Kapras et al. Prague: Národní Rada Československá. 1936.

Beneš, Václav L. "Czechoslovak Democracy and Its Problems, 1918-1920." *A History of the Czechoslovak Republic.* Edited by Mamatey and Luza.

Berlin, Isaiah. *Two Concepts of Liberty.* Oxford: Oxford University Press, 1958.

Betts, R.R. "Masaryk's Philosophy of History." *The Slavonic Review,* 26 (1947).

Birke, Ernst. "Das neue Europa in den Kriegsdenkenschriften T.G. Masaryks 1914 bis 1918." In *Zur Geschichte und Problematik der Demokratie: Festgabe für Hans Herzfeld.* Edited by Wilhelm Berges. Berlin: Duncker und Humbolt, 1958.

Bochkovs'kyi, O.I. *T.G. Masaryk. Natsional'na problema ta ukrains'ke pytannia (sproba kharakterystyky ta interpretatsii).* Podebrady: Ukrains'ka hospodars'ka akademiia v CSR, 1930.

Borman, Stuart A. "The Prague Student Zionist Movement, 1896-1914." Unpublished Ph.D. dissertation, University of Chicago, 1972.

Bosl, Karl, ed. Die "Burg." *Einflussreiche politische Kräfte um Masaryk und Beneš.* Munich and Vienna: Oldenbourg, 1973-1974.

_____, ed. *Handbuch der Geschichte der böhmischen Länder.* 4 vols. Stuttgart: A. Hiersemann, 1968-1970.

Brock, Peter, and Skilling, Gordon, eds. *The Czech Renascence of the Nineteenth Century.* Toronto: University of Toronto Press, 1970.

Calder, Kenneth J. *Britain and the Origins of the New Europe.* Cambridge: Cambridge University Press, 1976.

Campbell, F. Gregory. "Central Europe's Bastion of Democracy." *East European Quarterly,* XI (1977).

_____. *Confrontation in Central Europe: Weimar Germany and Czechoslovakia.* Chicago and London: University of Chicago Press, 1975.

Čapek, Karel. *President Masaryk Tells His Story.* London: George Allen and Unwin, 1934.

_____. *Hovory s T.G. Masarykem.* Prague: Československý spisovatel, 1946.

_____. *Masaryk on Thought and Life: Conversations with Karel Čapek.* London: George Allen and Unwin, 1938.

Čapek, Milič. "Současnost Masarykova myšlení." *Proměny.* 17 (1980).

Cathrein, V. *Moralphilosophie.* 2 vols. 6th ed., Leipzig: 1924.

Černý, Václav. "Nekolik portrétu." *Proměny,* 16 (1979).

Červinka, František. "The Hilsner Affair." *The Leo Baeck Institute Year Book,* XIII (1968).

_____. "Spor o smysl českých dějin 1912." *Plamen,* 1969, No. 1.

"Česká politika a Uhry." *Naše Doba,* XI (1903-1904).

Chlebowczyk, Józef. "Marks i Engels a problem małych narodów w Europie Środkowo-Wschodniej." *Z pola walki,* 1970, No. 2.

Chmelař, Josef. *The German Problem in Czechoslovakia.* Prague: Orbis, 1936.

Cohen, Gary B. "Recent Research on Czech Nation-Building." *Journal of Modern History,* 51 (December 1979).

Crossman, R.H.S. *The Charm of Politics.* London: Hamish Hamilton, 1958.

Czedik, Alois. *Zur Geschichte der k.k. österreichischen Ministerien, 1861-1916.* 4 vols. Teschen, Vienna, and Leipzig: K. Prochaska, 1917-1920.

Day, John. "Authority." *Political Studies.* XI (1963).

Denis, Ernest. *La Bôheme depuis la Montagne-Blanche.* Paris: E. Leroux, 1903.

Deutsch, Karl W. *Tides among Nations.* New York and London: The Free Press, 1979.

Dokumenty o protilidové a protinárodní činnosti T.G. Masaryka. Prague: Orbis, 1953.

Doležal, J. "Masaryk na studiích ve Vídni." In *Masarykuv Almanach.*

. *Masaryk osmdesátiletý.* Prague: Státní nakladatelství, 1931.

. *Masarykova cesta životem.* 2 vols. Brno: Polygrafie, 1920-1921.

Duncan, Graeme. *Marx and Mill: Two Views of Social Conflict and Social Harmony.* Cambridge: Cambridge University Press, 1973.

Fajfr, František. "Masarykova filosofie demokracie." *Masarykuv Sborník,* I, 3(1924-1925).

Falt'an, Samo. *Slovenská otázka v Československu.* Bratislava: Vydavatel'-stvo politickej literatúry, 1968.

Fest, Wilfried. *Peace or Partition: The Habsburg Monarchy and British Policy, 1914-1918.* London: George Prior, 1978.

Festschrift T.G. Masaryk zum 80. Geburtstage. Edited by B. Jakowenko. 2 vols. Bonn: F. Cohen, 1930.

Firt, Julius. "Die 'Burg' aus der Sicht eines Zeitgenossen." in *Die Burg.* Edited by Karl Bosl.

. "Die 'Burg' und die Zeitschrift Přítomnost." In *Die Burg.* Edited by Karl Bosl.

Fischer, J.L. "T.G. Masaryk. Počátky a vlivy." *Česká Mysl,* XXVI (1930).

Flint, Robert. *Philosophy as Scientia Scientiarum and a History of Classifications of the Sciences.* Edinburgh and London: W. Blackwood and Sons, 1904.

Foustka, R.N. "Otázka fašisace zákonodárství buržoasní Československé republiky," *Rozpravy Československé Akademie Věd,* Řada SV, 68, 8 (1958).

Frank, S. L. *Biografiia P.B. Struve.* New York: Izdatel'stvo im. Chekhova, 1956.

Franko, Ivan. "Moje styky s Masarykem." *Masarykuv Sborník,* IV (1930).

Garver, Bruce M. *The Young Czech Party 1874-1901 and the Emergence of a Multi-Party System.* New Haven and London: Yale University Press, 1978.

Gibian, George. "Masaryk and Dostoyevsky." In *Czechoslovakia Past and Present.* Edited by Rechcigl.

Gillies, A. "Herder and Masaryk: Some Points of Contact." *Modern Language Review,* XL (1945).

Gogalák, Ludwig von. "T.G. Masaryks slowakische und ungarländische Politik." *Jahrbuch des Collegium Carolinum,* IV (1963).

Golan, Galia. *Reform Rule in Czechoslovakia.* Cambridge: Cambridge University Press, 1973.

Green, Simon Rosengard. "Thomas Garrigue Masaryk: Educator of a Nation." Unpublished Ph.D. dissertation, University of California-Berkeley, 1976.

Griffith, William D. "Myth and Reality in Czechoslovak History." *East Europe,* XI (1962).

Hajda, Jan. "The Role of the Intelligentsia in the Development of Czechoslovak Society." In *The Czechoslovak Contribution.* Edited by Rechcigl.

Hauner, Milan. "Recasting Czech History." *Survey,* XXIV, 3 (Summer 1979).

Havránek, Jan. "The Development of Czech Nationalism." *Austrian History Yearbook,* III, part 2 (1967).

———. "Social Classes, Nationality Ratios and Demographic Trends in Prague, 1880-1900." *Historica,* XIII (1966).

Herben, Jan. *Kniha vzpomínek.* Prague: Družstvení práce, 1936.

———. *Masaryk.* Prague, 1910.

———. *T.G. Masaryk.* 3 vols. Prague: Nakladem spolku výtvarných umělcu Mánes v Praze, 1926-1927.

Hobsbawm, E.J. *Labouring Men: Studies in the History of Labour.* London: Weidenfeld and Nicholson, 1964.

Horna-Perman, Dagmar. "The Castle." *East Central Europe,* 4 (1977).

Hostovsky, Egon. "The Czech-Jewish Movement." In *The Jews of Czechoslovakia.*

Hromádka, J.L. *Masaryk as European.* Prague: International Philosophical Library, 1937.

Huber, Augustinus Kurt. "Die 'Burg' und die Kirchen." *Die Burg.* Edited by Bosl.

Hudečkova, Viera. "Príspevok k vymedzeniu vztahov T.G. Masaryka a F. Brentana." *Sborník Prací Filosofické Fakulty Brněnské University,* B 16 (1969).

Jaksch, Wenzel. *Europe's Road to Potsdam.* Translated by Kurt Glaser. New York and London: Praeger, 1963.

Jászi, Oscar. *The Dissolution of the Habsburg Monarchy.* Chicago: University of Chicago Press, 1961.

The Jews of Czechoslovakia: Historical Studies and Surveys. Philadelphia and New York: Jewish Publication Society of America, 1968 and 1971.

Jičínský, Z. *K politické ideologii buržoazní ČSR.* Prague: Nakl. politické literatury, 1965.

Jirasek, Josef. "Masarykovy dopisy Husserlovi (Dokumenty filosofického prátelství)." *Sborník Prací Filosofické Fakulty Brněnské University,* B 17 (1970).

Johnson, Owen V. "Sociocultural and National Development in Slovakia, 1918-1938. Education and Its Impact." Unpublished Ph.D. dissertation, The University of Michigan, 1978.

Kaizl, Josef. *České myšlenky.* Prague: 1896.

Kalvoda, Josef. "Masaryk in America in 1918." *Jahrbücher für Geschichte Osteuropas,* XXVII (1979).

Kann, Robert A. *The Multinational Empire: Nationalism and National Reform in the Habsburg Empire, 1848-1918.* 2 vols. New York: Columbia University Press, 1950.

Kann, Robert A., et al., eds. *The Habsburg Empire in World War I.* Boulder, Colorado: East European Quarterly, 1977.

Kárník, Zdeněk. Socialisté na rozcestí: *Habsburk, Masaryk či Šmeral?* Prague: Svoboda, 1968.

Kerner, R.J., ed. *Czechoslovakia: Twenty Years of Independence.* Berkeley: University of California Press, 1940.

Kestenberg-Gladstein. "The Jews between Czechs and Germans in the Historic Lands, 1898-1918." In *The Jews in Czechoslovakia.*

Kohák, Erazim V. "Masaryk and Plato in the 20th Century." In *The Czechoslovak Contribution.* Edited by M. Recheigl.

Kolegar, Ferdinand. "T.G. Masaryk's Contribution to Sociology." In *Czechoslovakia Past and Present.* Edited by Miloslav Rechcigl.

Korbel, Josef. *Twentieth Century Czechoslovakia.* New York: Columbia University Press, 1977.

Kozák, J.B. "Masaryk as Philosopher." *The Slavonic Review,* VIII (1930).
. "Masaryks Stellung zur Metaphysik." *Festschrift T.G. Masaryk,* II (1930).

Král, Josef. "Masaryk als Philosoph und Soziologe." *La pensée de T.G. Masaryk.* Prague: Internationale Bibliothek für Philosophie, 1937.

Kraus, Oskar. "Die Grundzüge der Welt- und Lebensanschauung T.G. Masaryks." In *La pensée T.G. Masaryk.*

Křížek, Jurij. *T.G. Masaryk a česká politika: Politické vystoupení českých "realistu" v letech 1887-1893.* Prague: Státní nakl. politické literatury, 1959.

Krofta, Kamil. *The Germans in the Czechoslovak Republic.* Prague: Orbis, 1937.
. *Masaryk's Political Democracy.* Prague: Orbis, 1935.
. "Masaryk und unser politisches Program." in *Masaryk–Staatsmann und Denker.* Prague: Orbis, 1930.

Kubka, František. *Mezi válkami: Masaryk a Beneš v mych vzpomínkách.* Prague: Svoboda, 1969.

Kulíšek, Vladimír. "O činnosti a významu Československanské jednoty před vznikem ČSR."*Historický časopis,* X (1962).

Kurczewska, Joanna. *Naród w socjologii i ideologii polskiej. Analiza porównawcza wybranych koncepcji z przelomu XIX i XX wieku.* Warsaw: Państwowe Wydawnictwo Naukowe, 1979.

Kusín, Vladimír V. *The Intellectual Origins of the Prague Spring.* Cambridge: Cambridge University Press, 1971.
. *Political Grouping in the Czechoslovak Reform Movement.* Cambridge: Cambridge University Press, 1972.

Kutnar, František. *Přehledné dějiny českého a slovenského dějepisectví,* II. Prague: Státní pedagogické nakladatelství, 1977.

Lichtheim, George. *Marxism: An Historical and Critical Study.* London: Routledge and Kegan Paul, 1961.
. *Marxism in Modern France.* New York: Columbia University Press, 1966.

Lijphart, Arend. *Democracy in Plural Societies: A Comparative Exploration.* New Haven and London: Yale University Press, 1980.

Lindsay, A.D. *The Modern Democratic State.* London, New York, and Toronto: Oxford University Press, 1943.

Lipscher, Ladislav. "Klub slovenskych poslancov v rokach 1918-1920." *Historicky časopis,* XVI (1968).

——. "Zur allgemeinen Analyse des politischen Mechanismus in der Tschechoslowakischen Republik." In *Die Burg.* Edited by Bosl.

Loužilová, Olga. "Masarykuv problém sebevraždy." *Acta Universitatis Carolinae,* Philosophica et Historica, I (1968).

——. "Masarykova filosofie člověka." *Acta Universitatis Carolinae,* Philosophica et Historica, Monographia XVII. Prague, 1967.

——. "Problém osobnosti v Masarykově filosofii člověka." *Filosoficky časopis,* XVI (1968).

Ludwig, Emil. *Defender of Democracy: Masaryk Speaks.* London: Mc Bride, 1936.

Macartney, C.A. *Hungary and Her Successors.* London, Oxford University Press, 1937.

Machovec, Milan. *Tomáš G. Masaryk.* Prague: Svobodné Slovo, 1968.

Magocsi, Paul Robert. *The Shaping of a National Identity: Subcarpathian Rus, 1848-1948.* Cambridge, Mass.: Harvard University Press, 1978.

Mamatey, Victor S. "The Establishment of the Republic." In *A History of the Czechoslovak Republic.* Edited by Mamatey and Luza.

——. "The Union of Czech Political Parties in the Reichsrat, 1916-1918." In *The Habsburg Empire.* Edited by R.A. Kann.

Mamatey, Victor S., and Luza, Radomir, eds. *A History of the Czechoslovak Republic.* Princeton, N.J.: Princeton University Press, 1973.

Mannheim, Karl. *Ideology and Utopia.* Translated by L. Wirth and E. Shils. New York: Harcourt, Brace & World, 1963.

Manuel, Frank E. *The Prophets of Paris.* Cambridge, Mass.: Harvard University Press, 1962.

Marx, Karl, and Engels, Friedrich. *The Holy Family or the Critique of Critical Critique.* Moscow: Foreign Languages Publishing House, 1956.

Marzik, T.D. "T.G. Masaryk and the Slovaks, 1882-1914." In *Columbia Essays in International Affairs: The Dean's Papers.* Edited by Andrew W. Cordier. New York and London: Columbia University Press, 1966.

Marzik, T.D. "Masaryk's National Background." In *The Czech Renascence of the Nineteenth Century*. Edited by Brock and Skilling.

Masaryk, T.G. *Der Agramer Hochverratsprozess and die Annexion von Bosnien und Herzegovina*. Vienna: S. Konegen, 1909.

———. *Die Bedeutung des Polnaer Verbrechens für den Ritualglauben*. Berlin: H.S. Hermann, 1900.

———. *Česká otázka*. Prague: Čas, 1895.

———. *Česká otázka. O naší nynější krisi. Jan Hus*. Edited by Zdeněk Franta. Prague: Státní nakladatelství, 1924.

———. *Cesta demokracie*. 2 vols. Prague: Čin, 1933-1934.

———. "Curriculum vitae." In *Masarykova cesta*. Edited by Doležal.

———. "Ernest Renan o židovství jako plemenu a náboženství." *Sborník Historický*, I (1883); reprinted in *Masarykuv Sborník*, I (1924-1925).

———. *Freie wissenschaftliche und kirchlich–gebundene Weltanschauung und Lebensauffaussung. Die kirchenpolitische Bedeutung der Wahrmundaffaire*. Vienna: S. Konegen, 1908.

———. *The Ideals of Humanity and How to Work*. London: George Allen and Unwin, 1938.

———. *Inteligence a náboženství*, Prague: Čas, 1906.

———. *Jan Hus*. Prague: Čas, 1896; Bursík a Kohout, 1923.

———. *Karel Havlíček*. Prague: J. Laichter, 1896.

———. "Ke klasifikaci věd," *Česká mysl*. III (1902).

———. "Lev XIII." *Naše Doba*, X (1902-1903).

———. *The Making of a State*. London: F.A. Stokes, 1927.

———. *Masaryk on Marx: An Abridged Edition of T.G. Masaryk, The Social Question: Philosophical and Sociological Foundations of Marxism*. Edited and translated by Erazim V. Kohák. Lewisburg: Bucknell University Press, 1972.

———. *The Meaning of Czech History*. Edited by René Wellek and translated by Peter Kussi. Chapel Hill: University of North Carolina Press, 1974.

———. *Modern Man and Religion*. Translated by A. Bibza and V. Beneš. London: George Allen and Unwin, 1938.

———. "Muj poměr k Jul. Grégrovi." In *Masarykova cesta*. Edited by Doležal.

———. *Národnostní filosofie doby novější*. Jičín: Fr. Holvek, 1905.

———. "Náš pan Fixl." *Besedy Času*, 24 February 1911. Reprinted in *Masarykova cesta*. Edited by Doležal.

Masaryk, T.G. *Naše nynější krise.* Prague: Čas, 1895.

. *Nesnáze demokracie.* Prague: Pokrok, 1913.

. *The New Europe: The Slav Standpoint.* Lewisburg: Bucknell University Press, 1972.

. *Die Nothwendigkeit der Revision des Polnaer Processes.* Vienna: Die Zeit, 1899.

. "O pokroku, vývoji a osvětě." In *Masarykova cesta.* Edited by Doležal.

. *O studiu děl básnických.* Prague: Voleský, 1926.

. *Otázka sociální: Zaklády marxismu filosofické a sociologické.* Prague: Jan Laichter, 1898.

. *Palackýs Idee des böhmischen Volkes.* Prague: Aug. Žalud, 1898.

. *Die philosophischen und sociologischen Grundlagen des Marxismus.* Vienna: S. Konegen, 1899.

. "Plato jako vlastenec." In *Masarykova cesta.* Edited by Doležal.

. *Poselství.* Prague: Orbis, 1930.

. "Potřeba pokrokové politiky." *Masarykuv Sborník,* I (1924-1925).

. *Právo přirozené a historické.* Prague: Čas, 1900.

. "Rukovět' sociologie." *Naše doba,* VIII (1900-1901).

. *Russland und Europa: Studien über die geistigen Strömungen in Russland.* 2 vols. Jena: E. Diederichs, 1913.

. *Der Selbstmord also sociale Massenerscheinung der modernen Civilisation.* Vienna: S. Konegen, 1881.

. *Slovanské studie 1. Slavjanofilství I.V. Kiřějevského.* Prague: Bursík a Kohout, 1889.

. "Slovenské vzpomienky." In *Masarykova cesta.* Edited by Doležal.

. *The Speech on the Tenth Anniversary.* Prague: Orbis, 1928.

. *The Spirit of Russia.* 3 vols. London: George Allen and Unwin, vols. I-II, 1919, vol. III, 1967.

. *Suicide and the Meaning of Civilization.* Translated by William B. Weist and Robert G. Bateson. Chicago and London: University of Chicago Press, 1970.

. *Světová revoluce za války a ve válce, 1914-1918.* Prague: Čin a Orbis, 1925.

. "Svobodomyslní Čechové v Americe." *Naše doba,* X (1902-1903).

. *Tak zvaný velezrádný proces v Záhřebe.* Prague: Pokrok, 1909.

. "Theorie a praxis." In *Masarykova cesta.* Edited by Doležal.

Masaryk, T.G. *V boji o náboženství.* Prague: Státní nakladatelství, 1927.

. *Vasič, Forgách, Aehrenthal.* Prague: Čas, 1911.

. *Věda a církev: Církevně politický význam Wahrmundovy aféry.* Prague: Čas, 1908.

. *Versuch einer concreten Logik.* Vienna: S. Konegen, 1887.

. *Základové konkretné logiky.* Prague: Bursík a Kohout, 1885.

. "Zur deutschböhmischen Ausgleichsfrage." *Die Zeit,* VIII, 82 (1896).

"Masarykovy dopisy." *Listy filologické, 56 (1929).*

Masarykovy projevy a řeči za války. Edited by P. Maxa. Smíchov: S. Minarík, 1919.

Masarykuv Almanach. Edited by Viktor Altmann et al. Vienna: Akademický spolek ve Vídni, 1925.

Masarykuv Sborník. Časopis pro studium života a díla T.G. Masaryka. 4 vols. Prague, 1924-1930. (Volume IV was a re-edition of *T.G. Masarykovi k šedesátým narozeninám,* edited by Edvard Beneš et al., Prague, 1910.)

Mayer, J.P. *Max Weber and German Politics.* London: Faber and Faber, 1956.

Mencl, Vojtěch and Menclová, Jarmila. "Náčrt podstaty a vývoje vrcholné sféry předmnichovské československé mocensko-politické struktury." *Československý časopis historický,* 16 (1968).

Meyer, Alfred G. *Marxism: The Unity of Theory and Practice.* Ann Arbor: University of Michigan Press, 1963.

Michels, Roberto. "Authority." *Encyclopedia of the Social Sciences.* Edited by Edwin R.A. Seligman. New York: Macmillan, II (1935).

Mill, J.S. *On Liberty and Considerations on Representative Government.* Oxford: Oxford University Press, 1946.

. *A System of Logic.* London: Parker and Bourn, 1865.

Munz, Sigmund. "Erinnungen an Thomas G. Masaryk." *Masarykuv Almanach.*

Nadolny, Rudolf. *Germanisierung oder Slavisierung? Eine Entgegnung auf Masaryks Buch Das neue Europa.* Berlin: O. Stollberg, 1923.

Namier, Lewis. *Vanished Supremacies: Essays on European History, 1812-1918.* New York: Harper and Row, 1963.

Nejedlý, Zdeněk. *T.G. Masaryk.* 4 vols. Prague: Melantrich, 1930-1937.

. "T.G. Masaryk a Revoluce." *Masarykuv Sborník,* II (1925-1926).

Nemec, Ludvik. *The Czechoslovak Heresy and Schism: The Emergence of a National Czechoslovak Church.* Philadelphia: American Philosophical Society, 1975.

Newman, Edward Polson. *Masaryk.* London and Dublin: Campion Press, 1960.

Newman, Karl J. *European Democracy between the Wars.* Translated by Keith Morgan. London: George Allen and Unwin, 1970.

Nový, Lubomír. *Filosofie T.G. Mararyka.* Prague: Státní pedagogické nakladatelství, 1962.

———. "Masaryk jako sociolog." *Sociologický časopis.* IV (1968).

———. "T.G. Masaryk v českém myšlení."*Filosofickýčasopis,* XIV (1966).

Nyíri, János Kristóf. "Philosophy and Suicide Statistics in Austria-Hungary." *East Central Europe,* V (1978).

O vzajomnych vzt'ahoch Čechov a Slovakov. Bratislava: Vydavatel'stvo Slovenskej Akademie Ved, 1956.

Odložilík, Otakar. "Enter Masaryk: A Prelude to His Political Career." *Journal of Central European Affairs,* X (1950).

Olivová, Vera. *The Doomed Democracy: Czechoslovakia in a Disrupted Europe.* Translated by George Theiner. London: Sidgwick and Jackson, 1972.

Oschliess, Wolf. "Masarykismus: Konservative und Progressisten in der Auseinandersetzung um das demokratische Vermächtnis des tschechoslowakischen Staatsgründers." *Politische Studien,* XXI, 194 (1970).

Palacek, Antonin. "The Good Genius of Czechoslovak Democracy: Masaryk and Beneš, or Švehla?" *East European Quarterly,* XIII (1979).

Palecek, Anthony. "Antonin Švehla: Czech Peasant Statesman," *Slavic Review,* 21 (1962).

Pamphilet, A. "A Corrective to the Principle of Nationality." *The New Europe,* XII (1917).

Patočka, Jan. *Dvě eseje o Masarykovi.* Toronto: Sixty-Eight Publishers, 1979.

———. "Pokus o českou národní filosofii a jeho nezdar." In *Hodina naděje: Almanach české literatury, 1968-1978.* Edited by Jiří Gruša et al. Toronto: Sixty-Eight Publishers, 1980.

Paul, David W. "Nationalism, Pluralism, and Schweikism in Czechoslovakia's Culture." Unpublished Ph.D. dissertation, Princeton University, 1973.

Pekař, Josef. "Masarykova česká filosofie." *Český časopis historický*, 18 (1912).

Perman, D. *The Shaping of the Czechoslovak State: A Diplomatic History of the Boundaries of Czechoslovakia.* Leiden: E.J. Brill, 1962.

Peroutka, Ferdinand. *Budování státu.* 4 vols. Prague: Fr. Borový, 1932-36.

Pichlík, Karel. "První projekt samostatného Československa z podzimu 1914." *Historie a vojenství,* 1966, no. 3.

. *Zahraniční odboj 1914-1918 bez legend.* Prague: Svododa, 1968.

Plaschka, R.G. *Von Palacký bis Pekař.* Graz-Cologne: H.Bohlaus Nachf., 1955.

Pogonowski, Jerzy. *T.G. Masaryk, Studjum.* Warsaw: F. Hoesick, 1927.

Polonsky, Antony. *Politics in Independent Poland, 1921-1939.* Oxford: Oxford University Press, 1972.

Popper, K.R. *The Open Society and Its Enemies.* London: Routledge and Kegan Paul, 1957.

Pražák, A. *Češi a Slováci.* Prague: Státní nakl., 1929.

Preston-Warren, W. *Masaryk's Democracy.* Chapel Hill: University of North Carolina Press, 1941.

Prinz, Friedrich. "Die böhmischen Länder im Zeitalter der modernen Industriegesellschaft." In *Handbuch der Geschichte der böhmischen Länder.* Edited by Bosl.

. "Die Burg: Ihre Entstehung und Struktur als Forschungsaufgabe." In *Die Burg.* Edited by Bosl.

Procházka, M. *Otázka dělnická.* Prague: 1898.

Pulzer, Peter G.J. *The Rise of Political Anti-Semitism in Germany and Austria.* New York: Wiley, 1964.

Rádl, Emanuel. *Der Kampf zwischen Tschechen und Deutschen.* Translated by Richard Brandeis. Reichenberg: Verlag Gebruder Stiepel, 1928.

Rámcový program české strany lidové (realistické). Prague: Čas, 1900.

Rechcigl, Miloslav, Jr., ed. *The Czechoslovak Contribution to World Culture.* The Hague: Mouton, 1964.

. *Czechoslovakia Past and Present.* The Hague and Paris: Mouton, 1968.

Renner, Karl. *Das nationale und das ökonomische Problem der Tschechoslowakei.* Prague: Verlag der Deutschen Sozialdemokratischen Arbeiterpartei in der Tschechoslowakei, 1926.

Richta, L. "O podstatě sociologické a filosofické soustavy 'masarykismu'." In *Filosofie v dějinach českého národa.* Prague: Nakladatelství Československé Akademie Věd, 1958.

Rokycana, Jaroslav. "Friends in Need." In *Masaryk and the Jews.* Edited by Rychnowsky.

Rothschild, Joseph. *East Central Europe Between the Two World Wars.* Seattle and London: University of Washington Press, 1974.

Rousseau, Jean Jacques. *The Social Contract, Discourses.* Translated by G.D.H. Cole. London: J.M. Dent, 1958.

Rychnowsky, Ernst. "The Struggle Against the Ritual Murder Superstition." In *Masaryk and the Jews.* Edited by Rychnowsky.

Rychnowsky, Ernst, ed. *Thomas G. Masaryk and the Jews.* Translated by Benjamin Epstein. New York: B. Pollak, 1941.

(Schauer), H.G. "Naše dvě otázky." *Čas,* I, 1 (December 20,1886).

Selver, Paul. *Masaryk: A Biography.* London: M. Joseph, 1940.

Seton-Watson, R.W. *Masaryk in England.* Cambridge: Cambridge University Press, 1943.

Shillinglaw, Draga B. *The Lectures of Professor T.G. Masaryk at the University of Chicago, Summer 1902.* Lewisburg and London: Bucknell University Press, 1978.

Skilling, H. Gordon. "Communism and Czechoslovak Traditions." *Journal of International Affairs,* XX (1966).

. *Czechoslovakia's Interrupted Revolution.* Princeton: Princeton University Press, 1976.

. "The Politics of the Czech Eighties." In *The Czech Renascence.* Edited by Brock and Skilling.

Slapnicka, Helmut. "Die Rechtsstellung des Prasidenten der Republik nach der Verfassungsurkunde und in der politischen Wirklichkeit." In *Die Burg.* Edited by K. Bosl.

Smith, Anthony D. *Theories of Nationalism.* New York: Harper and Row, 1971. *Nationalism in the 20th Century.* New York: New York University Press, 1979.

Steenson, Gary P. *Karl Kautsky, 1854-1938: Marxism in the Classical Years.* Pittsburgh: University of Pittsburgh Press, 1978.

Stern, Fritz. *The Politics of Cultural Despair: A Study in the Rise of the German Ideology.* Berkeley: University of California Press, 1961.

Stloukal, Karel. *Československý stat v představach T.G. Masaryka za války.* Prague: Politický Klub, 1930.

Stolzl, Christoph. "Die 'Burg' und die Juden." In *Die Burg*. Edited by Bosl.

Svítak, Ivan. *The Czechoslovak Experiment, 1968-1969*. New York and London: Columbia University Press, 1972.

Syllaba, Theodor. "Na okraj Masarykova 'Ruska a Evropy'." *Filosofický časopis*, 1958, no. 6.

Szporluk, Roman. "Aspects of T.G. Masaryk." *East Central Europe*. 4 (1977).

———. "Masaryk in Search of Authority." *Canadian Slavonic Papers*, VII (1965).

———, "Masaryk's Idea of Democracy." *Slavonic and East European Review*, XLI (1962).

———."Masarykova republika: Nacionalismus s lidskou tváří." *Proměny*, 17 (1980).

Taborsky, Edward. "The Roots of Czechoslovak Democracy." In *Czechoslovakia Past and Present*. Edited by Rechcigl.

———. *Czechoslovak Democracy at Work*. London: George Allen and Unwin, 1945.

Tapie, Victor-Lucien. *The Rise and Fall of the Habsburg Monarchy*. New York: Praeger, 1971.

Taylor, A.J.P. *The Habsburg Monarchy, 1809-1918*. London: Hamish Hamilton, 1948.

Thomas, Trevor Vaughan. "Bohumil Smeral and the Czech Question, 1900-1914." *Journal of Contemporary History*, XI (1976).

Thomson, S. Harrison. "T.G. Masaryk and Czech Historiography." *Journal of Central European Affairs*, X (1950).

Toennies, Ferdinand. *Community and Society*. Translated and edited by Charles P. Loomis. New York: Harper and Row, 1963.

Treadgold, Donald. *The West in Russia and China*. Cambridge: Cambridge University Press, 1973.

Trotsky, Leon. "Professor Masaryk uber Russland." *Der Kampf*, VII, 11-12 (1914).

Urban, Rudolf. *Die tschechoslowakische Hussitische Kirche*. Marburg/Lahn: J.G. Herder-Institut, 1973.

Urban, Zdeněk. *Problémy slovenského národniho hnuti na konci 19. stoleti*. Prague: Acta Universitatis Carolinae, Philosophica et historica, monographia XXXVII, 1971.

van den Beld, Antonie. *Humanity: The Political and Social Philosophy of Thomas G. Masaryk.* The Hague and Paris: Mouton, 1975.

Vico, Giambattista. *The New Science of Giambattista Vico.* Translated by T.G. Bergin and M.H. Fisch. New York: Cornell University Press, 1948.

Vienna, Kriegsarchiv. Militärkanzlei Franz Ferdinand. 5344 and 6300/ 1913, and 741 and 1604/1914. ("Nobel-Friedenspreis fur Professor Masaryk.")

Vienna, Kriegsarchiv. Militärkanzlei Seiner Majestät. 57-3/15-3 ex 1916. ("K.K. Militäranwalt des Militärkommandanten in Wien. Anklageschrift gegen Johann Hájek, Cyrill Dusěk . . . und Anna Beneš.")

Vlček, V. "Jan Herben et cie." *Osvěta* (1899).

Vojtěch, Tomáš. "Česká historiografie a pozitivismus do roku 1918," *Československý časopis historický*, 28 (1980).

Vorovka, K. *Dvě studie o Masarykově filosofii.* Prague: Nakl. vlastním, 1926.

Vudce generací. 2 vols. Prague, 1930-1931. (*Masarykuv Sborník,* vols. V-VI.)

Vyšný, Paul. *Neo-Slavism and the Czechs, 1898-1914.* Cambridge: Cambridge University Press, 1977.

Wandycz, Piotr. "Pierwsza Republika a Druga Rzeczpospolita." *Zeszyty historyczne,* 28 (1974).

Wellek, René. "Masaryk's Philosophy." In *Essays on Czech Literature.* The Hague: Mouton, 1963.

Weltsch, Felix. "Masaryk and Zionism." In *Masaryk and the Jews.* Edited by Rychnowsky.

Werner, A. *T.G. Masaryk: Bild seines Lebens.* Prague: 1934.

Werstadt, Jaroslav. *Odkazy dějin a dějepiscu.* Prague: Historický Klub, 1948.

Willars, Christian. *Die böhmische Zitadelle, CSR–Schicksal einer Staatsidee.* Vienna and Munich: Molden, 1965.

Winters, Stanley B. "Kramář, Kaizl, and the Hegemony of the Young Czech Party." In *The Czech Renascence.* Edited by Brock and Skilling.

Wiskemann, Elizabeth. *Czechs and Germans: A Study of the Struggles in the Historic Provinces of Bohemia and Moravia.* London: Oxford University Press, 1938.

Zacek, Joseph F. "Nationalism in Czechoslovakia." In *Nationalism in Eastern Europe.* Edited by Peter F. Sugar and Ivo J. Lederer. Seattle and London: University of Washington Press, 1969.

Žáček, Václav et al. *Češi a Jihoslované v minulosti: Od nejstarších dob do roku 1918.* Prague: Academia, 1975.

Zeman, Zbyněk. *The Breakup of the Habsburg Empire.* Oxford: Oxford University Press, 1963.

    . *The Masaryks: The Making of Czechoslovakia.* London: Weidenfeld and Nicolson, 1976.

Zorach, Jonathan. "The British View of the Czechs in the Era Before the Munich Crisis," *Slavonic and East European Review,* 57 (1979).

    . "The Enigma of the Gajda Affair in Czechoslovak Politics in 1926." *Slavic Review,* 35 (1976).

INDEX

EAST EUROPEAN MONOGRAPHS

The *East European Monographs* comprise scholarly books on the history and civilization of Eastern Europe. They are published by the *East European Quarterly* in the belief that these studies contribute substantially to the knowledge of the area and serve to stimulate scholarship and research.

Political Ideas and the Enlightenment in the Romanian Principalities, 1750-1831. By Vlad Georgescu. 1971.

America, Italy and the Birth of Yugoslavia, 1917-1919. By Dragan R. Zivjinovic. 1972.

Jewish Nobles and Geniuses in Modern Hungary. By William O. McCagg, Jr. 1972.

Mixail Soloxov in Yugoslavia: Reception and Literary Impact. By Robert F. Price. 1973.

The Historical and National Thought of Nicolae Iorga. By William O. Oldson. 1973.

Guide to Polish Libraries and Archives. By Richard C. Lewanski. 1974.

Vienna Broadcasts to Slovakia, 1938-1939: A Case Study in Subversion. By Henry Delfiner. 1974.

The 1917 Revolution in Latvia. By Andrew Ezergailis. 1974.

The Ukraine in the United Nations Organization: A Study in Soviet Foreign Policy. 1944-1950. By Konstantin Sawczuk. 1975.

The Bosnian Church: A New Interpretation. By John V. A. Fine, Jr., 1975.

Intellectual and Social Developments in the Habsburg Empire from Maria Theresa to World War I. Edited by Stanley B. Winters and Joseph Held. 1975.

Ljudevit Gaj and the Illyrian Movement. By Elinor Murray Despalatovic. 1975.

Tolerance and Movements of Religious Dissent in Eastern Europe. Edited by Bela K. Kiraly. 1975.

The Parish Republic: Hlinka's Slovak People's Party, 1939-1945. By Yeshayahu Jelinek. 1976.

The Russian Annexation of Bessarabia, 1774-1828. By George F. Jewsbury. 1976.

Modern Hungarian Historiography. By Steven Bela Vardy. 1976.

Values and Community in Multi-National Yugoslavia. By Gary K. Bertsch. 1976.

The Greek Socialist Movement and the First World War: The Road to Unity. By George B. Leon. 1976.

The Radical Left in the Hungarian Revolution of 1848. By Laszlo Deme. 1976.

Hungary between Wilson and Lenin: The Hungarian Revolution of 1918-1919 and the Big Three. By Peter Pastor. 1976.

The Crises of France's East-Central European Diplomacy, 1933-1938. By Anthony J. Komjathy. 1976.

Polish Politics and National Reform, 1775-1788. By Daniel Stone. 1976.

The Habsburg Empire in World War I. Robert A. Kann, Bela K. Kiraly, and Paula S. Fichtner, eds. 1977.

The Slovenes and Yugoslavism, 1890-1914. By Carole Rogel. 1977.

German-Hungarian Relations and the Swabian Problem. By Thomas Spira. 1977.

The Metamorphosis of a Social Class in Hungary During the Reign of Young Franz Joseph. By Peter I. Hidas. 1977.

Tax Reform in Eighteenth Century Lombardy. By Daniel M. Klang. 1977.

Tradition versus Revolution: Russia and the Balkans in 1917. By Robert H. Johnston. 1977.

Winter into Spring: The Czechoslovak Press and the Reform Movement 1963-1968. By Frank L. Kaplan. 1977.

The Catholic Church and the Soviet Government, 1939-1949. By Dennis J. Dunn. 1977.

The Hungarian Labor Service System, 1939-1945. By Randolph L Braham. 1977.

Consciousness and History: Nationalist Critics of Greek Society 1897-1914. By Gerasimos Augustinos. 1977.

Emigration in Polish Social and Political Thought, 1870-1914. By Benjamin P. Murdzek. 1977.

Serbian Poetry and Milutin Bojic. By Mihailo Dordevic. 1977.

The Baranya Dispute: Diplomacy in the Vortex of Ideologies, 1918-1921. By Leslie C. Tihany. 1978.

The United States in Prague, 1945-1948. By Walter Ullmann. 1978.

Rush to the Alps: The Evolution of Vacationing in Switzerland. By Paul P. Bernard. 1978.

Transportation in Eastern Europe: Empirical Findings. By Bogdan Mieczkowski. 1978.

The Polish Underground State: A Guide to the Underground, 1939-1945. By Stefan Korbonski. 1978.

The Hungarian Revolution of 1956 in Retrospect. Edited by Bela K. Kiraly and Paul Jonas. 1978.

Boleslaw Limanowski (1835-1935): A Study in Socialism and Nationalism. By Kazimiera Janina Cottam. 1978.

The Lingering Shadow of Nazism: The Austrian Independent Party Movement Since 1945. By Max E. Riedlsperger. 1978.

The Catholic Church, Dissent and Nationality in Soviet Lithuania. By V. Stanley Vardys. 1978.

The Development of Parliamentary Government in Serbia. By Alex N. Dragnich. 1978.

Divide and Conquer: German Efforts to Conclude a Separate Peace, 1914-1918. By L. L. Farrar, Jr. 1978.

The Prague Slav Congress of 1848. By Lawrence D. Orton. 1978.

The Nobility and the Making of the Hussite Revolution. By John M. Klassen. 1978.

The Cultural Limits of Revolutionary Politics: Change and Continuity in Socialist Czechoslovakia. By David W. Paul. 1979.

On the Border of War and Peace: Polish Intelligence and Diplomacy in 1937-1939 and the Origins of the Ultra Secret. By Richard A. Woytak. 1979.

Bear and Foxes: The International Relations of the East European States 1965-1969. By Ronald Haly Linden. 1979.

Czechoslovakia: The Heritage of Ages Past. Edited by Ivan Volgyes and Hans Brisch. 1979.

Prima Minister Gyula Andrassy's Influence on Habsburg Foreign Policy. By Janos Decsy. 1979.

Citizens for the Fatherland: Education, Educators, and Pedagogical Ideals in Eighteenth Century Russia. By J. L. Black. 1979.

A History of the "Proletariat": The Emergence of Marxism in the Kingdom of Poland, 1870-1887. By Norman M. Naimark. 1979.

The Slovak Autonomy Movement, 1935-1939: A Study in Unrelenting Nationalism. By Dorothea H. El Mallakh. 1979.

Diplomat in Exile: Francis Pulszky's Political Activities in England, 1849-1860. By Thomas Kabdebo. 1979.

The German Struggle Against the Yugoslav Guerrillas in World War II: German Counter-Insurgency in Yugoslavia, 1941-1943. By Paul N. Hehn. 1979.

The Emergence of the Romanian National State. By Gerald J. Bobango. 1979.

Stewards of the Land: The American Farm School and Modern Greece. By Brenda L. Marder. 1979.

Roman Dmowski: Party, Tactics, Ideology, 1895-1907. By Alvin M. Fountain, II. 1980.

International and Domestic Politics in Greece During the Crimean War. By Jon V. Kofas. 1980.

Fires on the Mountain: The Macedonian Revolutionary Movement and the Kidnapping of Ellen Stone. By Laura Beth Sherman. 1980.

The Modernization of Agriculture: Rural Transformation in Hungary, 1848-1975. Edited by Joseph Held. 1980.

Britain and the War for Yugoslavia, 1940-1943. By Mark C. Wheeler. 1980.

The Turn to the Right: The Ideological Origins and Development of Ukrainian Nationalism, 1919-1929. By Alexander J. Motyl. 1980.

The Maple Leaf and the White Eagle: Canadian-Polish Relations, 1918-1978. By Aloysius Balawyder. 1980.

Antecedents of Revolution: Alexander I and the Polish Congress Kingdom, 1815-1825. By Frank W. Thackeray. 1980.

Blood Libel at Tiszaeszlar. By Andrew Handler. 1980.

Democratic Centralism in Romania: A Study of Local Communist Politics. By Daniel N. Nelson. 1980.

The Challenge of Communist Education: A Look at the German Democratic Republic. By Margrete Siebert Klein. 1980.

The Fortifications and Defense of Constantinople. By Byron C.P. Tsangadas. 1980.

Balkan Cultural Studies. By Stavro Skendi. 1980.

Studies in Ethnicity: The East European Experience in America. Edited by Charles A. Ward, Philip Shahshko, and Donald E. Pienkos. 1980.

The Logic of "Normalization:" The Soviet Intervention in Czechoslovakia and the Czechoslovak Response. By Fred Eidlin. 1980.

Red Cross. Black Eagle: A Biography of Albania's American Schol. By Joan Fultz Kontos. 1981.

Nationalism in Contemporary Europe. By Franjo Tudjman. 1981.

Great Power Rivalry at the Turkish Straits: The Montreux Conference and Convention of 1936. By Anthony R. DeLuca. 1981.

Islam Under the Double Eagle: The Muslims of Bosnia and Hercegovina, 1878-1914. By Robert J. Donia. 1981.

Five Eleventh Century Hungarian Kings: Their Policies and Their Relations with Rome. By Z.J. Kosztolnyik. 1981.

Prelude to Appeasement: East European Central Diplomacy in the Early 1930's. By Lisanne Radice. 1981.

The Soviet Regime in Czechoslovakia. By Zdenek Krystufek. 1981.

School Strikes in Prussian Poland, 1901-1907: The Struggle Over Bilingual Education. By John J. Kulczycki. 1981.

Romantic Nationalism and Liberalism: Joachim Lelewel and the Polish National Idea. By Joan S. Skurnowicz. 1981.

The "Thaw" In Bulgarian Literature. By Atanas Slavov. 1981.

The Political Thought of Thomas G. Masaryk. By roman Szporluk. 1981.

Prussian Poland in the German Empire, 1871-1900. By Richard Blanke. 1981.

The Mazepists: Ukrainian Separatism in the Early Eighteenth Century. By Orest Subtelny. 1981.

The Battle for the Marchlands: The Russo-Polish Campaign of 1920. By Adam Zamoyski. 1981.

Milovan Djilas: A Revolutionary as a Writer. By Dennis Reinhartz. 1981.

DATE DUE

GAYLORD			PRINTED IN U.S.A.